JS.

Periods of European Literature

EDITED BY
PROFESSOR SAINTSBURY

VII.

THE FIRST HALF OF THE
SEVENTEENTH CENTURY

PERIODS OF EUROPEAN LITERATURE.

Edited by Professor SAINTSBURY.

A COMPLETE AND CONTINUOUS HISTORY OF THE SUBJECT.

In 12 Crown 8vo Volumes.

"*The criticism which alone can much help us for the future is a criticism which regards Europe as being, for intellectual and spiritual purposes, one great confederation, bound to a joint action and working to a common result.*"
—Matthew Arnold.

I. The DARK AGES	Professor W. P. Ker.	[*Ready.*
II. The FLOURISHING OF ROMANCE AND THE RISE OF ALLEGORY	The Editor.	[*Ready.*
III. The FOURTEENTH CENTURY	F. J. Snell.	[*Ready.*
IV. The TRANSITION PERIOD	G. Gregory Smith.	[*Ready.*
V. The EARLIER RENAISSANCE	The Editor.	[*Ready.*
VI. The LATER RENAISSANCE	David Hannay.	[*Ready.*
VII. The FIRST HALF OF THE SEVENTEENTH CENTURY	Professor H. J. C. Grierson.	[*Ready.*
VIII. The AUGUSTAN AGES	Professor O. Elton.	[*Ready.*
IX. The MID-EIGHTEENTH CENTURY	J. H. Millar.	[*Ready.*
X. The ROMANTIC REVOLT	Professor C. E. Vaughan.	
XI. The ROMANTIC TRIUMPH	T. S. Omond.	[*Ready.*
XII. The LATER NINETEENTH CENTURY	The Editor.	

CHARLES SCRIBNER'S SONS, New York.

THE FIRST HALF OF THE SEVENTEENTH CENTURY

BY

HERBERT J. C. GRIERSON, M.A.
CHALMERS PROFESSOR OF ENGLISH LITERATURE
IN THE UNIVERSITY OF ABERDEEN

NEW YORK
CHARLES SCRIBNER'S SONS
153-157 FIFTH AVENUE
1906

All Rights reserved

PREFACE.

A WORD by way of preface is requisite, if only to explain to the reader, who may take up this volume without recalling its place in a series, why there is no chapter on Spain in a history of European literature during the first half of the seventeenth century. The present writer undertook his task on the understanding that the Spanish literature of the epoch was covered by Mr Hannay's chapters in *The Later Renaissance*. It was explained there that the principle of overlapping, which must be admitted in any attempt to divide European literature into epochs, is specially applicable to the case of Spain; and the six chapters devoted to the literature of Spain in the sixteenth and seventeenth centuries in that volume preclude the necessity of treatment in this.

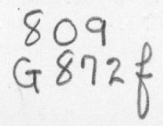

The same principle has been applied, to a certain extent, in the chapters on Dutch literature, with which this volume opens. Some passing references there have been to the literature of the Low Countries in previous volumes, but it has been thought well to give something of a connected sketch of the earlier literature at this point, when that literature forms an important and independent ganglion in the general European system. The mediæval literature of the Low Countries is doubtless sufficiently interesting to deserve fuller treatment; but it is, in the main, a literature of translation and imitation from the French, with some notable exceptions. This fact may serve as an excuse for the slight sketch of the subject given here—a sketch which, to be intelligible, should be read in close connection with what has been written about mediæval and fifteenth-century literature in earlier volumes of the series. I have reserved the larger portion of the space at my disposal for the period in which the Dutch, having shaken off the Spanish yoke, created for themselves a national literature and a national art.

My work in these chapters, as in those on other foreign literatures, is based on the researches of native scholars, whose results I have endeavoured to present in the light which seemed to me likely to prove most useful and interesting to the reader for whom this series is principally intended—the English student of comparative literature. I had begun my work before I realised that Dutch literature deserved a fuller treatment than had been given to it in other volumes, and it was perhaps rash to venture on the task. I felt tempted to undertake it from an interest in the Dutch people dating back to earliest years, when the harbour of my native town was crowded with Dutch fishing-boats every summer, and its narrow streets thronged with their picturesque costumes. If my chapters fail to satisfy a specialist, perhaps a less critical and exacting reader may derive interest from what, in its preparation, has given myself great pleasure. Holland has no Dante or Shakespeare or Goethe, for the sake of whom alone it would be worth while to study the language in which he wrote, but to the lover of lyrical poetry the work of Hooft and Vondel will give some fresh and intense experiences.

I have indicated in the bibliographical notes the authors on whose work mine is based. But I have received in addition personal encouragement and advice. On the occasion of two short calls, Professor Te Winkel of Amsterdam spoke to me regarding books that would be useful. But my chief debt is to Professor Kalff of Leyden. During two visits to Leyden —one of a fortnight's and one of a month's duration— he introduced me to the University library, in which are stored the books of the *Maatschaapij van Nederlandsche Letterkunde*, gave me the benefit of his advice on any point regarding which I consulted him, and every possible assistance. He has added to his kindness by reading my pages when in proof, and correcting some errors into which I had fallen. Imperfect as my chapters are, they would have been much more so without his advice and correction. My debt to his written work is clear from the notes. I only regret that the first volume of his new *Geschiedenis der Nederlandsche Letterkunde* did not reach me until my work was in type.

At the same time, Professor Kalff is not to be held in any way responsible either for the manner in which I have treated the subject, for my generalisations, or for my criticisms of individual authors and works, with which he would not always be in agreement. These, be they right or wrong, are the fruit of my own reading, at any rate in the case of the principal authors dealt with. When I have not had time or opportunity to make an independent study of lesser authors, I have tried to indicate in the text the source of any criticism passed upon them. As regards quotation, my plan has been to keep to the original when metre was what I wished to draw attention to. When the sentiment is of importance, I have ventured to translate, believing it would be merely pedantic to assume any such general knowledge of the Dutch language as of French and German, or even Italian. The translations are as close as I could make them, while endeavouring to retain something of the spirit and movement of the original.

As to other literatures, I have indicated in the notes my guides and authorities, and need here only mention some personal aiders. My debt to my teacher, the late Professor Minto, is not covered by the references to his printed work. I have known no one with saner views of the aim and methods of literary history. In him the æsthetic, the historical, and the philosophical critic were happily blended, no one usurping upon the other. In studying the Italian literature of the period, I received much assistance, and advice as to recent work on the subject, from Professor John Purves of the Technical Institute, Johannesburg, formerly English Assistant in the University of Aberdeen, who came to Aberdeen straight from Italy, where he had studied for two years, in Rome and Siena, as Carnegie Scholar. To him, and to others who helped me by reading the proofs, I would express my gratitude. If I do not name them all, it is for fear of making them appear in any way responsible for my errors and oversights. From the outset I have been indebted to the unwearied patience and invaluable criticisms of the general editor. My former pupil, Mr George Herbert Mair, Scholar of Christ Church, Oxford, has supplied the index.

In the last chapter I have endeavoured to indicate some of the forces at work in the period. But I have not felt able to open with a general view, for the epoch does not seem to admit of any such clear general description as does, say, that which follows. All the literatures touched on here have a common debt to Italy and the Classics. In the development, however, which followed the stimulating influence of the Renaissance, each is, in the earlier seventeenth century, at a very different stage. Italy herself is falling into the background, though the superficial influence of Marino is so widespread that a reader might do well to turn to the chapter on Italy among the first. In France, the influence of the Renaissance is practically exhausted, and, despite a taste for Italian and Spanish fashions, the distinctively national movement towards clear thought and symmetrical form proceeds apace. During the first ten years of the century, English literature is still in the full flush of the late Elizabethan efflorescence, but passes, as the century goes on, through a period of very independent and complex changes, determined in great measure by the religious and political history of the time, which it seems to me impossible to describe by any single term, be it disintegration with Mr Barrett Wendell, or decadence with Mr Gosse. Elizabethan literature was never integral, notwithstanding Spenser's effort at reconciliation; and decadence seems a term hardly applicable to a period which opens with Shakespeare and Bacon, and closes with Locke and Milton. For Holland, the period is that of the rapid ripening—to be followed by a too rapid decay — of a literature inspired, as English had been earlier, by admiration of Italy and France as well as the Classics, but thoroughly national in all its essential features. In Germany, a similar movement is too early checked by "inauspicious stars." I have tried to outline these different movements, but to bring them under any single expression of real value is beyond my philosophic capacity.

P.S.—The dates in brackets appended to the names of works are those of first publication, except in the case of Corneille's plays, when they are those of performance as given by Marty-Laveaux. Bacon's *Advertisement touching the Controversies of the Church*, though written probably in 1589, when the Martin-Marprelate controversy was at its height, was first issued, as a pamphlet, in 1640, when the quarrel was renewed.

ABERDEEN, *May* 10, 1906.

CONTENTS.

CHAPTER I.

HOLLAND—VERSE AND PROSE.

PAGE

Introductory — Mediæval romance and lyric — The fourteenth century—Maerlant and other didactic poets—Dirk Potter—Fifteenth century—The Chambers of Rhetoric—Anna Bijns—Renaissance—Marnix and Coornhert—Spieghel and Roemer Visscher — The "Eglantine" or "Oude Kamer"—Hooft—Song-books—Brederoo and Starter—Vondel—Life and work—Criticism — Literature outside Amsterdam — The Hague: Huyghens — Zeeland: Jacob Cats — Camphuyzen — Stalpert van der Wiele—Followers of Vondel and Hooft—Latin prose and verse — Heinsius and Grotius — Dutch prose — Hooft—Brandt 1

CHAPTER II.

HOLLAND—DRAMA.

Introductory—Mediæval drama—Problem connected therewith—The Moralities, Histories, and Farces of the Chambers—Renaissance secular drama—The "Eglantine"—Coster and Rodenburg—Brederoo—Hooft—"Quarrel of the Players"—Coster's Academy—The "Amsterdamsche Kamer" and new theatre — Vondel — Development of his drama — Individual tragedies — Characterisation and criticism — Failure of the romantic and classical drama—Jan Vos's *Aran en Titus*—Later plays 49

CHAPTER III.

ENGLISH DRAMA.

Introductory — George Chapman — Ben Jonson — His theory of comedy — Earlier comedies — Tragedies — Mature comedies — Last plays — Masques — *Sad Shepherd* — Achievement — Marston — Dekker — Middleton — Heywood — Webster — His two tragedies — Tourneur — Beaumont and Fletcher — Last phase of Elizabethan drama — Sentimental tragedy and romance — Comedy of incident and manners — Massinger — Ford — Shirley — Lesser dramatists — Conclusion . . 84

CHAPTER IV.

ENGLISH POETRY.

Introductory — George Chapman — The younger Spenserians — Protestant and bourgeois — The Fletchers — Browne and Wither — Quarles, More, Beaumont, &c. — Drummond and Sir John Beaumont — Donne and Jonson — Characteristics and influence — Caroline courtly poetry, religious and secular — Herbert, Vaughan, Crashaw, and Traherne — Carew, Lovelace, Suckling, Herrick — Andrew Marvell — Milton's life and early poems — Poetry of the Commonwealth — Waller and Denham — Davenant and Chamberlayne — Cowley — Milton's later poems — *Paradise Lost* — *Paradise Regained* — *Samson Agonistes* — Conclusion 135

CHAPTER V.

ENGLISH PROSE.

"An immoderate hydroptic thirst of learning." Bacon — Jonson. Divines — Anglo-Catholic: Andrewes — Donne — Jeremy Taylor; Puritan: Adams; Latitudinarian: Hales — Chillingworth. Controversialists: Hall — Taylor — Milton. "Characters": Hall — Overbury — Earle. Burton — Drummond — Browne — Urquhart — Fuller. Philosophy: Hobbes. History: Clarendon. Biography: Walton 202

CONTENTS.   xiii

CHAPTER VI.

FRENCH VERSE AND PROSE.

Waning of the Pleiad. Malherbe—Purity and correctness—Verse.
Disciples—Maynard—Racan. Social forces—Hôtel de Rambouillet — Academy. Independents — Théophile de Viau—
Saint-Amant — Mlle. de Gournay and Mathurin Régnier.
Vincent Voiture. Heroic poems. Prose-romances—D'Urfé
—*L'Astrée;* Camus — Exemplary tales; Heroic romance—
Gombauld's *Endymion*—Gomberville's *Polexandre*—La Calprenède—Elimination of the marvellous—Romantic history
—Madeleine de Scudéry — Culmination of "Préciosité"—
Boileau's dialogue *Les Héros de Roman.* Realism and burlesque in romance—Sorel—*Le Berger Extravagant*—*Francion*
—Lannel — Cyrano — Scarron. Shapers of modern French
prose—Balzac and the cult of style; Descartes—Rationalism
and lucidity; Pascal—The way of the intellect and the way
of the heart. The *Memoirs*—De Retz and La Rochefoucauld
—Philosophy of the *Fronde*—*Les Maximes*   .   .   .   244

CHAPTER VII.

FRENCH DRAMA.

The formation of French tragedy and comedy—Sixteenth-century
drama—Larivey and Montchrestien—The popular drama—
Experiments in the provinces—Hardy and Valleran Lecomte
—Hardy's tragedies, tragi-comedies, pastorals, and mythological plays — Beginning of polite drama — Théophile and
Racan—Influence of Italian pastoral, and of Spanish tragicomedy—Mairet—The Unities—*Sophonisbe* and the revival of
tragedy—Corneille—*Mélite* and the development of comedy—
Early plays—The *Cid* and the flowering of tragedy—Battle of
the *Cid*—Triumph of the Unities—Corneille's great tragedies
—*Le Menteur*—Comedy under Spanish influence—Corneille's
last plays — Relation of French tragedy of Corneille and
Racine to Greek tragedy and to romantic tragi-comedy—
Rotrou—Burlesque comedy—*Les Visionnaires*   .   .   285

CHAPTER VIII.

ITALY AND GERMANY.

"Secentismo." Marino—*La Lira*—*L'Adone*. Followers. Chiabrera—The Italian *canzone* and the classical ode—Bernardo Tasso—Chiabrera's Pindarics and *canzonette*. Testi. Tassoni—Criticism of Aristotle and Petrarch—*La Secchia Rapita*—Prose — Galileo — D'Avila — Bentivoglio. Germany — Late influence of Renaissance. Precursors. Opitz—Theory and practice. Followers—Fleming. Hymns. Drama—Gryphius. Satire—Logau 325

CHAPTER IX.

CONCLUSION.

Forces at work—End of the enaissance—The Counter-Reformation—Rationalism and classicism 361

INDEX 380

THE FIRST HALF OF THE SEVENTEENTH CENTURY.

CHAPTER I.

HOLLAND—VERSE AND PROSE.

INTRODUCTORY — MEDIÆVAL ROMANCE AND LYRIC — THE FOURTEENTH CENTURY—MAERLANT AND OTHER DIDACTIC POETS—DIRK POTTER—FIFTEENTH CENTURY—THE CHAMBERS OF RHETORIC—ANNA BIJNS—RENAISSANCE—MARNIX AND COORNHERT—SPIEGHEL AND ROEMER VISSCHER—THE "EGLANTINE" OR "OUDE KAMER"—HOOFT—SONG-BOOKS—BREDEROO AND STARTER—VONDEL—LIFE AND WORK—CRITICISM—LITERATURE OUTSIDE AMSTERDAM—THE HAGUE: HUYGHENS—ZEELAND: JACOB CATS—CAMPHUYZEN—STALPERT VAN DER WIELE—FOLLOWERS OF VONDEL AND HOOFT—LATIN PROSE AND VERSE—HEINSIUS AND GROTIUS—DUTCH PROSE—HOOFT—BRANDT.

ON no country in Europe did the two main influences of the sixteenth century—the Renaissance and the Reformation—set a deeper mark than on the Netherlands. The country which produced Erasmus is not the least important contributor to the revival of learning, while the revolt of the Netherlands was, in Motley's words, "the longest, the

Introductory.

darkest, the bloodiest, the most important episode in the history of the religious reformation in Europe." Of the greatness of the people which emerged victorious from this struggle, of the high level of culture and learning to which they had attained, of the range and magnificence of their achievement in the art of painting, there has never been any question. But of the Dutch literature of the seventeenth century little is known outside Holland except by a few scholars,[1]

[1] Jonckbloet's *Geschiedenis der Nederlandsche Letterkunde* (4th ed., 1889, C. Honigh), an epoch-making work, is still the fullest history of Dutch literature. The arrangement is at times confusing, and much work has been done since. Penon's *Nederlandsche Dicht-en-Proza-werken*, 1886, forms a companion set of volumes to Jonckbloet's *Geschiedenis*, and contains carefully edited texts, but not always of the works one would most wish to have. A popular sketch is Jan ten Brink's *Geschiedenis der Nederlandsche Letterkunde*, 1897. A very interesting sketch, from a Catholic point of view, is the late J. A. Alberdingk Thijm's *De la Littérature néerlandaise à ses Différentes Epoques*, 1854. Of the earlier literature a condensed and learned sketch by Professor Te Winkel is contained in Paul's *Grundriss der Deutschen Philologie*, 1900. Delightfully written and indispensable works by Professor Kalff are *Nederlandsche Letterkunde in de XVI^{de} Eeuw*, Brill, n.d. ; *Literatuur en Tooneel te Amsterdam in de Zeventiende Eeuw*, Haarlem, 1895,—biographical and critical sketches of Hooft, Vondel, Cats, Huyghens, &c. The first volume of a history of Dutch literature in eight volumes by the same writer has appeared, Groningen, 1905. Busken-Huet's brilliant *Het Land van Rembrandt* and *Litterarische Fantasien* are well worth reading. The work of many scholars is contained in *De Gids*, the great literary periodical founded in 1837. Excellently annotated seventeenth-century texts—and the language presents difficulties which require elucidation—have been issued in the *Nederlandsche Klassieken*, general editor Dr Eelco Verwys, Versluys, Amsterdam, and the *Klassiek Letterkundig Pantheon*, W. J. Thieme & Co., Zutphen. An interesting and representative though small Anthology is Professor Kalff's *Dichters van den Ouden Tijd*, Amsterdam, n.d. English works are some essays in Gosse's *Studies in the Literature of*

and it has not been unusual to speak of Dutch literature as an entirely negligible quantity, because the Netherlands produced no creative genius of that highest class to which Shakespeare and Cervantes belong. But geniuses of such world-wide recognition are the exception. The degree to which a country's literature is studied abroad depends not on intrinsic merit alone, but on the country's political importance and familiarity with its language. The student of Dutch literature in the seventeenth century will not find a drama comparable, strictly as drama, with that of England or France or Spain, nor an epic and narrative poetry comparable to that of Italy, and of England as represented by Milton. But he will find and enjoy a lyrical poetry of singular depth and richness, characterised by that feeling for nature which is such a striking feature of Dutch painting, by what the Dutch critic J. A. Alberdingk Thijm justly entitles "le naturel, la naïveté, la franchise, et le sentiment de la couleur qui paraissent être inhérents au caractère néerlandais." In naturalness, in the sense attached to the word when we speak of the "return to nature," feeling for external nature, interest in the life of the people, the inclination to discard convention and make poetry the simple, direct, and vibrating utterance of the poet's own emotions, Dutch poetry, taken as a whole, partly because it is

Northern Europe, Lond., 1879, and the same writer's article in the *Encyclopædia Britannica;* Bowring and Van Dyk's *Batavian Anthology*, Lond., 1824; Longfellow's *Poets and Poetry of Europe*, Philadelphia, 1849; an article in the *Foreign Quarterly Review*, 1829.

a bourgeois or middle-class product, seems to me in advance of the poetry of any country with which this volume deals. For this simplicity and directness is not characteristic of Renaissance lyric poetry in Italy or the countries which caught their inspiration from Italy. Even in the case of Shakespeare's sonnets it is notoriously difficult to say how far the feeling is sincere, how far conventional. In English poetry one might say that lyrical poetry, as we have come to understand the phrase since Wordsworth, Byron, and Shelley wrote, begins with *Lycidas*—in the personal digressions—and Milton's sonnets. But poetry of this self-revealing outspoken character abounds in the literature with which this chapter deals, and although of course in form and style Dutch poetry is not unaffected by the conventions of the century, yet only one poet, Hooft, really mastered the courtly style, and caught the tone of the Italian Petrarchians and the Pléiade. Vondel and Brederoo and Huyghens are most effective when most natural and direct, not least so when they express themselves in dialect. The natural runs easily into the commonplace, and of the commonplace there is not a little in Dutch poetry. Its apostle is Jacob Cats; yet even in Cats there is a vein of racy narrative, while in ardour and elevation there are few lyrical poets superior to Vondel.

The space at our disposal to deal even with this greatest period in Dutch literature is so limited that *Mediæval Romances.* it is impossible to say more than a word concerning the earlier poetry. Mediæval literature is represented in the Low Countries by all the usual forms—romances, Carlovingian, Arthurian, and Oriental (Alexander and Troy), versified saints' legends, shorter tales or *sproken*, lyrics, and a considerable body of didactic literature. Of the drama something will be said in the following chapter. The Dutch romances of the thirteenth century are mainly, if not entirely, translated from the French. *Moriaen* is probably an exception, and Professor Kalff defends the originality of *Karel ende Elegast* and the fine *Roman van Walewein*. Most interesting of all is the popular *Reinaert*,[1] based on a French work, but much superior to the original, and admittedly the finest version of the Reynard stories.

It was, naturally, the nobility and their followers who were the principal readers of the romances, as *Religious and* it was the "religious" who composed and *Didactic Poetry.* studied poems such as *Vanden Leven ons Heeren*, *Beatrijs*, and other saints' legends. The taste of the middle classes, which began to assert itself as the thirteenth century drew to a close, is represented by the didactic writers, at the head of whom stands the prolific Jacob van Maerlant, author of versions of the Alexander, Merlin, and Troy stories, and of various didactic works such as the *Rijmbijbel* and *Spieghel Historiael* (*Mirror of History*). He was followed by a number of verse chroniclers and didactic writers, as Melis Stoke and Jan van Boendale or de Clerk, author of a *Lekenspieghel* (*Mirror for Laymen*), whom it is impossible to enumerate here. The *Roman*

---

[1] The twentieth branch, *Le Plaid*, of the *Roman du Renart*, ed. Meon and Chabaille. See Jonckbloet's *Geschied*, i. xii.

de la Rose, the tone of the second part of which is that of this cultured middle class, was translated in the fourteenth century by Hein van Aken.

The same century produced abundance of short tales or *sproken,* a few courtly, very many didactic, and some in the humorous popular vein of the French *fabliau.* They were recited in banqueting halls by the *Sprekers* or *Zeggers,* and many of the more humorous and coarse of them have probably been lost. A collection of stories, serious and humorous, very much in the style of Gower's *Confessio Amantis,* from which indeed the Dutch poet borrows, was made by Dirk Potter (1370-1428) under the title *Minnenloop.* Potter, like Chaucer, visited Italy, but he learnt nothing from Italian poetry, and stands much closer to Gower and Cats than to the author of the Canterbury Tales. To the fourteenth century belong also the oldest extant Dutch songs, ballads, and love-poems, such as the famous *Het daget in den Oosten, Halewijn, Graaf Floris, Een liedeken vanden Mey, De Leeuwerik,* and others. The lyrics of Zuster Hadewijch — in which the language of the Minnesingers is employed to express a mystical passion for Christ—belong to the thirteenth century. Other religious songs are the charming Kerstliederen or Christmas songs, the Maria-liederen, and the Liederen der Minnende Ziele. No part of Mediæval Dutch or Flemish literature is more entirely delightful than the songs.

Lyrical Poetry.

The centres or nuclei of literature in the Low Countries during the fifteenth and sixteenth cen-

HOLLAND—VERSE AND PROSE.

turies were the Chambers of Rhetoric.[1] Indeed to the end of the seventeenth century the conditions of dramatic production were determined by the old customs of these celebrated institutions. The name, and possibly to some extent the institution, of "Rederijkers-kamers" came from France, where these secular and literary developments of the religious guilds were known as "Chambres de Rhétorique," "Puys," "Cours d'amour"; but in no country did they thrive more vigorously than in Flanders, Brabant, Zeeland, and Holland. Every town, and almost every village, had its chamber. They combined the functions and attractions of a dramatic company, a literary society, and a convivial club. "Rederijker, Kannekijker" became a proverb, and Jan Steen's picture in Brussels is characteristic of at any rate their later developments. They instituted competitions—*Landjuweelen* or smaller *Haagspelen*— at which prizes were offered for the most magnificent procession into town and the most elaborate decoration of the hostel where a chamber lodged, as well as for the best dramatic or poetic work. This work was not, however, of a high order. The dramatic *Zinnespelen* (Moralities) and *Kluchten* (Farces)—of which we shall have something to say in the next chapter—and the lyrical *Refereinen* and *Liedekens* of the chambers, were the last colourless products of the Middle Ages touched with the pedantry of the revival of learning, and composed in a style corrupted by bastard French words.

---

[1] *Vide* Jonckbloet, *Geschiedenis*, ii.; Kalff, *XVI^{de} Eeuw*, i.; also van Duyse and Potter, *History of the Chambers of Rhetoric*.

The loosely rhythmical metre easily passes into doggerel. The best lyrics of the sixteenth century are not those of the "rederijkers," but the people's songs or "volksliederen," which handled the old courtly themes in a more free and homely spirit. In the second half of the sixteenth century these songs became, as in the famous "Geuzenliederen," the most potent expression of religious and political sentiment. The war-songs of the English Puritans a century later were the Psalms of David. The Dutch Calvinists expressed their feelings more directly in simple and moving descriptions of the sufferings of martyrs to the cause, and in fierce onslaughts upon Philip and the Pope. It was the spirit of an unconquerable people which breathed in their rude verses:—

> "Help now yourself and you shall see
> God from the tyrant set you free,
>   Oppressèd Netherland!
> The rope that's round your neck must be
>   Torn by your own right hand."

The national anthem of Holland is still the grave and resolute—

> "Wilhelmus van Nassouwen
>   ben ik van duytschen bloed :
> Het vaterland getrouwe
>   blijf ik tot in den dood."

It is impossible, and hardly necessary, to mention individual "Rederijkers," even the fairly important Matthijs de Casteleyn (1488 ?-1550), author of a *Const van Rhetoriken*, in which, using the common device of a dream, he gives rules for the

De Casteleyn.

art of rhetoric or poetry. Above all, the poet must use "aureate" terms or "schuim," for as the sun illumines the day and the moon the night, "alsoo verlicht schuym eene schoone oratie." He must begin with easier compositions, as "balladen" and "rondeelen," before attempting what is most difficult—namely, the Morality. Only one poet, whose work is definitely "Rederijkers" poetry, succeeded in impressing upon it a distinct individuality, and that was the Antwerp poetess Anna Bijns,[1]

Anna Bijns.

who lived about the same time as De Casteleyn. Of her life we know only what can be gathered from her "refereinen,"—that she had known the pleasures and gaieties of the world, had loved and had been disappointed, and, like others of her sex, found consolation in religion, becoming a fiery champion of the Catholic Church against the new heresies of Luther. Of her early life she writes with the hyperbole to which the language of religious remorse has always tended. The tone of her poetry is that of the burgher class, far removed from the refined and mystical style of Zuster Hadewijch and the mediæval religious poets. She is a woman of her class and of her people, looking out on the world of everyday life with shrewd gaze, and describing it with vigour and even coarseness in images drawn

[1] *Refereinen van Anna Bijns, uitg. Bogaers en van Helten,* 1875. *Nieuwe Refereinen van A. B., uitg. Jonckbloet en van Helten,* 1880. *Nieuwe Refereinen,* Gent, 1886. On her life see Jonckbloet (*Geschiedenis,* &c., ii. 6), who takes very literally her expressions of remorse, and Kalff (*XVI^{de} Eeuw*), who qualifies Jonckbloet's account.

from familiar objects and experiences. What exalts and distinguishes her "refereinen" is the intense feeling with which they glow, whether religious or erotic, lyrical or didactic.

The poetry of the chambers was not of a kind which could long satisfy those who had once tasted of the sweets of classical and Italian poetry, and as the sixteenth century drew to a close men of culture made strenuous efforts to reproduce in their own language what they admired in Virgil and Horace, Seneca and Cicero, Petrarch and Marot and Ronsard. One of the first and best results of these efforts was the purification of the language; and the second was the gradual substitution of a more regular metre for the loose, often doggerel, rhythm of the *zinnespelen* and *refereinen*. The first translations of the classics were in the style and verse still in vogue; but in 1597 Karel van Mander, a Flemish poet and painter, produced a version of Virgil's *Eclogues* and *Georgics* which Professor Kalff describes as fairly faithful, pure in language, and written in metrical, at times even flowing, verse. Jan van der Noot (1538 ?-1595 ?), a native of Antwerp, but driven for a time to wander in other lands, and familiar with the works of Dante, Petrarch, and the Pléiade, wrote odes, sonnets, and epigrams, as well as an elaborate allegory in more than one metre. Their poetic merit is not great, but they show a significant striving after form, and some dignity of style. But the most important predecessors of the "bloeitijd" in the literature of Holland

Renaissance.

were Philip van Marnix van St Aldegond, the fiery Calvinistic statesman and friend of William the Silent, Dirck Volckertz. Coornhert (1522 - 1590), Henrick Laurensz. Spieghel (1549-1612), and Roemer Visscher.

Of these Marnix[1] was the greatest. He was a man of culture, ardent faith, and ardent patriotism, and at the same time stood outside the circle of the chambers. The *Wilhelmuslied*, the most famous of the "Geuzenliederen," is probably by him, and his metrical version of the Psalms marks the highest level reached by Dutch poetry in the sixteenth century. The rhythm and stanza-structure is in each adapted to the feeling of the psalm in a manner which is characteristic of Dutch lyrical poetry in the following century:—

Marnix.

> "Straf doch niet in ongenaden
>   Mijn misdaden,
> Heer ! maer heb met mij gedult !
> Wil niet zynd in toorn ontsteken,
>   Aen my wreken
> Mijne sonde en sware schuldt."

De Byenkorf der Heiligh Roomsche Kerk (1569), a savage satire on the Church of Rome, is the first work in which Dutch prose showed itself an instrument of sufficient power and pliability to do the work hitherto assigned to Latin. In Holland, as in France and England, it is to the Reformation's requirement of a polemic, addressed not only to scholars but to

[1] See Kalff's *XVI*^{de} *Eeuw*, ii. 270, and works cited there, including Motley's *Rise of the Dutch Republic*.

"the man in the street," that we owe the evolution of modern prose.

Coornhert, Visscher, and Spieghel[1] were men of more culture than genius. They differ from Marnix also in their attitude towards religion. All of them represent the growth in cultured circles, towards the close of the century, of a more liberal sentiment and a distaste of Calvinistic tyranny. Coornhert's life was spent in controversy, and his own independent position (he was dubbed a "libertine") was the outcome of the study of the Bible and the Fathers on the one hand, and the ancient philosophers on the other. He translated Boethius and Cicero's *De Officiis*, and composed an eclectic treatise on ethics, *Zedekunst dat is Welleven-skunst* (1586), in which Stoic morality is illumined by Christian faith, and which, as a piece of pure, clear, and often striking prose, stands next to Marnix's *Byenkorf*. Spieghel and Visscher were more entirely men of letters than Marnix and Coornhert. As Catholics—though liberal Catholics—they held aloof from public life, but they were both members of the Amsterdam Chamber of Rhetoric, known from its blazon as the "Eglantine."[2] Since 1578 the Eglantine, known also as "De Oude Kamer," had been one of the most important of the chambers, and as

Coornhert.

[1] See Kalff, *XVI^{de} Eeuw*, pp. 295-368, and Penon's *Nederl. Dicht-en-Proza-werken*, iii.

[2] Its motto was *In liefde bloeyende* (blossoming in love), in reference primarily to the Cross, which in an old engraving of the chamber's full coat-of-arms is represented breaking into flower. The blazon was presented to the chambers by Charles V.

the century drew to a close, was much concerned about the purification of the language and the advance of rhetoric. Spieghel and Visscher were leading members, and their houses centres of literary culture. To Visscher's house an additional charm was given by his cultured daughters, Anna and Tesselschade, themselves much admired, if not really distinguished, poetesses, and the friends of Hooft and Huyghens, Brederoo and Vondel. Neither Visscher nor Spieghel was a great poet. Visscher's *Brabbelingh* (1614) and *Sinne-en-Minnepoppen* (1614) consist mainly of epigrams and poems of a half-humorous, half-didactic caste. Spieghel wrote some sonnets and songs which have a little of the grace of their Italian originals, but in later life he grew serious and composed moral and religious lyrics, as well as an elaborate ethical poem in Alexandrines—*Hert-spieghel*—didactic, even prosaic, in spirit, harsh and obscure in style.

Visscher.

Spieghel.

Thus by the close of the sixteenth century the study of classical and Italian literature had done much for the purification of the language, and had quickened a desire for improvement in style and verse. But poetry was still didactic and heavy: no artist had yet appeared to do for Dutch poetry what Spenser by *The Shepheardes Kalender* did for English in 1579,—no poet capable of transplanting the flower of Renaissance poetry from Italian or French soil and naturalising it in Holland. But the seventeenth century had not long to wait before such a poet appeared in Pieter Cornelisz

Hooft,[1] not certainly a poet of the creative genius of Spenser, but a true poet, an artist to the finger-tips, and a man of no less vigour and independence of mind than varied and complete culture.

Hooft.

The oldest son of a wealthy Amsterdam burgher, Hooft was at sixteen a member of the "Oude Kamer," and author of a classical play—*Achilles en Polyxena*—in "rederijkers" style. From June 1598 to May 1601 he was abroad visiting Germany, France, and Italy, studying especially the classical historians, but also doubtless the poets of Italy and France, Petrarch, Ariosto, and Ronsard. His first play that shows Italian influence—*Granida*—appeared in 1605. Meantime he was studying letters and law at Leyden preparatory to official work. In 1609 he was appointed Drost of Muiden and Bailiff of Gooiland, with an official residence, the Muider Slot on the Zuyder Zee, which he occupied in summer, and which he made the centre of a brilliant literary and learned circle known as the "Muiderkring." Here he wrote love-poems in the style which he had begun to cultivate at Leyden, where he celebrated his first love, Brechtje Spieghel, and mourned her early death. His later verses are addressed to his first and second wives, Christina van Erp and Eleonora Hellemans, or to Susanna van Baerle, who married Huyghens, or to

---

[1] *Gedichten*, ed. F. A. Stoett, Amsterdam, 1899. For appreciations see Busken-Huet's brilliant article, *Hooft's Poezie*, in his *Litterarische Fantasien*, and Kalff's *Hooft's Lyriek*, Haarlem, 1901. Stoett's edition has an interesting appendix on the airs to which Hooft's songs were written.

Anna and Tesselschade Visscher. Here he composed his best plays, and in the last years of his life, having prepared himself for the task by a careful study of Tacitus, his historical works, including the great *Nederlandsche Historien*, begun in 1628 and published, but not completed, in 1642. Hooft died in 1648.

Hooft's love-poetry is the most complete representative in Holland of the love-poetry of the Renaissance, with all its conventions—Petrarchian, mythological, and pastoral. He gathered the flower in Italy and France, but he grafted it on a healthy native or naturalised stock of popular airs and rhythms, and coloured it with his own full-blooded Epicurean temperament. He wrote sonnets and wrote them well, whether purely complimentary and conventional, or passionate,—as once at any rate, in "Mijn lief, mijn lief, mijn lief"—or best of all, when the thought is weighty and dignified, as that to Hugo Grotius, which Mr Gosse has translated, or the following sonnet to a newly-born child, his nephew:—

"O fresh young fruit, that from the quiet night
   Of slumber in the womb awaked, must go—
   Time that lets nothing rest hath willed it so—
Forth to the whirl of sense, the realms of light !
Lo ! birth hath given thee o'er to Fortune's might.
   Her school is change. She mingles joy with woe,
   And woe with joy, exalts and hurls below,
Till dazed with hope and fear we darkling fight.
May He Who giveth all things grant thee a heart
Undaunted to withstand the fiercest dart
   Fate in her anger at thy life may speed :
Her gifts too when in milder mood she pours
Riches and joys and honour from full stores,
   Be it thine to use grateful and with good heed."

But it is in lyrical measures of all kinds, especially light and tripping, that Hooft excels, and they are the best expression of his seldom passionate but Epicurean and often playful moods. He can use a stately iambic to express a luxurious melancholy, as in the delightful memories of early love, which Goethe might have written—

"'T gemoedt herwenscht verlooren vrolijckheden,
En wentelt in den schijn des tijts voorleden,
Wanneer 't de stappen siet die 't heeft getreden.

Hoor jck haer naem, of comt me Min mij tegen,
Het bloedt comt, uit mijn teen, nae 't hooft gestegen.
U hartje, Lief, en voelt het geen bewegen?"—

but more commonly a tripping trochaic, dactylic, or anapæstic measure is employed, as in the delightful pastoral—

" Vluchtige nymph waer heen soo snel?
Galathea wacht u wel,
Dat u vlechten
Niet en hechten,
Met haer opgesnoerde goudt
Onder de tacken van dit hout";

or—

" Amaril, had ick hair uit uw tuitjen,
'K wed ick vleughelde' het goodtjen, het guitjen,
Dat met sijn brandt, met sijn boogh, met sijn flitsen,
Landt tegen landt over einde kan hitsen,
En beroofde den listighen stoocker,
Van sijn toorts, sijn geschut en sijn koocker";

or—

" Rosemont, hoordij speelen noch singen?
Siet den daegheraedt op koomen dringen";

or, one of his favourite stanzas, used by Constable—

> "Op's winters endt,
> Wanneer de lent,
> Dat puick en pit der tijen,
> Elck aengenaem
> Voortdoet de kraem
> Van haer kleenooderijen";

and many other rhythms impossible to describe here. No poet in Holland caught so much of the grace and elegance of Renaissance song. And yet Hooft is still a Dutchman. There are no "metaphysics" in his love-poetry, no super-refined idealism. Nature is never far away, and he is capable occasionally of deviating into the prosaic. Nor was he only an Epicurean lover of good verses and beautiful women, but also a scholar and thinker, the disciple of Seneca and Montaigne as well as Petrarch and Ronsard. In one of his epithalamia he turns aside to write an appreciation of Montaigne, which contains the gist of Pascal's famous disquisition on that writer and Epictetus. His *Stichtrijmen en Zededichten*, epigrams, inscriptions, and addresses, are condensed in style and weighty in thought. He was a staunch patriot, though more stoical in his outlook than the sensitive and sympathetic Vondel, and his patriotism finds expression in some noble occasional poems, such as the *Lykklacht van Pieter Dirckz. Hasselaer*, as well as in his tragedies. Vondel is a greater poet than Hooft, but not a more finished artist; and in virtue of his deeper culture and varied achievements—lyric poet, tragedian, comic poet, and historian, the greatest prose-writer of the century—Hooft was regarded as the more eminent man of letters.

The seventeenth century in Holland was prolific of song-books,—collections, generally, of songs by different "hands," the members of some chamber of rhetoric. *Den Nieuwen Lusthof* (1602) and *Den Bloemhof van de Nederlandsche Jeught* were the work principally of members of the Eglantine, *Den Nederduytsche Helicon* (1610) of exiles from the southern Netherlands. The poems in these collections are mainly "refereinen," and their poetic worth is slight. The first collection in which a newer and finer vein appeared, both courtly Italianate love-poetry, and poetry of a more popular character but written with fresh art and vigour, was the *Apollo of ghesang der Muzen wiens lieflijcke stemmen meerendeels in vrolijcke en eerlycke ghescelschappen werden ghesongen* (1615). The best of the courtly songs in this collection were the work of Hooft; the best of the popular songs, the comic or "boertige liedjes," were by the editor of the collection

Brederoo. —the young romantic and comic dramatist, Gerbrand Adriaensz Brederoo (1585-1618).[1] Like Marlowe, the son of a shoemaker but a man of substance, the young Brederoo was educated, not without success, as a painter, but his poetic genius

[1] *De Werken van G. A. Brederoo*, Amst., 1890, in three volumes, with a preface by Dr Kalff, and the poems and different plays edited with notes and introductions by Kalff, Ten Brink, Moltzer, Te Winkel, &c. See also Ten Brink's *Gerbrand Adriaensz Brederoo*, Utrecht, 1858, and the *Brederoo Album*, a special number of *Oud-Holland* issued for the tercentenary of Brederoo's birth in 1885. An excellent edition of *De Spaenschen Brabander* in the *Nederlandsche Klassieken*.

soon made him one of the most brilliant members of
the "Oude Kamer" and of the circle which met at
the house of Hooft and Roemer Visscher. He was
one of Tesselschade's many admirers and suitors, but
his humble birth and convivial tastes did not recommend him to her father. But his experiences as a
"lustig gezel," and an ensign in the Town Guard, made
him intimately acquainted with the life of the people,
and his best work in drama and song is that which
reflects their life and moods.

Of Brederoo's comedies we shall speak later. His
Boertigh amoreus en aendachtigh Groot Liedt-Boeck
(1622) contains, as the name indicates, humorous, love,
and religious songs. The first are by far the best, and
it is only regrettable that he did not write more of
them instead of essaying the more artificial and conventional love-poetry, in which he could not vie with
the cultured Hooft. The *Boerengezelschap*, beginning—

"Arent Pieter Gysen, met Mieuwes, Jaap en Leen,
En Klaasjen, en Kloentjen, die trocken t's amen heen
Na 't Dorp van Vinckeveen
Wangt ouwe Frangs, die gaf sen Gangs
Die worden of ereen"; [1]

---

[1] "Arent Pieter Gysen, with Mieuwes, Jaap, &c., went all together out to the village of Vinckeveen; for old Frans gave his geese to be ridden off." This barbarous sport consisted in riding under a live goose hung on a line by the feet, and pulling off its head in passing. It might be done from a punt carried swiftly under the rope stretched across the stream. Brederoo's poem has all the phases presented in *Christ's Kirk on the Green* and similar popular poems—the gathering in the morning, the jollification, the quarrel, and the dispersion. *Wangt, Frangs, gangs* for *want, Frans* and *gans*, are due to the Amsterdam pronunciation.

and describing how a peasants' meeting for jollification ended in drawn knives and blood, has the swing and animation of a poem by Burns, the spirit of a picture by Jan Steen. None of the others are quite so vigorous, but there are some admirable pieces of peasant moralising on themes familiar to readers of Burns, as "What can a young lassie do wi' an auld man?" the comparative claims of love and a comfortable "tocher," and the dangers of rejecting too often some ardent Duncan Gray. The simpler love-poems, too, written in a frank peasant strain, are often excellent, passionate, and flowing.

Equally gay and fresh—if never showing quite the same passion and descriptive vigour—are the songs of the Dutch poet of English birth, Jan Janszen Starter,[1] who, born in London of Brownist parents, was a member of the "Oude Kamer," but spent several years of his wandering irregular life at Leeuwarden in Friesland, and at Franeker. He finally enlisted with Mansfeld, and seems to have died worn out on a march some time before 1628. He was a dramatist and a facile writer of occasional verses—epithalamia, songs on victories, visits, deaths, &c., as well as love- and drinking-ditties. His employment of the courtly conventions is, of course, less graceful than Hooft's, but his gayer love-poems and his drinking-songs are spirited and

Starter.

---

[1] *De Friesche Lusthof* was republished in 1864. There is a *Bloemlezing* (anthology), ed. by Dr C. H. P. Meier, in the *Klassiek Letterkundig Pantheon*.

rhythmical. His metres seem to me even lighter and more dancing than Brederoo's—

" Doen ik was in 't bloeyen van mijn tyd, in 't groeyen van mijn jaren
In 't groenst, in 't soetst, in 't sotst, in 't boertigst van mijn jeught
Docht ik noyt myn selven met een vrouw of vrouws gelijck te paren,
Maar te leven vry onghebonden in de vreught
        Och, ick wurpt soo veer
        En docht altyd weer
Die een vrouw heeft heeft in 't gemeen een heer."

or,
        " Sult ghy dan niet beginnen een reys ?
        Waarna begheert ghy doch langer te beyen ?
        Naaste Gebuyrtje voldoet ghy mijn eys
        Heft op een Liedtjen, men sal u geleyen."

As Professor Kalff says, Starter's songs sing themselves. Those in a patriotic strain are of the fierce breed of the *Geuzenliederen*.

Starter never forgot altogether his English origin. It betrays itself in occasional phrases; many of his songs are written to English airs; and two at any rate are translations — *Is Bommelalire zoo groote geneughd* and the *Menniste Vryagie*, the latter from the "Wooing of a Puritan" in the old comedy *How a man may choose a good wife from a bad*.[1] Starter's songs were collected in 1621 and 1622 in a volume entitled *De Friesche Lusthof*.

The greatest of Dutch poets united a large measure of the culture of Hooft to the racy vigour of Brederoo,

[1] Dodsley's *Old English Plays*, vol. ix.

and a lyric inspiration as deep and full as that possessed by any poet of the seventeenth century. Joost van den Vondel[1] (1587-1679) was by birth a South Netherlander, which probably explains in part the peculiar ardour of his temperament. His parents were natives of Antwerp, pious Baptists, who were driven by religious persecution to Cologne, where the poet was born in the year, as he said, of the murder of Mary. While he was still a child they migrated to Utrecht and finally to Amsterdam, where his father soon acquired a considerable business in the stocking trade. Vondel's brother received a classical education, but he himself was bred to his father's business—a circumstance, as it proved, by no means unfortunate. The stocking trade conducted by his wife secured him a competence such as he could never have gained from poetry or plays. The only remuneration which the former brought to a Dutch poet were gifts from corporations or individuals, made in return for occasional poems, as epithalamia, poems on victories and state-entries, and others of the kind that the chambers had cultivated. Starter was offered a fixed sum by a group of mer-

Vondel.

---

[1] *De Werken van Joost van den Vondel uitgegeven door Mr J. van Lennep, Herzien en bijgewerkt door J. H. W. Unger*, Leiden, n.d., in thirty volumes. All the works are arranged in chronological order, and there are illustrations, notes, and interesting reprints of contemporary replies to Vondel's satires. The oldest life is Brandt's *Leven van Vondel*, 1683. Kalff's *Vondel's Leven*, 1902, is an interesting study of the man. A. Fischel: *The Life and the Writings of J. v. d. Vondel*, 1854, I have not seen. Most of his tragedies and the satires have been edited in the two series mentioned above.

chants on condition that he would remain in Amsterdam and provide them with songs as required, for each of which he was to receive further two florins. Such a livelihood as Marlowe, Shakespeare, and Jonson obtained from the theatre was not available for a Dutch poet where the actors were the members of the guilds, paid a small sum for their trouble, and a large part of the profits were handed over by the chambers to charitable institutions.

The education which his father denied him Vondel secured for himself, sharing to the full the opinion of his age, which his biographer Brandt lays down with emphasis, that no genius can dispense with learning and especially familiarity with the Greek and Latin poets, "that from their thyme they may suck honey." His earliest noteworthy works, a poem on the death of Henri IV. (1610), the finer *Lofzang over de Scheepsvaert der vereenighde Nederlanden* (1613), and the drama *Het Pascha* (1612), bear traces of his reading of Du Bartas—as popular in Holland as in England—and of Garnier's choruses. He was already grown-up and an author when he began the study of Latin, and later in life he acquired sufficient Greek to translate from that language with the help of more scholarly friends, and to recognise, to the advantage of his later plays, the superiority of the Greek tragedians to Seneca. His successive poems show the effect of his studies on his maturing art, but he never became a scholar such as Milton was, and it is not altogether to be regretted. He was not tempted to Latinise his idiom. The purity of Vondel's language is as much the boast of his people as its richness.

While the form of Vondel's poetry was modified by classical and other literary influences, its spirit was quickened by the events happening around him. Love of God and of his fellow-men was the inspiration of all Vondel's poetry; and he was still a young man, brought up in the particular sect of the Baptists known as the "Waterlanderen," when his sensitive and ardent nature was stirred to its depths by the conflict between the Calvinists and Arminians that ended in the Synod of Dort and the execution of Oldenbarneveldt. At what date some of his earliest satires were written is difficult to say, as they were not published at once. The condensed and pithy *Op de Waegschael van Holland*, beginning

Inspiration.

> "Gommar en Armijn te Hoof
> Dongen om het recht geloof,"

and telling how Maurice's sword turned the scale, is assigned by Brandt to 1618, and the fiery *Geuse Vesper* may belong to the same time; but the first of his works which arrested attention, and may be said to inaugurate his active poetical career, was the Senecan tragedy *Palamedes of Vermoorde Onnoozelheid*, a veiled attack on the intolerance of the Calvinist preachers and the ambition of Prince Maurice, which had brought Oldenbarneveldt to the scaffold. The publication placed Vondel in considerable danger, from which he ultimately escaped with a fine; but it also indicated the appearance of a new and great poet. Readers recognised, Brandt says, a purity of language, an elevation of thought, and a flow of verse superior to anything which Dutch poetry had yet achieved. From the publication of *Palamedes* onwards to the end of his life Vondel poured forth poetry in a never-failing stream, lyric and didactic, satiric and narrative, as well as dramas and translations.

Translation was to Vondel a means of preparing for original work as well as an interest in itself.
Translations. Before he composed *Palamedes* he had put into verse a translation of the *Troades* of Seneca made by himself and some scholarly friends. When he learned Greek he made versions of plays of Euripides and Sophocles, and his works include complete translations in prose and verse of Virgil and Horace, as well as a metrical version of the Psalms and a prose rendering—still in manuscript—of Tasso's *Gerusalemme Liberata*.

The longer didactic poems were the fruit of his conversion to Rome, and include, besides the *Brieven der Heilige Maeghden* (1642), which is
Didactics. not strictly didactic, being the "heroical epistles" of martyred maidens, the *Altaergeheimenissen* (1645), on the Mass, *De Heerlyckheit der Kerke* (1663), on the Church, and the *Bespiegelingen van Godt en Godtsdienst* (1662), on the divine attributes. Before he finally, in 1636, adopted tragedy as the most fitting form for great and grave poetry, he meditated an epic on the subject of Constantine, but the death of his wife broke his purpose, and his only narrative poem, *Johannes de Boetgezant*, is a short epic of six

books, suggested by the *Strage degli Innocenti*, which, like *Paradise Regained*, is in part didactic, the narrative being interrupted by long discourses.

Of the innumerable lyrical poems which he wrote, ranging in length from over thirteen hundred to a couple of lines, *Groote Lofdichten, Zegezangen, Bruiloftdichten*, &c., the great majority were, like the satires or *Hekeldichten*, occasional poems, written to celebrate the sea-power of Holland, the birth of a prince of the House of Orange, the victories of Frederick Henry by land or van Tromp and Ruiter by sea, the building of a new Stadhuis, or the visit of Henrietta Maria, the marriages and deaths of his friends. The poetry of the Chambers of Rhetoric had been of this occasional character, and Vondel's poetry, more than Hooft's, represents the final flower of the Rederijkers' poetry, enriched by the culture of the Renaissance and the strong air of freedom and commercial prosperity. He was the Laureate of Amsterdam, when that city was the heart of the Netherlands, and the Netherlands stood at the very centre of the movements of Western Europe, responsive to all that took place from Sweden to Spain, from Turkey to England, and looking out over the seas, of which her control was just beginning to be disputed, to the Indies, East and West. To Vondel's ardent patriotism, humanity, and piety these themes were far more congenial than the refinements of love which Hooft sang in courtly and Italianate style. Early and happily married, Vondel hardly touched on love except in the Epithalamia he wrote for his friends, and it is only occasionally that the current of his private life rises to the surface in his verse.

Apart from this large and varied literary activity, the chief events of Vondel's life were his conversion to Rome, which took place finally in 1641, though the symptoms of what was going on in the poet's mind can be traced much earlier, and the tragic events which overshadowed his closing years. Vondel's conversion was a result of the same wave of reaction which produced the Anglo-Catholicism of Laud, and which carried Crashaw, with whose ardent and mystical temperament Vondel had much in common, out of the *via media* altogether. Personal ties with Rome Vondel had through his only and much-loved brother, his friends Anna and Tesselschade Visscher, and his daughter, who had preceded him. The Arminians, with whom he fought his first battle against Calvinism, were liberally inclined, moving in the same direction as Hales and Chillingworth. Vondel's profoundly religious nature required more definite dogma, and it is clear from all his later poetry that he found in the faith and practice of the Church of Rome full and intense satisfaction of heart and imagination. Grotius, whom he loved and admired, was carried in the same direction by his study of antiquity.

Conversion.

The closing years of Vondel's life were saddened, though not embittered, by the folly of the son to whom he had transferred his business. He not only failed, but made away with

Last Years.

large sums entrusted to his care. The aged poet came to the rescue, and with the savings of a lifetime cleared his name. Left thus penniless, he was granted a post in the Amsterdam *Mont de Piété*, from which he was allowed to retire on his full salary after ten years' service. He made no complaint, his biographer says, and there is no reference to the circumstances in his work such as we find to Milton's private as well as public misfortunes in *Samson Agonistes*. Vondel had not the sublime egotism of Milton, and his religion was more essentially Christian. He was, like the English poet, a good hater, but his nature was less stern. His hatred of the Gomarists was the reflection from his love of God and his fellow-men, a detestation of the intolerance which brought a father of his country to the scaffold, and of a doctrine which, stated with the logical severity of the seventeenth century, seemed to him an outrage on God and the human heart. But he could no more have written some of the fiercest passages of Milton's episcopal pamphlets than he could have attained to the stern and majestic sublimity of *Paradise Lost*. Vondel's highest flights are on the wings of adoration and love, and recall Crashaw rather than Milton.

Born more than twenty years before Milton, Vondel outlived him by five, dying in 1679, the acknowledged head of Dutch poets, yet alienated to some extent from his people by his change of faith, and never so widely popular as the homely and garrulous Cats.

Death.

Vondel's greatest success was achieved in lyrical poems — under which head his satires fall — and lyrical tragedy, and it will be sufficient here to indicate some aspects of the first of these. Of what I have called his laureate lyrics—pæans and eulogies—time has evaporated some of the interest, and poems of this sort produced in such abundance were necessarily unequal. Much of the content is conventional (whether mythological or pastoral), and Vondel handles the conventional with less art than Hooft. Nor had he the architectonic skill with which Milton builds an elaborate ode. His inspiration ebbs and flows, and the style with it, becoming at times harsh, bombastic, and prosaic. Yet, though unequal, these poems are wonderfully vital. Even such an elaborate and detailed description of Amsterdam and its commercial activity as is given in the *Inwyding van het Stadhuis* (1655) sustains the reader's interest to the end by its wonderfully animated and sympathetic picture of the stress of life in what was the greatest mercantile city in the world. In his short tractate on poetry, *Aenleyding ter Nederduitsche Dichtkunst* (1650), Vondel condemns emptiness above all faults. "If you are engaged on a work demanding sustained inspiration (*van eenen langen adem*), see to it that it flag neither in the middle nor at the close, but keep full sail throughout." These glowing and flowing poems, though certainly "long - winded," surprise by their sustained ardour, fertility of thought, and broad, full rhythm.

But Vondel is more effective and felicitous in the shorter and intenser satires. These were not, like Huyghens', composed on the classical model, but are rather political squibs, popular songs and ballads, often in the nasal Amsterdam dialect, or short, pithy, epigrammatic copies of verses. Indignation has seldom inspired more burning lines than the short and famous *Geuse Vesper of Sieckentroost* on the execution of Oldenbarneveldt:—

Justice.

> " Did he bear the fate of Holland
>   On his heart,
> To the latest breath he drew
>   With bitter smart;
> Thus to lave a perjured sword
>   With stainless blood,
> And to batten crow and raven
>   On his good?
>
> Was it well to carve that neck
>   Within whose veins
> Age the loyal blood had withered?
>   'Mong his gains
> Were not found the Spanish pistoles
>   Foul with treason,
> Strewn to whet the mob's wild hate,
>   That knows no reason.
>
> But the Cruelty and Greed
>   Which plucked the sword
> Ruthless from the sheath, now mourns
>   With bitter word;
> What avails for us, alas! that
>   Blood and gain
> Now to dull Remorse's cruel
>   Gnawing pain?

> Ay! content you now all preachers
>   East and West,
> Pray the saints of Dort to find your
>   Conscience rest!
> 'Tis in vain! the Lord stands knocking
>   At the door,
> And that blood will plead for vengeance
>   Evermore!"

The *Decretum Horribile* is an impassioned expression of his abhorrence of the doctrine which consigned newly-born infants to eternal perdition. The lofty strain of consolation in which the poem closes indicates clearly what it was in Romanism—its appeal to the heart and the imagination—which charmed him as it did Crashaw. These two poems are probably the finest expression of the mingled indignation and sorrow which is the purest note in Vondel's satire. *Roskam* (1630) and *Harpoen* (1630) are more quiet and argumentative expostulations against endless theological hatred and strife. His humour and his command of the racy dialect of Amsterdam are well shown in *Rommelpot van 't Hanekot* (1627), where the mutual amenities of the Contra-Remonstrant clergy are portrayed under the figure of a roost full of gobbling, scratching, fighting cocks. More purely poetic and lyric are the two strange ballads he wrote, to some popular air, when in 1654 his *Lucifer* was driven from the stage by the fury of the clergy. In an almost Shelleyan strain he sings of the fate of Orpheus, torn by the "rout that made the hideous roar"—

> "Toen Orfeus met zyn keel,
> Toen Orfeus met zyn keel, en veel
> In 't mastbosch zong en speelde
> Tierelier, tierelier
> Dat schoone, lustprieel."

None of Vondel's poems stand higher to-day than the satires in the estimation of his countrymen. "As satirist," says Professor Moltzer, "Vondel is a phœnix. In him Dutch poetry attained her zenith,—that is what we may say in thinking of by far the most of his satirical poems and verses." The reason is in part that in none of his poems is Vondel's peculiar ardour of feeling combined with so much of sanity and humour, so free from pedantry and the note of overstrained ecstasy which one may detect in his as in Crashaw's religious poetry.

But making allowance for this strain, the intensity of the satirical poems is only heightened and purified in the best of Vondel's religious poems. *Religion.* Such are, leaving the tragedies aside, the beautiful dedication to the Virgin of the *Brieven der Heilige Maeghden*, the *De Koningklyke Harp*, — a rhapsody on the Psalms of David,—and the best of the consolatory *Lykklachten*. Even in reading the longer didactic poems, though there is in them much that is hardly suitable for poetry, one is amazed by the poet's unflagging ardour, the range of his study, and the fertility of his thought.

The tenderness of Vondel's feeling is as marked as its ardour. He has written of nature with delicacy and freshness in his *Wiltzang, Lantghezang*, and other lyrics and choruses, including the stately flowing *Rynstroom*. The Dutch poets played a little with the usual pastoral convention, but the sincerity of their feeling for nature as they saw it around them is as clear from their poems as from their pictures. An intenser tenderness animates the few poems in which Vondel wrote of his private sorrows, notably the *Uitvaert van mijn Dochterken* (1633), so modern in its simplicity and discarding of seventeenth-century conventions, so artistic in its evolution and metre. It is difficult to imagine an English or French poet of the period describing a child's games without mythology or periphrasis or conceit, as Vondel ventured to do:—

Nature and Sorrow.

> "Or followed by her friends, a lusty troop,
>   Trundled her hoop
> Along the street, or swung shouting with glee,
>   Or dandled on her knee
>   Her doll with graver airs,
>   Foretaste of woman's cares."

In the similar poem which he wrote thirty years later, on the death of his grandchild, sorrow yields to a lofty strain of devout resignation—

> "When this our life on earth hath ended,
>   Begins an endless life above;
>   A life of God and angels tended,
>   His gift to those that earn His love."

Ardour, elevation, tenderness, music, these are the great qualities of Vondel's poetry, and they place him, in spite of defects which will appear more clearly when we come to speak of his drama, at the head of Dutch poets.

The poets of whom we have spoken hitherto belong all more or less closely to the Amsterdam circle of which the "Oude Kamer" was the general, Hooft's residence the more select, centre. Of lesser lights, such as Anna and Tesselschade Visscher, it is impossible to speak here. Outside Amsterdam there were of course other chambers, centres of dramatic and poetic activity. Zeeland was "a nest of singing-birds." The *Zeeuwsche Nachtegaal*, published at Middelburg in 1623, contained poems "door verscheyden treffelicke Zeeuwsche Poeten." And the song-books mentioned earlier are but some of many which were issued, and not in Amsterdam alone.

Outside Amsterdam.

The most distinguished, if not the most popular, of the poets not connected with Amsterdam is the poet and statesman of The Hague, Constantijn Huyghens[1] (1596-1687), the famous father of a more famous son. French was the language of the Court, and Huyghens, who was all his life in the active service of the House of Orange, as well as one of the most cultured men of his day, was

Huyghens.

---

[1] *Gedichten*, ed. Dr J. A. Worp, in nine volumes. All the poems, Latin, French, Dutch, &c., are arranged in chronological order. Huyghens' own arrangement is preserved in the *Pantheon* edition of the *Korenbloemen*, edited by Dr J. van Vloten, and revised in parts by H. J. Eymael and J. Heinsius. Much has been written of late on Huyghens as man and poet by Potgieter, Jonckbloet, Kalff, Eymael, and others.

almost as prolific a composer in French and Latin as in Dutch. He tried his hand, like Milton, at Italian verses, and he translated from Guarini and Marino, as well as some thirteen hundred Spanish proverbs and about twenty of Donne's songs and elegies. Huyghens visited England three or four times in the service of his country, was knighted by James, and seems to have seen something of English men of letters at the house of Sir Robert Killigrew.

For his courtly and politer poetry Huyghens used French by preference. His French poems are quite in the affected, Marinistic, complimentary vein of the day. In Dutch his tone becomes more homely, his style more masculine,—not without affectations, but affectations which recall Jonson and Donne rather than Marino. He used his native language to correspond in playful and delightful verses with intimate friends, such as Hooft and Tesselschade Visscher, and to compose epigrams and longer poems of a satiric, didactic, and reflective character. The *Otia* (1625) included poems in various languages. In the *Korenbloemen* (flowers gathered from among the grain of a busy life), published towards the close of his long life (1672), he collected his Dutch poems alone in twenty-seven books. Of these, fifteen contain epigrams (*Sneldichten*), one translations, two lighter lyrics and epistles. The longer poems include *'t Kostelyck Mal* (1622), a satire on the dress of the day in the usual Alexandrines; *'t Voorhout* (1621), a fresh and sparkling eulogy of the forest outside The Hague, written in stanzas of eight trochaic dimeters, catalectic and acatalectic, and rhyming alternately; *Dagh-Werck*, an unfinished description of a day in his life, in the same metre, but one of the most affected and obscure in style of his poems; *Euphrasia of Ooghen-Troost* (1647); *Hofwyck* (1652); and *Zeestraet* (1672),—all moralising, chatty poems, called forth by incidents in his life, as a lady friend's losing her eye, the building of a "Buitenplaats" or country-house, the construction of the road from The Hague to Schevening. A poem in the same key, a survey of his life written in the evening of his days, *Cluyswerck*, was printed by Jonckbloet in 1841, and did much to revive interest in Huyghens, Potgieter, the poet and critic, making it the occasion of an enthusiastic appreciation.

Huyghens has neither the ardour and tenderness of Vondel nor the artistic instinct of Hooft. He could only be called the first metrist among his contemporaries if Praed were allowed the same distinction among his. Huyghens' more playful verses are exceedingly clever:—

> "Tessel-schaetge
> Cameraedtge
> Die dit praedtge
> Uit mijn hert
> En van binnen
> Uit het spinnen
> Van mijn sinnen
> Hebt ontwert."

But Vondel does the same thing with more feeling in *Kinderlyck*, beginning—

> "Constantijntje
> 't Zalig kijndje
> Cherubijntje
>   Van omhoog
> d'ijdelheden
> hier beneden
> Uitlacht met een lodderoog."

And Huyghens has none of the grander music of Vondel,[1] nor the charming Ronsardist strain of Hooft.

Huyghens is a poetic moralist. His poems are as occasional as Vondel's, but the occasion is generally personal, and he uses it to talk at large about himself, his work, his enjoyment of nature, of music, of books, and domestic life, and to moralise in a satirical or more elevated and pious strain. At times he sinks almost to the level of Cats in his homely didactic prattle, but usually his outlook is less bourgeois and popular, his knowledge of humanity finer, and his poems better seasoned with wit and humour. His style is, in some works especially, harsh and obscure. Donne has been made responsible for this defect, but Mr Eymael has shown that Huyghens had probably not read Donne's poems before 1630, when his own style was formed and beginning to grow simpler; and indeed the resemblance is very

---

[1] One of Huyghens' poems has some of the combined intensity and homeliness of Vondel's satires, namely, *Scheeps-Praat* (*Ship's Talk*) on the death of Prince Maurice, the stout "schipper zonder weerga," which tells how Frederick Henry rebuked the disconsolate sailors, reminding them that he too was an experienced pilot—

> "North and South too many an hour
>   I've by the skipper held the wheel;
> Seen too many a hissing shower
>   O'er my old sou'-wester reel."

superficial between Donne's subtle mind and bizarre imagination and the fundamental simplicity of Huyghens' character. In poetry such as Huyghens' much depends upon the personality of the author, and it is the simplicity and freshness of his nature, combined with wide culture, insight, and a noble piety, which made Potgieter call him "one of the most lovable men that ever lived."

Huyghens' friend, the first of Zeeland poets, and for long the most popular of Dutch poets, Jacob Cats[1] (1577-1660), is a difficult author for a foreigner to appreciate. He is the incarnation of all that is most bourgeois and practical in the Dutch character. He was, like Huyghens, a man of means. He grew rich by reclaiming "polders" from the sea, and was a sharp—at times, Huyghens affirmed, too sharp—business man. He acknowledges that—

Cats.

"Het is een deftigh [difficult] werk en waert te zijn gepresen
Godtzalig en met een oock rijck te mogen wezen."

Cats was a learned man, and served his country as Raedpensionaris, visiting England twice as an am-

[1] Many old and handsome editions, with finely-engraved emblems and illustrations. Most of his works have been republished in the *Pantheon*. Cats' long-established reputation as the most popular and edifying of Dutch poets was assailed by Potgieter in his *Rijks-Museum*, 1844. He was followed by Busken-Huet in *De Gids*, 1863, who made great sport of the "God-fearing money-maker and his low-toned morality." Jonckbloet was more judicial but equally severe. Cats has been defended by Dr A. Kuyper—recently Prime Minister of Holland—in *Het Kalvinisme en de Kunst*, 1888. All that can be said for Cats as a poet by a discriminating critic will be found in Professor Kalff's *Jacob Cats*, Haarlem, 1901.

bassador. Like Huyghens, he was an ardent Calvinist, and had come under the influence of English "pietism," which had taken root in Zeeland.

Cats was a voluminous poet. Beginning with Emblems,—all the Dutch poets wrote Emblems,—he poured forth poems in a didactic strain, and written in a monotonous Alexandrine couplet, of which the best known are *Houwelick* (1625) and *'s Werelts Begin, Midden, Eynde besloten in den Trou-ring* (1634). He is as profoundly interested in the subject of marriage as Coventry Patmore; but if the latter occasionally approaches Cats in his descent to homely details, Cats has none of Patmore's delicacy of feeling and soaring flights. Practical advice, enforced by diffusely narrated stories—not always of the chastest, for as the moral is coming to set all right, why omit piquant details?— prattle about himself, these are the staple of Cats' poems. His language is pure, and many of his proverbial sayings have passed into current use, but his work is of interest for the student of national thought and morality rather than of literature.

There is much greater depth of feeling and music of verse in the *Stichtelyke Rymen* of another religious poet, Dirk Rafaelsz Camphuysen[1] (1586-1627). Born at Gorkum, educated at Leyden, a teacher for some time at Utrecht, he became a "predikant," and was for a short time an exceedingly popular preacher in Vleuten. But his sympathies

Camphuysen.

[1] See Kalff's *Camphuysen Herdacht*, 1901. A selection edited by Van Vloten is included in the *Pantheon*.

were too liberal. He was turned out as an Arminian, and led a wandering and troubled life till his death at Dokkum, where he had worked as a flax-spinner. Camphuysen's poems are all religious, and include a paraphrase of the Psalms. His aim is like Cats', "te stichten en met een vermaken," to edify while pleasing; but his religion was of the more inward and finer type of our own Herbert's and Vaughan's, though he expresses his feelings in a less conceited style and in simpler melody. His poems are written to be sung as well as read: "Zoo wel leezelijk als zingelijk, zoo wel zingelijk als leezelijk," are his own words. His *Maysche Morgenstond*, a beautiful song of returning spring, and the *Christelijk Gevecht*, are the best known of his poems to-day, but they are not the only ones in which feeling and melody are both alike arresting, and void of conceit or convention as his art is, it is by no means naïve. Witness the structure of such a verse as this:—

> "Hoe lang, ach Heer!
> Hoe lang noch mist mijn ziel den zoeten stand
>   Van 'twaar verheugen!
>   Helaas, wanneer
> Wanneer zal ik eens 'teeuwig vaderland
>   Bestreden meugen?
> Jeruzalem des hoogsten Konings stad
> Des deugd-betrachters hoop en hartenschat
> Die u maar kend is licht des levens zat
>   Te lang, te lang valt bang!"

This power of writing flowing musical verse echoing each mood of feeling belongs to another religious poet, the Catholic Johannes Stalpert van der

Wiele[1] (1579-1630). Of noble parentage, born in The
Hague, for a short time an advocate in that
Van der Wiele. city, Stalpert van der Wiele soon abandoned
the world for the Church, and after studying divinity
at Louvain was ordained deacon at Malines. He
was at Brussels for some time, and visited Paris and
Rome, but his ultimate sphere of duty was in Delft,
Rotterdam, and Schiedam. His poems, issued at
Delft, Hertogenbosch, and Antwerp, were written for
the edification of his Catholic flock. The longer
are mostly legends of saints and martyrs. *Hemelryck*
(1621) tells in flowing Alexandrines how the persecuting
Adrian of Nicomedia was converted by the description
which the martyrs gave him of the joys of
heaven. Others deal with the martyrdom of Laurence
and Hippolytus, St Agnes' denunciation of gorgeous
clothing, and the points at issue between Rome and
Calvin. But Stalpert van der Wiele's best-known
and best poems are the religious songs he wrote
to old and frequently secular airs. *Den Schat der
geestelijcke Lofsangen, gemaeckt op de feest-daegen van
'tgeheele jaer* (1634), is a Roman *Christian Year*. Of
the deeper thought and more elaborate art of Keble
there is as little in Van der Wiele's songs as of the
conceits, quaint or imaginative, of our seventeenth-
century devotional poets. His songs are written for
the people, and express the simplest Catholic piety
with the naturalness and music of the folk-songs on

[1] *Leven en Uitgelezen Dichten*, by Van Vloten, K. L. Pantheon,
1865. The first critic to do justice to Van der Wiele was J. A.
Alberdingk Thijm.

which they are based, and have enjoyed, Alberdingk Thijm says, the fate of such songs—to be printed in various collections without the collector or printer knowing by whom they were composed.

It is impossible here to do more than mention the names of some of the poets of the second generation, the followers and imitators of Hooft and Vondel. The pastoral and mythological conventions were generally rather clumsily handled in the song-books. The patriotic and laureate lyrics, into which Vondel put so much music and colour, were essayed with no great success by Reyer Ansloo[1] (1626-1669) and Gheeraerdt Brandt (1626-1685), more famous as a historian and biographer, whose *Uitvaert van Hugo Groot* and similar poems have a fair measure of rhetorical vigour; Joachim Oudaen (1628-1692); Johannes Vollenhove (1631-1708), whom Vondel called his son; and Johannes Antonides van der Goes (1647-1684), whose *Ystroom* is the most ambitious of these Vondelian pieces. But it needed all the ardour of Vondel's lyrical temperament to give vitality and interest to these long poems with their blend of matter-of-fact details and pedantic mythology.

Followers of Vondel and Hooft.

The last poet whose verses have the naturalness and music of the best Dutch lyrical poetry was a disciple of Hooft rather than Vondel. In Jan Luiken's[2] *Duytse Lier* (1672) ends that

Luiken.

[1] Extracts from Ansloo, Brandt, &c., in Penon, *op. cit.*, iv.
[2] *Duitsche Lier opnieuw uitgegeven door Dr Maurits Sabbe*, K. L. Pantheon.

lyrical stream which, beginning in the Middle Ages, preserved in the folk-songs of the fifteenth and sixteenth centuries rather than in the "rijmelarij" of the "Rederijkers," was by Hooft and Vondel purified, deepened, and enlarged. Born in Amsterdam in 1649, Luiken was trained as an etcher, and wrote his love-songs while a young man. At the age of twenty-six he became a pious and mystical Christian, and his later works, *Het Leerzaam Huisraad, Byekorf des Gemoeds, d'Onwaerdige Wereld,* are written in a didactic strain, lightened by occasional flashes of his purer lyrical gift. But the *Duytse Lier* contains the finest love-songs after Hooft's. Luiken reproduces some of Hooft's metres, especially his iambic quatrains and the "Galatea" stanza quoted above; but he has many of his own, light and musical. He was the only Dutch poet who learnt from Hooft the secret of that fresh and charming artifice which the latter, and so many others, were taught by Ronsard—

> "De dageraat begint te blinken
> De Roosjes zijn aan't open gaan;
> De Nucht're Zon komt peerlen drinken,
> De zuyde wind speelt met de blaan:
> Het Nachtegaaltjen fluyt,
> En't Schaapje scheert het kruyt;
>   Hoe zoet
>   Is een gemoet,
>   Met zulk een vreugd gevoet."

With such music the great period in Dutch poetry ended, and the lyrical began to give way, as elsewhere, to the prosaic and rhetorical.

To a comparatively small country like Holland the use of Latin as an international language of scholarship was an even more obvious convenience than to larger countries. The most distinguished Hollander of the Renaissance, Erasmus, is not thought of as a Dutch author, and the same is true, in a somewhat less degree, of several notable Dutchmen of the seventeenth century, distinguished not only by their learning but by their contributions to the *belles lettres* of humanism, such as Daniel Heinsius, Isaac Vossius, and Hugo Grotius. Both Heinsius and Grotius wrote some poems in their native tongue, but their fame rests on their Latin lyrics and tragedies, and still more securely on the treatises of the former on criticism, of the latter on international law. Grotius, indeed, was one of the great men of the century, and were this primarily a history of thought and scholarship would require specially full treatment. In the present chapter he must yield to those who cultivated their native tongue.

Latin Prose.

The principal writer of artistic prose in the earlier seventeenth century—the successor of Coornhert in the modelling of Dutch upon Latin prose—was Hooft. To the writing of prose Hooft brought all, and more than all, the careful study and elaborate art which he bestowed upon his poems. Some of his letters to his friends show that he could write in a simple and playful style, though in general they, too, smell of the lamp. But the stately Muse of History was to be served in the seventeenth century

Dutch—Hooft.

only in costly, brocaded robes. Hooft's model was Tacitus. Virgil he accounted, Brandt tells us, the first of Latin poets, Tacitus of historians and prose-writers. He had read his works fifty-two times, and had made at different periods of his life a complete translation of them. Following in the footsteps of his master, he prepared for his greater task by composing a *Leven van Hendrik den Groote* (1626), for which he was ennobled by Louis XI., and the *Rampzaaligheden der Verheffinge van den Huize van Medicis* (1649).

While he was thus elaborating his style, he was also gathering materials for his great work on the liberation of Holland. He spared no pains to arrive at the truth, and submitted the work as it proceeded to friends to be criticised. For the military portions especially he sought the help of qualified persons; and he endeavoured above all things to be just—to acknowledge the shortcomings of his countrymen and the virtues of the foe. The misfortune attending this elaboration is that the work was never finished, and that an unnecessary degree of artificiality was given to the style. The imaginary speeches delivered on critical occasions, after the manner of Thucydides and Tacitus, are the chief blots in the eye of a modern critic; but to a native ear Hooft's coinages—the result of his zeal for the purification of the language from words of French origin, his occasional harsh and too condensed constructions, his Latin idiom and sentence order—are more obvious. But these are flaws in a dignified and impressive narrative. It is impossible to read any of the greater episodes without recognising and admiring the vigour, the compression, the loftiness, and the fire with which Hooft tells his moving story. His deep interest in the events he narrates recalls Clarendon, but he is not so constantly the advocate of one side; and the condensation of his style and his frequent felicitous figures are more in the manner of Bacon in the *Henry VII.*, although he has not the same detached interest in Macchiavelian kingcraft. A figure like that which follows is quite in Bacon's style: "But these considerations weighed little with that oppressor who had already set his heart upon the desolating of cities, the stamping out of liberty, and the confiscation of property. 'I have ere this,' said he, 'tamed a people of iron, and shall I not now be able to tame a people of butter?' For he did not bethink him that hard metal may be hammered, but not soft curd, which he that would handle must deal gently withal." And the following might have come out of the essay *Of Dissimulation:* "Sparing of words indeed was this Prince, and wont to say that no craft of concealment can cover his steps that lets himself be taken a-prattling."

Of other prose work in the period there is not much to say. Attempts to imitate the French pastoral and heroic romance were unsuccessful. Hooft's dignified historical prose was most successfully cultivated by Gheeraert Brandt, whose poetry has been mentioned. The son of a watchmaker in Amsterdam, whose family, like Vondel's, came from

Brandt.

Antwerp, Brandt was at seventeen the author of a tragedy, and at twenty he composed a funeral oration on the death of Hooft, which was recited by an actor in the theatre and received with immense applause. As a fact, the speech was simply a translation of Du Perron's *Oraison Funèbre* for Ronsard. Later, when he had left watchmaking and become a Predikant, he composed his *Historie van de Reformatie* (1668-74), the second part of which, dealing with the Arminian controversy, provoked the bitter hostility of the Calvinists. He composed short and sympathetic biographies of Hooft and Vondel for editions of their works, and a *Leven van de Ruiter* (1687), which is the finest example of his prose.

Brandt's model is quite clearly the dignified prose of Hooft with its elaborate periods. "The perception of this," he begins his Life of Van Ruiter, "and the utility for the state involved, has moved me to devote some of my hours to the description of his praiseworthy life and valiant achievements, with the firm purpose in this work, which may God bless, of confining myself strictly within the bounds prescribed by the supreme law for historians, and, in the service of truth alone, of narrating as well the errors of friends as the praise of enemies; ever bearing in mind that I write not of olden times whose memory has grown dim, but of things that happened but yesterday, and, as it were, under the eyes of many who took part in them, assisting or being present, friends and strangers, who without doubt should I, in this wide sea of manifold events, wander from the course of truth, misled by favour or hatred, would punish me and expose me to shame." Brandt's diction, however, is simpler than Hooft's, his style generally clearer, and at its best not less vivid and impressive. A lighter and more conversational prose was developed by Van Effen under French and English influence.

CHAPTER II.

HOLLAND—DRAMA.

INTRODUCTORY—MEDIÆVAL DRAMA—PROBLEM CONNECTED THEREWITH—THE MORALITIES, HISTORIES, AND FARCES OF THE CHAMBERS—RENAISSANCE SECULAR DRAMA — THE EGLANTINE — COSTER AND RODENBURG—BREDEROO—HOOFT—"QUARREL OF THE PLAYERS"—COSTER'S ACADEMY — THE "AMSTERDAMSCHE KAMER" AND NEW THEATRE — VONDEL — DEVELOPMENT OF HIS DRAMA — INDIVIDUAL TRAGEDIES—CHARACTERISATION AND CRITICISM—FAILURE OF THE ROMANTIC AND CLASSICAL DRAMA—JAN VOS'S 'ARAN EN TITUS'—LATER PLAYS.

THE history of the drama in Holland in the seventeenth century is the history of an effort which was not fully successful. The same elements were present as in England and France. The Morality gave way to the tragi-comedy or dramatised story-play, romantic and historical. The classical drama, represented especially by Seneca, Plautus, and Terence, was studied, admired, and imitated by a band of young men eager to elevate and refine the literature of their country. But the elements never succeeded in combining to produce a living and great drama, on either the English

Introductory.

romantic or the French classical model. Vondel and Hooft put some of their best poetry into dramatic form, but neither of them ever clearly grasped the fact that the essence of drama is neither the incident of the popular plays nor the sentiment, style, and morality of the scholarly, but the vivid presentation of the agitations and conflicts of the human soul, revealed in a motived and naturally evolved action. The history of the experiment is, however, not without interest and significance, and in comedy some humorous and realistic work was produced not unworthy of the countrymen of Jan Steen and Adriaen van Ostade.

The oldest Mediæval plays in Dutch which have survived are of a purely secular character, four serious, so-called *abele Spelen*, and six farces —*kluchten* or *sotternien*—belonging to the later fourteenth century.[1] Of the serious plays, three —*Esmoreit, Gloriant, Lanseloet van Denemarken*—are romances dramatised in simple and naïve manner, but by no means ineffectively. In *Esmoreit* a prince is sold by his ambitious cousin to the Turks, but returns at the right moment to rescue his mother,

Mediæval Plays.

---

[1] They were edited for the first time by Hoffmann von Fallersleben from the single manuscript in which they are all preserved (the Hulthemsche MS. of the early fifteenth century, the *répertoire* of some guild or company) in that scholar's *Horæ Belgicæ*, and were later included by Professor H. E. Moltzer in his *Bibliotheek van Middelnederlandsche Letterkunde* (Groningen, 1868-75), of which a new edition is in course of publication. For the questions raised see Jonckbloet's *Geschiedenis*, ii. 6. 1, and works cited there; also Creizenach, *Geschichte des neueren Dramas*, Fünftes Buch (Halle, 1901).

who has been imprisoned for years by her husband's jealousy, and marries the daughter of the Turkish king. *Lanseloet* tells of a lady, Sandrijn, wronged by her princely lover at his mother's instance, of her marriage, and her first lover's repentance and death. Parts of the story are narrated, not dramatised, and the whole is closed with a moral. *Gloriant*, the longest, is a story of a Christian Duke of Brunswick's love for a Saracen maiden, the daughter of a bitter foe of the Duke's family. They are well-constructed little plays—none is longer than 1142 lines—and evidently written for a stage with fixed stations and its own conventions. *Winter ende Somer* is more of a simple "débat" or "estrif," a dispute between Summer and Winter as to their respective merits, in which some boers and a beggar take part, and which is closed by Venus. The "sotternien," or farces, which followed the "abele spelen"—

> "Nu swight en maeckt een ghestille
> Dit voorspel is ghedaen
> Men sal u eene sotternie spelen gaan"—

were dramatised short stories of humorous and coarse incidents in the life of the people.

These purely secular plays are older than any religious plays which have survived in Dutch. The *Maastrichtsche Paaschspel*, written in the dialect of Limburg, dates possibly from the second quarter of the fourteenth century, but the oldest extant Flemish Mystery, *De eerste Bliscap van Marie*, was performed at Brussels in 1444.

Their Source (?).

Still later is the *Spel van den Heiligen Sacrament vander Nyeuwervaert*, performed at Breda about 1500. The relation in which the secular and religious plays stand to each other in time led Mone in 1838 to claim for the drama of the Netherlands a unique secular origin. It was descended, he argued, not from the religious drama but from the dialogues recited by one or more "sprekers," of whose performances we hear in old account-books. The question has been much debated, the descent from the religious plays under French influence being urged by Wybrands and Jonckbloet, the native and independent by Moltzer and J. H. Gallée. It cannot be discussed at length in a chapter whose subject is only in passing the Mediæval drama. It is not possible in any case to get beyond conjecture, as the plays form an isolated group. How far the "tweespraken" or dialogues (occasionally even "driespraken") referred to in account books were dramatic in character and were represented by more than one "zegger," is matter solely of conjecture. Wybrands and Jonckbloet consider that the statements of Maerlant, and other evidence, point to their having been recited by one person representing the different speakers. On the other hand, the descent of the "abele spelen" from the mysteries under French influence is equally conjectural, or more so, for the only French secular serious play which is older than the fifteenth century — the *Griseldis* — stands, as Creizenach points out, in obviously close relationship to the Virgin Mary Miracle-plays, which the Dutch plays as obviously do not, being entirely secular in tone. As Professor Moltzer says, if the Dutch "abele spelen" are descended from the French, there must have existed in France before the fifteenth century a highly developed secular drama alongside the ecclesiastical, of which these plays give us our only conception. The pieces of Adam de la Halle—described by Mr Gregory Smith in an earlier volume —stand quite by themselves, and were probably composed for private performance.

Mysteries and Miracle-plays were produced in abundance in the fifteenth century; but in the sixteenth the favourite plays of the chambers of rhetoric were the Moralities or *Zinnespelen*, the seriousness of which they relieved with *Esbattementen* or farces. The chambers which issued the challenge for a *Landjuweel* propounded the subject of the plays to be performed—*e.g.*, "What is the greatest mystery or grace provided by God for the salvation of man?" "What is Man's greatest consolation in death?" "What best prompts Man to the cultivation of art?" The *Zinnespelen* lent themselves readily to Catholic and anti-Catholic propagandism. At a great *Landjuweel* held at Ghent in 1539 the Protestant doctrines of Justification, and the superiority of the Bible and St Augustine to Thomas Aquinas and Scotus, were set forth in the boldest terms. The tone of the Ghent plays was serious, but in *Den boom der schrifturen*, performed at Middelburg in the same year, Romanism was bitterly satirised. Philip the Second naturally forbade this sort of thing, and the song became in

Moralities.

North Holland a more potent instrument than the play.

Besides the pure Morality, the "rederijkers" produced plays of the kind which in the Netherlands, as in England, formed a bridge from the abstract Morality to the more concrete history or tragi-comedy — plays which used as a vehicle for moral instruction a story taken from the Bible, from national history, or from classical history and mythology, and brought on the stage together concrete persons and abstractions. *Spel van Sinne van Charon*, *Spel van Jason*, *Spel van den Koninck van Frankrike*, *Abraham's Utganck*, are examples of plays not unlike Bale's *Kyng Johan* and Preston's *Cambyses*. It is perhaps interesting to remember that Bale was for several years an exile in the Low Countries. One well-known and impressive Morality was composed in Holland, *Den Spiegel der Salicheit van Elkerlyck* (our *Everyman*), which was possibly the work of a South-Netherland cleric and mystical writer, Pieter Dorland (1454-1507). Many of the clergy were members of the Chambers, some of them holding the post of "facteur" or poet to the Chamber. The literary and dramatic worth of *Elkerlyck*, however, is far above the average of the usual "Rederijkers'" poetry. The *Zinnespelen* and Scriptural Moralities are in general, from a dramatic and literary point of view, wearisome and worthless performances. There is more life in the farces such as Cornelis Everaert (1509-1533) produced in abundance. *Van den Visscher, van Stout en Onbescaemt, 't Spel van den hoogen Wint*

Transition Plays.

en den zoeten Reyn, are significant titles, and recall the names of Heywood's *Merry Interludes*.

Both Moralities and Scripture-plays continued to be composed and performed by the chambers in the seventeenth century. In the southern and Catholic Low Countries especially they were popular, and in the Brabantian Chamber at Amsterdam, whose members came from the southern provinces, they continued in fashion when the "Oude Kamer" or "Eglantine" was experimenting in secular romantic and classical plays. Vondel's earliest work was a "rederijker's" Biblical drama, and his religious tragedies thus stand in a direct line of descent from the Mediæval Mysteries, however much their final form may have been influenced by Garnier, Seneca, Grotius, and Sophocles. But though the *Zinnespelen* lingered, the movement in the opening seventeenth century was towards the secular drama, and this movement, as elsewhere, manifested itself in two distinct but often quaintly blended results. The one was the so-called tragi-comedies (*treur-bly-einde-spelen*), the dramatised *novelle* or romances which are found everywhere at the Renaissance, full of incident, regardless of the "unities," and mingling serious with farcical scenes. Even in these the influence of the classical drama is traceable in the occasionally Senecan character of the story, in the division into acts, and the oddly tagged-on choruses. The other result is the more regular imitation of Seneca, Plautus, and Terence. The plays of the first kind in Holland show unmistakably the

Secularisation.

influence of Lope de Vega and also of the English drama; those of the latter equally clearly that of Garnier and the Pléiade.

The leaders in the dramatic activity of the Eglantine were Hooft—whose work from the first took a classical direction — Dr Samuel Coster,[1] Brederoo, and Theodore Rodenburg. Coster (1579-1660 ?), a leading spirit in the life of the chamber, was a mediocre dramatist and poet. His best work is found in his farces, the *Boerenklucht van Teeuwijs de Boer en men Juffer van Grevelinckhuysen* (1612) and *Tysken van der Schilden* (1613), coarse but vigorous and genial plays. His later and more serious plays, as *Isabella* and the would-be classical *Itys* (1615), *Polyxena* (1619), and *Iphigenia* (1617 ?), an attack upon the Calvinist clergy, are crude and melodramatic.

The "Eglantine" Dramatists.

Rodenburg's[2] numerous tragi-comedies abound in incident, and his characters — *e.g.*, in *Jaloersche Studenten*—are drawn with some sympathy, but his style is pedantic and affected. He had visited both Spain and England, and of his extant plays some are adaptations from Lope, one a translation of Cyril Tourneur's *Revenger's Tragedy*. He might, like Hardy, have had historic interest if his work had led to important developments, but Rodenburg and Coster, with Hardy's fatal deficiency in style, have even less dramatic power.

Rodenburg (1580?-1638).

Brederoo[3] and Hooft alone wrote plays which deserve

[1] *Samuel Coster's Werken uitg. R. A. Kollewijn*, Haarlem, 1883.
[2] No modern edition.
[3] Editions, *vid. sup.*, p. 18 note.

to be dignified with the name of literature. After his
first crude essays Hooft took for his models
Brederoo. Italian pastoral drama and French Senecan
tragedy. Brederoo followed in his earliest plays the
more romantic and popular line of Rodenburg, of
Hardy, and of the English dramatists, blending scenes
from popular romances or *novelle* with humorous and
realistic pictures of servants and peasants. But
nothing is more characteristic of the difference
between the English and the Dutch drama than the
complete failure of the romantic part of Brederoo's
plays and of those of his fellow-dramatists. His
three first plays, *Treurspel van Rodderick en Alphonsus*
(1611-16), *Griane* (1612), and *Lucelle* (1616), are dramatised Spanish romances or love-stories, but the serious
scenes lack entirely that poetic and romantic spirit
with which not only Shakespeare, but lesser men
like Greene and Dekker, Middleton and Fletcher, in-
vested their versions of Italian and Spanish novellas.
The serious part of a Shakespearean comedy is, Hazlitt
says, generally better than the comic. Be that as it
may, the exact opposite is the case with Brederoo,
whose dramatic reputation rests entirely upon the
comic interludes in the above-mentioned plays, the
three farces, *Klucht van de Koe*, *Klucht van Symen
sonder Soeticheyt*, and *Klucht van den Molenaer*, which
he wrote between 1612 and 1613, and his two more
regular and elaborate comedies, *'t Moortje* (1615-17)
and *De Spaensche Brabander* (1617-18).

The reason of Brederoo's failure to rise on the
ethereal wings of romance is to be found doubtless

in his own genius and that of his people, but perhaps also in another circumstance which explains a good deal in the history of Dutch drama and poetry. Dutch literature is from the fourteenth century onward a bourgeois literature. The Dutch poets and dramatists never enjoyed the courtly audiences whose influence did so much for the English drama in the sixteenth century, and helped the French in the seventeenth century to throw off the barbarism of Hardy's plays and the pedantry of Garnier's. It is among the highest and lowest classes of society that art is able to develop least impeded by the restrictions of practical morality. That freedom Dutch literature obtained in farce and popular song, never completely in higher and more serious literature, which accordingly retained to the end something of the bourgeois and didactic tone it acquired with Maerlant.

Dutch Plays not romantic.

The servants and peasants in Brederoo's comedies are drawn to the life. Coarse humour, racy description, proverbial wisdom, jest, and sarcasm flow from their lips in a rich stream of "Amsterdamsch" dialect. The three farces are also little masterpieces—the traditional themes of the "Sotternien" handled with the *verve* and range of expression of a man of genius. A peasant is tricked into selling his own cow by the thief who has "lifted" it the night before, and that for the sole benefit of the thief. The miller artfully cuckolds himself. The morality is on a level with that of the Miller's and the Reeve's tale, but so is the

Brederoo's Comedy.

comic art. In the more elaborate comedies, which Brederoo, who was no scholar himself, wrote at the instance of his cultured and pedantic friends, the construction and character-drawing are weak, but there is the same wealth of language and the same power of vivid description. The best things in *'t Moortje* (1617), a not altogether successful attempt to adapt the *Eunuchus* of Terence to the conditions of life in Holland, are the long digressions, in one of which he describes, with a Rabelaisian extravagance of racy detail, a stroll through the markets of his native town; in another a skating party on the canals; while in a third an old servant details her recollections of life in a wealthy burgher's house. He was even happier in the picture of Amsterdam life which he gave in *De Spaensche Brabander* (1617), a dramatisation and adaptation of the picaresque romance *Lazarillo de Tormes*. The hero of Brederoo's play is a boastful Brabander, a bankrupt fugitive from Antwerp, living on the trustful "botte Hollanders" of Amsterdam. His servant is an adroit beggar whose wits bring in more than his master's boasts. The story is slight, and the connection between the scenes loose. It is a study of humours, not in the analytic, microscopic style of Jonson, but vivid and genial. The realism of the Spanish original was quite in the Dutch taste, and some of the scenes, as that in which two courtesans relate their history, has a realism unrelieved by poetry which is quite foreign to the Elizabethan drama, and hardly appears in our literature before Defoe. A comic dramatist such as Molière, a compeller of thoughtful laughter, Brederoo was not, nor had he any large measure of the creative genius and all-comprehending humour of Shakespeare; but he could paint with a masterly hand, and with some of Aristophanes', Rabelais', and Shakespeare's wealth of phrase, the life and conversation of the people.

The scholarly Hooft naturally shared the taste of his age for classical tragedy and comedy and Italian pastoral. His earliest plays hardly count. *Achilles en Polyxena* and *Theseus en Ariadne* are "rederijkers'" plays, though the language is purer and more poetic, and the latter contains one lovely song—

Hooft's Classical Plays.

> "Ick schouw de werelt aen,
> En nae gewoonte gaen
> Sie ick vast alle dingen,
> Sij sijn dan groot of cleen ;
> Maer ick helas ! alleen
> Blijf vol veranderingen."

Granida (1605)—a pastoral, the plot of which was apparently derived from the English *Mucedorus*, the spirit and language, especially of the charming opening scenes, from Tasso and Guarini — is the first artistic Dutch play, and its art is, characteristically, poetic rather than dramatic. The same is true of his Senecan historical tragedies, *Geeraert van Velsen* (1613) and *Baeto* (1617, pr. 1626). They both have a political interest,—*Geeraert* patriotic, the *Baeto* a noble and poetic plea for peace without and within, written a year before the execution of Oldenbarneveldt and the outbreak of the Thirty Years' War. The subject of the first, chosen partly from the association of the story with the Muider Slot, is the tale told by Melis Stoke, and in a fine old ballad, of the vengeance executed on Count Floris V. for his violation of the wife of Geeraert van Velsen, and its national consequences. The patriotic note is struck in the character of Gysbrecht van Amstel, who resists the proposal to call in English aid against the Count, and in the eloquent, although dramatically irrelevant, closing prophecy of the liberation of Holland, the rise of the House of Nassau, the daring of Dutch navigators, and the greatness of Amsterdam. The *Baeto* dramatises a mythical story of the origin of Batavia, and emphasises in the hero the "pietas," the courage, and the love of peace which Hooft would have to be the fundamental virtues of his people. This political motive lends his tragedies a warmth which is too often lacking to the Renaissance plays on classical subjects, but the interest and beauty appear in the poetry alone. Dramatically they have all the faults of their kind, but they contain fine descriptions, elevated speeches, and musical choruses. Hooft's master in the latter was Garnier. In *Geeraert* he adopts two or three of that poet's metres, and handles them with skill. In the *Baeto* he put some of his weightiest thought and sincerest feeling into delightful lyrical measures. There is a chorus on the return of spring which has some of the music of Mr Swinburne's "The hounds of spring are on winter's traces"; one on the blessings of peace which throbs with noble emotion; and the most mov-

ing thing in either of the plays is the antiphonal song
of exile, chanted by bands of maidens:—

> "O soete beecken! waer nevens in swang
> Te gaen eendraghtig plagh onse sang
>   Hoogheffende 't doen
>   Der helden koen
>   Van overlang."

In the *Cluchtige Comedy van Warenar, dat is, Aulularia van Plautus nae's lants gelegentheid verduitscht* (1616), which Hooft was stimulated to write by the success of Brederoo's *'t Moortje*, he showed that he knew the people and their speech as well almost as Brederoo himself, and had more constructive though less descriptive power, and less wealth of humorous phrase. Besides these longer plays, Hooft wrote *Tafelspelen*, and he adapted Aretino's *lo Ipocrito* as *Schijnheyligh*, not softening the realistic details.

The literary and dramatic reforms which Coster, Hooft, and Brederoo initiated in the Eglantine soon led, as such movements often do, to disagreements.[1] The reasons were in part personal. Rodenburg's tragi-comedies, which he produced with something of the fertility of Hardy —twenty-two have survived — were regarded as barbarous by the admirers of the classical drama, while at the same time their popularity, and the vanity of Rodenburg, excited disgust. But there were other and less personal reasons. The growth of a more artistic drama necessitated some change in the

Dissensions in the "Eglantine."

[1] Jonckbloet gives a full account of the quarrel, *Geschiedenis*, ii. p. 101 f.

HOLLAND—DRAMA.

system by which the parts for representation were distributed among the members of the chamber, and the time had also come for the separation of the educational from the artistic functions of the chambers. The time was past for giving instruction in theology and science through the medium of plays. Rodenburg continued the tradition, but Brederoo scoffed at philosophising ostlers and servant-girls. The result of the dissension was a schism led by Coster, under whom the more brilliant and learned members swarmed off and founded the famous "Coster's Academy," whose blazon was a beehive and motto *Yver*. The intention of the founders was to separate and yet retain both the functions of the older chambers. The Academy was to be a college and a theatre—an "Extension College" giving instruction in the vernacular, whereas the universities allowed only the use of Latin—and a theatre for the production of plays composed in accordance with the "rules" of Aristotle and Horace.

In the first of their purposes—

"de burgery te stichten
En met de fackel van de duytsche taal te lichten"—

they were defeated by the jealousy of the clergy, and the fact was not forgotten by the dramatists. The years immediately following the opening of the Academy were years of great dramatic activity. Coster's *Polyxena*, Hooft's *Warenar*, and Brederoo's *Spaensche Brabander* were all Academy plays, and war was waged not only with Rodenburg but with the clergy. But in 1620 the strife ended.

Coster's Academy.

Brederoo was dead; Coster and Hooft became silent; gradually the old breach was healed, and the Academy and Eglantine united in the "Amsterdamsche Kamer," for which a new theatre was built, and opened in 1638 with the performance of Vondel's *Gysbrecht van Amstel*.

But the year 1620 marked not only the close of the "quarrel of the players," but the end of the first movement towards the creation of a new drama. Hooft, Brederoo, and Coster had certainly done much to raise the serious drama above the level of "rederijkers'" work, as may be clearly seen by comparing their plays with those of writers for the Brabantian Chamber such as Kolm and De Koning. Still, they had not succeeded in creating a drama at once poetic and dramatically interesting. The popular plays continued to be tragi-comedies— plays half history, half morality—and farces. Van der Eembd's *Harlemse Belegeringh* and *Sophonisba* (1620), Jan Harmensz. Krul's *Diana* (1628), Jacob Struys's *Romeo en Juliette* (based on Bandello's novel, but showing no acquaintance with Shakespeare's play), H. Roelandt's *Biron* (1629), are the names of one or two through which the present writer has struggled without finding much to reward the trouble. The style varies between bombast and utter banality. Roelandt's Biron has the brag of Chapman's hero, but not the lofty poetic eloquence. The best popular plays are the farces, often unspeakably coarse. The scholarly drama, on the other hand, passed from Hooft to Vondel,—a great lyrical poet certainly, but not the man to do what Shakespeare effected for the romantic, or Corneille for the classical, drama.

Vondel formed his dramatic style slowly, and it was not until 1635 that he selected tragedy as the principal vehicle for the expression of his sentiments, religious and political. His earliest play, *Het Pascha ofte de Verlossinge Israels uit Egypten* (published 1612), produced by the Brabantian Chamber, where Biblical plays were still in vogue, has the naïve structure and dramatic weakness of the Chamber plays; but the death of the first-born is well described, and the style and versification show already the hand of a poet. *Hierusalem Verwoest* (1620), with which Vondel made his *début* at Coster's Academy, is not stronger dramatically, but the language is purer, and the choruses have the fire and pulse of his best poetry. Neither of these plays, however, was later included by Vondel among his works. They were "'prentice" pieces, written before he had made acquaintance with the classics. The first fruit of his self-imposed study of Latin was a translation, made in collaboration with Hooft and Laurens Reael, of the *Troades* of Seneca, which Grotius had entitled the "Queen of tragedies." This was followed in 1625 by his first important tragedy, the *Palamedes*, — of whose political significance we have spoken already, — a play thoroughly Senecan in structure, spirit, and machinery.

For seven years after the appearance of the *Palamedes* Vondel was better known as a poet than a dramatist. Like Milton, he hesitated as he became

familiar with classical models whether he should
<small>Return to the stage.</small> express his religious sentiments in epic or tragic form. It was in part his admiration for Grotius which brought him back to the stage. In 1635 Grotius published his Latin tragedy *Sophompaneas*. Vondel, with the help of two friends, translated the play, and, to judge from the number of times it was subsequently performed at the new theatre, it must have been received with favour from the beginning. It was possibly the success of this translation, as well as Vondel's reputation as the first poet of the Academy, — now merged in the new Amsterdam Chamber,—which led to his being invited to compose the play with which the new theatre was opened in the following year. The subject he chose—
<small>Gysbrecht van Amstel.</small> *Gysbrecht van Amstel* (1637)—was suggested by Hooft's *Geeraerdt van Velzen*, and has the same patriotic motive,—to sing the praises of Amsterdam, her greatness material and spiritual. The device Vondel adopted is characteristic of the strange blend in Dutch poetry at this period of intense patriotism, national and local, with the devout and pedantic admiration of the classics. In substance the *Gysbrecht* is a dramatisation of the fall of Troy as narrated in the second book of the Æneid, adapted to Amsterdam, and that the Amsterdam not of the twelfth century, but of the poet's own day. The story is essentially an epic one, and the most striking scenes have to be narrated in detailed picturesque descriptions, appropriate enough in the mouth of Æneas as he sits at Dido's table while the shadows fall, and renews past

griefs, not equally so when delivered in the midst of the scene itself, while the roar of flames and fighting and the crash of falling buildings are audible in the background. But Vondel's conception of a dramatic action was neither Shakespeare's nor Corneille's. His exercise in satirical and lyrical-descriptive poetry had matured his style, and the narrations are glowing, the Alexandrines stately and musical, while two of the choruses—in which another note, the Catholic, that was soon to become dominant in his poetry, appears for the first time—are among the finest of Vondel's lyrics,—the beautiful Christmas song—

"O kerstnacht schooner dan de dagen,"

and the noble ode to married love—

"Waer werd oprechter trouw
Dan tusschen man en vrouw
Ter wereld oit gevonden."

The Catholic atmosphere of the *Gysbrecht*—its glorification of Christmas and of martyrdom—excited the suspicions of the Amsterdam clergy, and in fact Vondel three years later became a Catholic, and that with all the zeal and devotion of his South Netherland and poetic temperament. The change affected all his subsequent work, colouring even his political sentiments, for the Catholics of Holland were in much closer sympathy than the Protestants with the inhabitants of the southern provinces.

The *Gysbrecht* was followed by thirty years of strenuous activity as a dramatist on Vondel's part, which did not exclude the composition of long didactic and narrative poems, as well as translations and lyrics in abundance. The number of his original tragedies—excluding translations—is twenty-three, of which only a few can be mentioned here, preliminary to a word or two on Vondel's tragic art generally.

Dramatic activity.

The *Maeghden*, with which he followed up *Gysbrecht* in 1639, is practically a Miracle-play, on the traditional martyrdom of Saint Ursula at Cologne, and interests only by its Catholic and patriotic sentiment. Vondel's love of Cologne, the city of his birth, is beautifully expressed in one of the finest of his personal lyrics, the *Olyftack aan Gustaaf Adolf* (1632).

The *Gebroeders* of the same year handles with considerable dramatic power the difficult subject of the expiatory murder of Saul's sons, which attracted other dramatists of the Renaissance. Conflicting passions are portrayed with more than usual power, but the impression produced by the play as a whole is confused and weakened by the division of the author's sympathies as man and poet on the one hand, as pious exponent of the Bible on the other. Jonckbloet's theory, that in the person of the Archpriest, who persuades David to comply with the demand of the Gibeonites, Vondel was attacking the Calvinist clergy, is not admissible in view of the poet's religious and ecclesiastical sympathies at this stage. He approves David's act though he commiserates the victims. In the dedication to Vossius he places the conduct of David on a level with Abraham's sacrifice of Isaac. David was a favourite character with Vondel as the ancestor and type of Christ, and the play was written to celebrate his eminent piety, and because of the tragic character of the story—as "tragic" was understood by admirers of Seneca like Vossius and Grotius. They praised the play enthusiastically, and it was performed forty-six times before the poet's death. An interesting record of the actors who performed, and of the staging prepared for the representation, has been preserved. The altar, candlestick, and priest's robes were all accurately and gorgeously reproduced, and the description emphasises the strangeness of the phenomenon presented by these sacred plays in so Protestant a country —the large element of the Middle Ages which the Chambers of Rhetoric preserved.

In the following year (1640) Vondel composed a couple of plays intended to form, with his translations of *Sophompaneas*, a trilogy on the story of Joseph— *Joseph in Dothan* and *Joseph in Egypten*. Characters of the pure and simple piety of Joseph, as Vondel portrays him, or saints and martyrs like Ursula and Jephtha's daughter, were specially dear to Vondel's heart, and are drawn with considerable charm. With his wicked characters he was too entirely out of sympathy to lend them strength and dignity. But the voluptuous passion of Jempsar, the wife of Potiphar, in *Joseph in Egypten*, and of Urania in *Noah*, is painted with colour and power. *Pieter en Pauwel* (1641) is another saints' play, more edifying to believers than dramatic, and so is *Marie Stuart* (1646). Mary dies a stainless martyr for the Catholic faith. Vondel was a zealous champion of the Queen of Scots and of her grandson Charles. But the saint, a favourite hero or heroine with Vondel, is perhaps the least dramatic of characters, for in the saint's mind all conflict is over. Even in Corneille's great tragedy, it is not the lyrical Polyeucte who most interests, but the more human and agitated Pauline and Sévère.

Vondel returned to more solid ground in the *Leeuwendaelers* (1648), a pastoral drama written to celebrate the Treaty of Munster, which closed the eighty years' war. Peace was the note which Vondel, like Hooft in the *Baeto*, desired to strike. He had no wish to exult over Spain or to keep alive proud memories of the war. He regretted the final separation of the northern from the southern Netherlands, and was inclined to think that there had been wrong on both sides, and that the war had been prolonged by those who wished to fish in troubled waters. Instead of exalting the Netherlands or the House of Orange, he preferred to describe the evils of dissension and the blessings of peace. He took the plot of his pastoral allegory from the *Pastor Fido*, with suggestions from the *Aminta*, but the sentiments are Dutch, bourgeois, not courtly, and so are the scenes, green pastures and cows, canals and sluices,— a people for whom the mere glory of war has no attraction, which loves above all things peace and prosperity. In this play and those which followed Vondel's dramatic art attained maturity.

In *Salomon* (1648) he dealt with the falling away

to idolatry of the old king under the influence of his Phenician wife, Sidonia. The hero is too weak and unimpressive for a tragedy, but Sidonia has greater power, the best scenes are dramatic, and the workmanship in every respect—invention, arrangement, verse—is admirable.

Salomon.

Still finer and greater is *Lucifer*[1] (1654), which has been described as the shining summit of Dutch poetry of the seventeenth century. Vondel was not fettered here by having to follow too closely a story narrated in Scripture. The references to the fall of Lucifer, on which this and other works on the subject rest, are few, short, and not a little obscure. The poet was free to invent his own incidents and motives. In doing so, he drew upon his memory and observation of events which had moved him passionately. That he intended to write a political allegory—like *Palamedes*, or even *De Leeuwendaelers*—is, apart from other considerations, incompatible with the poet's reverential attitude towards sacred and Scriptural subjects. But in describing a great mutiny in heaven, a rising of the angels to vindicate their "rights," and the leaders who use it to further personal ambition, he recalled the use Prince Maurice had made of popular feeling against Oldenbarneveldt, and the progress of the contemporary rebellion in England with the rise of Cromwell. The result was a play more dramatic and moving, in action

Lucifer.

---

[1] The *Lucifer* has been translated by Mr Leonard Charles van Noppen, an American student. For relation to *Paradise Lost*, see chap. iv., note.

and character, than anything he had written. Lucifer's deeply wounded pride, Belial's Iago-like instigations, Beelzebub's "policy," Michael's stern and unbending loyalty, Raphael's pleading, are clearly and grandly drawn. The interviews are not mere interchanges of argumentative platitudes, but show us the clash of contending passions. It is not so much with Milton's epic treatment of the same theme that Vondel's play invites comparison, except in the descriptive passages, —and even here the differences are as great as the resemblances, — but, one is tempted to say, with Shakespeare's earlier Marlowesque histories, their comparatively simple but intense characters and vehement eloquence. Even the choral odes are not undramatic excrescences. The chorus of angels takes an active part in the debates, and their songs are evoked naturally and directly by the events of the moment. The faults of the tragedy are the necessary exclusion of God from direct participation in the action, and the inclusion of the fall of Adam in what might be called a postscript. The latter action should have been left for another play, and Vondel felt this, for he wrote another on the subject.

In none of his subsequent plays does Vondel come so near to a dramatic and tragic as well as a literary and poetic masterpiece. Excluding trans-
Later Plays. lations from Sophocles and Euripides, he wrote eleven more tragedies. *Jeptha* (1659), *Koning David in Ballingschap* (1660), *Koning David Herstelt* (1660), *Samson* (1660), *Adonias* (1661), *Adam in Ballingschap* (1664), and *Noah* (1667), are Biblical;

Salmoneus (1656) and *Faeton of Reuckeloze Stoutheit* (1663), mythological; *Zungchin of Ondergang der Sineesche Heerschappye* (1666) was inspired by his enthusiasm for the Jesuit missions to China; and *Batavische Gebroeders* (1662) is on a patriotic theme similar to Hooft's *Baeto*. Of these we need mention only four.

In *Jeptha* (1659) Vondel boasted that he had produced a tragedy which complied exactly with the requirements of the critics from Aristotle to Vossius and La Mesnardières, while adhering closer to Scripture than Buchanan; but the chief interest of the play, apart from the poetry, is the ingenuity with which Vondel has used the story to propagate the Catholic condemnation of private judgment. In Buchanan's play Jephtha represents uninstructed religious feeling. A man must keep his oath, cost what it may. The priest who dissuades him from the sacrifice voices a more enlightened religion, which forbids to keep an oath when to do so involves a crime. In Vondel's play the conflict is between the conscience of the individual and the power and authority of the priest. Pressed to consult the High Priest before sacrificing his daughter, Jephtha justifies the appeal to his own conscience, and cries in Luther's words—

"Godt is mijn burgh en vaste toeverlaet."

But Vondel fails to make Jephtha's conflict tragic. His sorrow and remorse when he realises his error are wanting in dignity. The poet's favourite character is the maiden martyr Iphis, who comes to the sacrifice arrayed as a bride, and with the words of the Psalmist on her lips—

> "Geen hygend hart, vervolgt en afgeronnen,
> Verlangde oit meer naer koele waterbronnen,
> Als mijne ziel, na zoo veel strijts, verlangt
> En hyght naar Godt, waeraen mijn leven hangt."

Vondel's *Samson* (1660) will not bear comparison for a moment with *Samson Agonistes*. His hero has none of the grandeur of Milton's, and the play is inferior both in unity of interest and elevation of sentiment. Vondel had not Milton's intense personal sympathy with the Old Testament hero. He fills up his drama with irrelevant discussions of the attitude of the Church to the stage, and the relation between Church and State. Samson interests him only as a type of a greater deliverer.

Samson.

The *Adam in Ballingschap* (1664) is dramatically a weak and bourgeois presentation of the story of the Fall. Adam is scolded into participation in Eve's action. But it contains some lyrical antiphonies (an angel's song of the Creation, and songs of adoration and joy between Adam and Eve) which remind an English reader of the *Prometheus Unbound*. This poetic and lyric interest Vondel's dramas retained to the end. *Noah*, composed when he was eighty, has lyrical choruses as light and fresh as the work of a poet in the first flush of his power. The song on the death of the swan is a perfect harmony of feeling and rhythm—

Adam.

Noah.

"Stervende zingtze een vrolijk liet
　　In 't suikerriet
　　In 't suikerriet.
Zy tart de nijdighe doot uit lust
　　Met quinckeleeren
　　En triomfeeren
　　En sterft gerust."

The dramatic weakness of Vondel's tragedies, the failure of any one of them to present quite adequately a great dramatic action or impressive characters, was pointed out in an unsparing review by Jonckbloet, who was acutely out of sympathy with both the classical pedantry of the seventeenth century and Vondel's religious sentiment. Much of what he said is undeniable, and applies not only to Vondel's plays but to the whole range of Renaissance classical tragedy, under which head I do not include the tragedies of Corneille and Racine. Yet the fact remains that Vondel's plays were written to be acted; that they enjoyed a considerable measure of popularity; and, moreover, that they were the work of a poet of genius — even if that genius was lyrical rather than dramatic — and a poet who, despite a touch of the pedantry of his age, was inspired in general, not by pedantic but by personal, patriotic, and religious motives. It is worth while, therefore, to try and look at Vondel's tragedies not from the point of view of any hard and fast æsthetic theory of the drama, whether classical or romantic, but from the poet's own point of view; not comparing them with the very different tragedies of Shakespeare or Racine, but trying to discover whether they have any special feature which distinguishes them from the purely artificial Senecan tragedy of the Renaissance. Such an aspect has been indicated by Professor Te Winkel.[1] In an interesting and exhaustive study of Vondel's tragedies, he has pointed out that in spirit and intention Vondel's dramas are a direct continuation of the Mysteries and Miracle-plays of the Middle Ages, and may be as justly styled the last flowering of the sacred drama in the north as Calderon's religious pieces were in the south. This statement applies to the form as well as the content of Vondel's earlier attempts, *Het Pascha* and *Hierusalem Verwoest*. Similar Biblical plays were composed by other members of the Brabantian Chamber, and both their spirit and naïve structure are those of the Mysteries, though the style is that of the Rederijkers. Vondel, however, as we have seen, rejected these plays, and his later tragedies were shaped by his study of Seneca, of the school drama of Buchanan and Hugo Grotius, of Sophocles and Euripides, as well as of the classical critics interpreted for him by Heinsius and Vossius. But none of these altered radically his conception of the character of a dramatic action, and none of them affected the spirit and motive with which he wrote his plays.

Vondel's Plays descended from the Mysteries.

The mode in which an action was presented in a classical play of the Renaissance was, after all, despite

[1] *Bladzijden uit de Geschiedenis der Nederlandsche Letterkunde* Haarlem, 1882, pp. 135-343.

the Unities, not very different from that of the Mysteries and Moralities. In both cases the story was generally familiar, the plot a series of episodes. There was — as I will indicate more fully in the chapter on the French drama—little or no endeavour to develop a story from the interaction of character and circumstance in such a way as to excite suspense. The finest tragedies consist of a series of statuesque scenes draped in oratorical and lyrical verse. Vondel's tragedies are built on the same plan. He takes a well-known story, generally from the Bible, and presents it in a series of scenes filled with long speeches or balanced dialogue. Single scenes are dramatically written, and in some of the best plays — *Salomon*, *Joseph in Dothan*, *Leeuwendaelers*—the story is simply and naturally conducted. But only in *Lucifer* is our interest aroused as to the final choice and consequent fate of the hero; and even in *Lucifer* the attention is, for dramatic effect, too frequently distracted from the central figure.

But dramatic effect is not the end which Vondel had first of all in view. If the classical drama modified the form of his tragedies, the spirit remained unaltered. With all their faults, his tragedies are no frigid classical reconstructions, but the expression of his deepest feelings, and their purpose is that of the Mysteries—edification and exaltation. He would doubtless, like Grotius, have chosen for his chief play the central theme of the Mysteries, but Vondel wrote in the vernacular and for the stage, and the reception of the *Lucifer*, which dealt with the first act in the great drama, warned him from venturing on dangerous ground. It was driven from the stage by the Amsterdam preachers after three performances, and the *Salmoneus*, one of his two plays on classical subjects, was written to make use of the artificial heaven prepared for the *Lucifer*. But though he did not venture on the subject of the Passion, not only are the great majority of his plays taken from the Bible, but, as Professor Te Winkel points out, those subjects are generally selected (as in the Mysteries) which were regarded as typifying the death and resurrection of Christ—the sacrifice of Jephtha's daughter, the death of Samson type of Him

"Who in His death gave death a mortal wound,"

the stories of Noah, Joseph, and David.

This devotional purpose set rigid limits to Vondel's dramatic art. He could not handle his stories as Shakespeare did Holinshed, or Corneille Roman and Byzantine history, altering the record and supplying the motives. He stood with bowed head before the incidents and the persons as he found them in Scripture. He expressly accepts Vossius' rule, "What God's Book says, of necessity; what it does not say, sparingly; what conflicts with it, on no account." He does best work, therefore, where the story is already well motived, or where the record is scanty. But Vondel's dramas, to be fully appreciated, need to be read in the devotional spirit in which they were written,—a difficult task for readers

who have become critical even of Vondel's sources,
and are not prepared to accept the execution of
Saul's sons as an instance of Divine justice. The
difficulty has led critics like Dr Jonckbloet to find
political allegory in plays such as *Gebroeders* and
Lucifer, where the poet's devotional feeling would
never have admitted it. And another barrier to the
enjoyment of Vondel's plays as such is the not in-
frequently bourgeois tone of his piety. His characters
are sometimes almost ludicrously unheroic in act and
speech. The Dutch as a people have, it may be, no
great love for the dramatically heroic—the fine point
of honour, splendid but desolating passions. No
nation has done more heroic deeds; none has cared
less for mere glory in comparison with duty, material
prosperity, and domestic happiness.

Vondel's plays are therefore not much read to-day,
except by students and by generous lovers of poetry,
Their lyrical features. of which there is abundance, especially in the choral odes. The late Dr
Nicholas Beets,[1] himself a poet, and the most
humorous painter of Dutch life, has enumerated
and illustrated the beauties of Vondel's choruses,
and they are those of all his best lyric poetry, ardour
and sweetness, fertility and subtlety of thought, learning and moral nobility, and with all and above all a
music of verse which is at every turn the full and
resonant counterpart of the feeling. In this, the
supreme gift of the lyrical poet, possessed by Dutch
poetry in an extraordinarily high degree, Vondel ex-

[1] *Verscheidenheden*, Haarlem, 1885.

cels all his countrymen. Vague in thought at times, in ardour and sustained rhythmical flight the chorus on God in *Lucifer* could not be easily surpassed. No translation can do justice to the original, but a single strophe may give some impression of the tone of Vondel's religious verse:—

> "Who is it that, enthroned on high,
>   Deep in unfathomable light,
> Nor time nor time's eternity
>   May measure being infinite?
> The Self-existent, Self-sustaining,
>   By and in whom all things that are,
> Their course prescribed unchanged retaining,
>   Move round as round their central star:
> The Sun of suns, His life that lendeth
>   To all our soul conceives, and all
> Conception's limit that transcendeth,
>   The Fount, the Sea whence on us fall
> Blessings unnumbered from Him flowing,
>   Proof of His wisdom, power, and grace,
> Evoked from nought ere yet this glowing
>   Palace of Heaven arose in space;
> Where we our eyes with our wings veiling
>   Before His radiant Majesty,
> Chanting the hymn of praise unfailing,
>   Bend as we chant the adoring knee,
> And, falling on our face in prayer,
>   Cry, 'Who is He? Oh! tell, proclaim!
> With tongue of Seraphim declare—
>   Or knows no tongue no thought that Name?'"

The antiphonal song of the six days' creation in *Adam*, the description of morning and the country in *Palamedes*, the Phœnix chorus in *Joseph*, the already-mentioned Christmas and marriage songs in

Gysbrecht, are others of the many pieces which, when all has been said that can be of his dramatic weakness, leave Vondel still the pride of his countrymen.

It is maintained in a subsequent chapter that there is no conclusive evidence that Milton was in any way influenced by Vondel. There is no room here to compare them in detail. Milton was both a more perfect artist and a greater creative genius. No single character in all Vondel's plays lives in the imagination like Milton's Satan. Vondel is more purely the lyric poet at the mercy of his inspiration. Yet there are some notes in Vondel's lyre of which Milton never learned the secret. A less finished artist, a less sublime and overawing poet of the supernatural, there is a sweetness, a charm, in Vondel's poetry which Milton's too soon lost, and his religious verse glows with a purer flame of love for God and his fellow-men.

Milton and Vondel.

It is not difficult to understand that Vondel's dramas failed to achieve for the Dutch drama what Corneille's effected for the French. They might be admired by men of taste and scholarship who were not repelled by the Catholic atmosphere, but they could never thrill a crowded theatre like *Hamlet* or the *Cid.* Their failure in this respect is proved by the resurgence in 1641 of the romantic drama in a crude and barbaric form. In that year Jan Vos (*c.* 1620-1667), a glazier in Amsterdam, created a sensation, which affected even scholars like Barlaeus, and poets such as Hooft and Vondel, by his *Aran en Titus, of Wraek*

Jan Vos.

en Weerwraek, a vigorous but bombastic and melodramatic version of the *Titus Andronicus* story, which the Dutch poet may have derived from Shakespeare's play. If he did he was careful to exclude the poetry with which Shakespeare relieved his painful scenes. The impression which this melodramatic piece produced was due to the fact that, so far as it goes, melodrama is drama, which stately pageants, long speeches, and choral odes are not. The taste of scholars was not shocked by horrors which Seneca had taught them were appropriate to tragedy so long as crime ended in punishment, and learned and unlearned alike enjoyed the interest of incident and suspense. But *Aran en Titus* indicated unmistakably the failure of the effort inaugurated by the Eglantine—the miscarriage of the Dutch drama. The popular and the scholarly had failed to blend in a living and cultured drama. The classical remained a school drama, the romantic degenerated rapidly. Vos's *Medea*, with which the second new theatre in Amsterdam was opened in 1662, was a melodrama furnished with elaborate stage-effects, and "Konst en vliegh-werck" were soon reckoned to be of more importance than characters and poetry. It is unnecessary to speak of slipshod translations from Spanish and French. The society whose motto was "Nil volentibus arduum" spoke much in the closing years of the century about the reform of the stage; but their vanity was greater than their genius, and they did not rise above translation.

It fared a little better with that vigorous native

growth, the farce, the coarseness and general slack morality of which shows how much of a popular growth it continued to be. One of Brederoo's closest imitators was Willem Diederickz. Hooft, author of five farcical pieces; but the best writers of comedy and farce in the latter years of the century were Dr Pieter Bernagie (1650-1699), who wrote some fifteen tragedies and comedies, "free and natural pictures of the native manners of his time," which have not yet disappeared from the stage, and Thomas Asselijn, whose *Jan Klaaszen* (1682), *Stiefmoer* (1684), *Stiefvaar* (1690), and *Spilpenning* (1690), are brilliant comic pictures of life and manners in the last days of the century. *Jan Klaaszen of Gewaande Dienstmaagd* is his masterpiece, inferior in comic spirit to Brederoo's best work, but superior in construction, owing, doubtless, in some measure to the beneficial influence of Molière. Asselijn and Langendijk, who followed, lie somewhat outside the period covered in this volume.

Later Comedy.

CHAPTER III.

ENGLISH DRAMA.

INTRODUCTORY — GEORGE CHAPMAN — BEN JONSON — HIS THEORY OF COMEDY — EARLIER COMEDIES — TRAGEDIES — MATURE COMEDIES — LAST PLAYS — MASQUES — 'SAD SHEPHERD' — ACHIEVEMENT — MARSTON — DEKKER — MIDDLETON — HEYWOOD — WEBSTER — HIS TWO TRAGEDIES — TOURNEUR — BEAUMONT AND FLETCHER — LAST PHASE OF ELIZABETHAN DRAMA — SENTIMENTAL TRAGEDY AND ROMANCE — COMEDY OF INCIDENT AND MANNERS — MASSINGER — FORD — SHIRLEY — LESSER DRAMATISTS — CONCLUSION.

THE first ten years of the century witnessed the crowning splendour of the Elizabethan drama.[1] The genial and mature comedies and heroic histories with which Shakespeare had illumined the closing years of the sixteenth century

Introductory.

---

[1] Minto, *Characteristics of English Poets*, Edin., 1885; Saintsbury, *Elizabethan Literature*, Lond., 1887-1903; Fleay, *Biographical Chronicle of the English Drama*, Lond., 1891; Mezières, *Predecesseurs et Contemporains de Shakespeare*, Paris, 1894, and *Contemporains et Successeurs de Shakespeare*, 1897; Courthope, *History of English Poetry*, vol. iv., Lond., 1903; Jusserand, *Histoire Littéraire du Peuple Anglais*, Paris, 1904; Emil Koeppel, *Quellen-studien zu den Dramen Ben Jonson's, John Marston's und Beaumont's und Fletcher's*, Erlangen und Leipzig, 1895; *Id. zu den Dramen George Chapman's, Philip Massinger's, und John Ford's*, Strassburg, 1897; *Transactions of the New Shakespeare Society*, 1874-92; *Jahrbuch der Deutschen Shakespeare-Gesellschaft*, Berlin, 1865-1905; *Englische Studien*, Heilbronn, 1877-1906; *Anglia*, Halle, 1878-1906; *Dictionary of National Biography*, Lond.

were succeeded by the great tragedies of thought and
passion; and when the second decade opened he was
taking farewell of the stage in the more slightly
constructed romances, full of pathos and poetry, in
which we can trace not only an alteration in the
poet's mood, but it may be also that more general
change in taste to which the romantic and sentimental drama of Beaumont and Fletcher conduced
and ministered. During these same years Jonson
was working with all the vigour of his gigantic
powers; and the best plays of Chapman, Marston,
Dekker, Middleton, and Webster date from this
decade or a few years later. The ruling spirits of
the next two decades are Beaumont and Fletcher,
and it is in the work of their followers and imitators
—Massinger, Ford, and Shirley—that the flame which
had been kindled by Marlowe and the other "university wits" burned itself out in the years immediately preceding the close of the theatres.

Shakespeare is, by the plan of this series, excluded
from the scope of the present volume, so that it
remains to sketch briefly the work of the other
dramatists who flourished during the years from 1600
to 1640.

The oldest of them all was the veteran scholar,
poet, and dramatist, George Chapman[1]. Born some

[1] *The Comedies and Tragedies of George Chapman, with Notes
and a Memoir*, 3 vols., London, 1873 (a literal reprint from the old
copies); *The Works of Chapman*, ed. R. H. Shepherd, 3 vols., London,
1874-5; *All Fools* and the "Bussy" and "Byron" plays, ed. W. L.
Phelps of Yale College, in *Mermaid Series*, London, 1895. Text in
all these corrupt. The "Bussy" plays have been edited carefully
by F. S. Boas, *Belles Lettres Series*, Boston and London, 1905.

eight years before Shakespeare, educated at Oxford, Chapman does not come before our notice as a poet until 1594, as a dramatist until 1595-96. How he spent the interval we do not know. There may be truth in Mr Swinburne's conjecture that he visited the Low Countries, with which he seems familiar, not, like Jonson, trailing a pike, but with the actors who went over in "Lecester's tijen," from which the peasants in Dutch comedy frequently date events, as the same comedies contain repeated reference to such companies. In 1598 he is mentioned by Meres as one of the best writers of comedies and tragedies, which would point to his being the author of plays now lost. Of plays certainly written before the close of the century we have only the worthless *Blind Beggar of Alexandria* (1598) and *A Humorous Day's Mirth* (1599), with the fine, though exaggerated and grotesque, adaptation from Terence's *Heautontimorumenos*, the comedy of *All Fools* (1600), so eloquently praised by Mr Swinburne. The majority of the plays which have survived belong to the early years of the new century. They include the comedies *The Gentleman Usher* (1606), *Monsieur D'Olive* (1606), *May Day* (1611), and *The Widow's Tears* (1612), with the tragedies *Bussy D'Ambois* (1607), *Byron's Conspiracy, The Tragedy of Charles, Duke of Byron* (1608), and *The Revenge of Bussy D'Ambois* (1613), to which falls to be added the later published tragedy of *Cæsar and Pompey* (1631) and *The Tragedy of Philip Chabot, Admiral of France* (1639). If Shirley had any hand in the latter, it was probably confined to the pathetic closing scene. I cannot myself discover Chapman's style in the crude plays *Revenge for Honour* (1654) and the *Tragedy of Alphonsus* (1654).

In Chapman's comedy the influence of Jonson is obvious. His comic characters are grotesque and absurd humourists, his comic incidents clumsy feats of gulling. But Chapman does not attempt to imitate Jonson's careful structure and his singleness of satiric purpose. His comic scenes are interwoven with romantic story. The romantic incidents are extravagant and grotesque, but are relieved by outbursts of the same splendid poetry as illumines the tragedies — passages of the same glowing enthusiasm for the spirit which can rise superior to mortal limitations and social conventions. Perhaps of all his comedies — in spite of the high praise given to *All Fools* — the most readable as comedy, but for the close, is the sardonic *Widow's Tears*.[1]

Comedy.

Chapman's tragedies bear an interesting family resemblance to one another. They are taken from French history, and Mr Boas has shown that Chapman's *Holinshed* was Edward Grimeston's *Inventorie of the Historie of France*, published in 1611. Dramatically and poetically they recall the tragedies of Marlowe. Their hero is a man "like his desires, lift upward and divine."

Tragedy.

[1] Mr A. L. Stiefel, who has tracked so many French plays to their source in Italian Novella-Comedies, has discovered Chapman's footsteps in the same snow, and shown that his *May-Day* is an adaptation of the *Alessandro* of Alessandro Piccolomini (1508-1578).

But Chapman is more of a philosopher and less of a dramatist than Marlowe. His turbid style is lightened by magnificent flashes of poetry, but never burns with the clear and lovely radiance of Marlowe's finest passages. His heroes, both rebels such as Bussy and Byron, and Senecan men such as Clermont in the *Revenge,* Cato, and Chabot, are all philosophers, reasoning in language which is often harsh, obscure, and bombastic, but which is often also intense and glowing, of "fate, free-will, foreknowledge absolute." Their motives are not elucidated in the sympathetic manner in which Marlowe delineates the ambition, the lust of gold and beauty, the hates and loves of his characters. From all the thunder and cloud and lightning of the speeches of Bussy or Byron it is not easy to gather what they would be at or why. Their deeds are not in proportion to their words; they may be violent but are not great. What remains in the mind is the sentiments of men of dauntless courage and unyielding resolution rising superior to all material and prudential considerations.[1]

A more interesting and important figure in the history of the drama than Chapman is the poet who alone of his compeers has enjoyed the honour of being at any time set in rivalry to Shakespeare. When the century opened, when the latter had perfected the romantic drama created

Ben Jonson.

[1] Many of the sentiments put into Clermont D'Ambois' mouth are translated from Epictetus' *Discourses.* See Boas's edition cited above.

by himself and the "university wits," Ben Jonson[1] had already turned his eyes in another direction, and begun what he trusted would prove a revolution in English play-writing. Single-handed he had begun to "correct" English comedy, and was preparing to render the same service to tragedy.

The lack of biographical material for the history of the Elizabethan drama prevents us from tracing the process by which Jonson reached his clear-cut and resolutely sustained conception of the proper end of comedy, and the means by which that end was to be attained; for the plays which embody this conception, and which alone he acknowledged, were by no means all he wrote. Of Scottish ancestry, born at Westminster in 1573, educated under Camden,—

Life.

> "Most reverent head to whom I owe
> All that I am in arts, all that I know,"—

for some time perhaps a bricklayer apprenticed to his stepfather, certainly a soldier in the Low Countries, Jonson was in 1597 a player and playwright to the "Admiral's Men." His fatal duel in 1598, his imprisonment, conversion to Romanism and re-conversion, are familiar to every reader of literary history.

---

[1] First folio (revised by the author), 1616; second, 1631-41. Later editions were superseded by Gifford's *Works of Ben Jonson*, 9 vols., Lond., 1816; rev. by Col. F. Cunningham, 1875. Select plays in *Mermaid Series*, with preface by C. H. Herford. The first folio is being reprinted by Professor Bang, Louvain, in his *Materialien zur Kunde des älteren Englischen Dramas*, Louvain, 1905. Swinburne, *Study of Ben Jonson*, 1889; J. A. Symonds, *Ben Jonson*, 1886; Phil. Aronstein, *Ben Jonson's Theorie des Lustspiels*, Anglia xvii., 1895.

For Henslowe he patched old plays (*The Spanish Tragedy* in 1610-12), and wrote plays singly and in collaboration, of some of which the names have survived, as the *Page of Plymouth* and *Richard Crookback*. *The Case is Altered* (1609), in whatever year it was composed, represents perhaps a survival of this joint work, perhaps an early experiment of his own in comedy, romantic and fanciful in story and spirit, but regular in structure, careful in character-drawing, and touched with satire. The story is woven from the plots of the *Aulularia* and the *Captivi*, and Mr Swinburne has justly regretted "that the influence of Plautus on the style and method of Jonson was not more permanent and more profound."

But no poet except Milton ever knew his own mind better than Jonson. With *Every Man in his Humour* (1601), which was produced at the Globe in 1597 or 1598 (the characters bearing then Italian names), his style appeared fully formed, and thereafter he could hardly think of the romantic *novella* comedy but with impatience and contempt. "I travail with another objection, Signor," says Mitis in *Every Man out of his Humour*, "which I fear will be enforced against the author ere I can be delivered of it." "What's that, sir?" replies Cordatus. *Mitis*. "That the argument of his comedy might have been of some other nature, as of a duke to be in love with a countess, and that countess to be in love with the duke's son, and the son to love the lady's waiting-maid; some such cross-wooing, with a clown to their serving-man, better than to be thus near and famil-

Theory of Comedy.

iarly allied to the times." *Cordatus.* "You say well, but I would fain hear one of these autumn-judgments define once *Quid sit comœdia?* If he cannot, let him concern himself with Cicero's definition, till he have strength to propose to himself a better, who would have a comedy to be *imitatio vitæ, speculum consuetudinis, imago veritatis;* a thing throughout pleasant and ridiculous, and accommodated to the correction of manners. If the maker have failed in any particular of this, they may worthily task him, but if not, why! be you that are for them silent." So Jonson condemns the comedy which had, with all its frequent absurdity, produced *Much Ado about Nothing* and *Twelfth Night,* and defines his own endeavour. Comedy was to be, in Mr Elton's happy phrase, "medicinal"; its work to purge the evil "humours" of society—its follies in the first instance, but in the greatest of his plays the scope was enlarged to include folly that has festered into crime. Of the means by which this end was to be achieved Jonson's conception was equally definite. A regular and elaborately constructed plot — deferential but not slavishly obedient to the Unities—exhibits a variety of characters, each the embodiment of a single humour or folly, suddenly, and when the "humours" are at the top of their bent, outwitted, befooled, and exposed. The style, whether verse or prose be the medium, is a style "such as men do use," not heightened with poetical bombast; reproducing current slang, the technicalities of particular arts and professions, the cant of the beggar and the Puritan; but showing

in every line, in the coarsest outbursts and the most
sustained speeches, the labour of a perhaps too conscientious artist, and the defective harmony inevitable
in verse superinduced upon what has been originally
drafted in prose.

The result of Jonson's definitely formed and resolutely pursued purpose was at first apparently—as is
usual in such cases—an outburst of hostility, which his arrogant temper did little
to allay, or rather much to provoke. *Every Man in
his Humour* is a comparatively genial play. The less
satirically drawn characters are not unamiable—the
young men who collect and exhibit "humourists,"
their old-school father, merry Cob, and genial Justice
Clements. The fools themselves evoke nothing stronger
than laughter and contempt. But apparently the
hostility awakened by the new departure, and by the
combative tone of the Prologue, irritated the poet's
own scornful humour, with the result of intensifying
his arrogance and hardening his style. *Every Man out
of his Humour* (1599) was hurled at the head of its
audience furnished with an induction and running
comment, to teach them the proper end of comedy—
what to admire, and why. Probability, the easy elaboration and interest of the story, are all lost sight of.
Everything is subordinated to the vivid and detailed
presentation of a set of characters quite too feeble
and lacking in interest to justify the storm of hatred
and scorn with which they are overwhelmed. In
Cynthia's Revels (1600), directed generally against the
affectations of court life and speech, but including, it

would seem, savage hits at individuals, the sacrifice of interest to satiric purpose and pedantic display was carried still further. Allegory, to which Jonson returned in his last plays, is added to the other elements of tediousness—foolish gulling and diffuse dialogue. The play was acted by the children of the Queen's Chapel, a fact significant of the terms on which the author stood with his fellow-actors and playwrights, and the scornful closing words betray a consciousness of fighting a difficult battle—

> "I'll only speak what I have heard him say,
> 'By God! 'tis good; and if you like it you may.'"

They were long remembered against him. All the incidents of the quarrel we shall never know—whether, for example, Shakespeare took part in it. He certainly refers to it in *Hamlet;* and *The Return from Parnassus* seems to imply that he had taken a leading part, although the words are ambiguous. It culminated in the production of *The Poetaster* and Dekker's *Satiromastix*. *The Poetaster* stands alone among Jonson's comedies, not only in its personal intention, but in virtue of its general plan. Jonson's conception of a comedy as the careful weaving of a plot in which folly is exposed, is here crossed by another idea of the duty of a dramatist, which appears most fully in his tragedies — namely, that in dealing with history he must be faithful to his authorities. The result in Jonson's work is a complete violation of Aristotle's rule that a play should not be episodic. In *The Poetaster*, Ovid's amour with

Julia, Propertius' sorrow, Augustus' interest in Virgil's *Æneid*, are connected in the loosest way with scenes satirising the citizen's wife, the swaggering soldier, and the jealousy of bad poets. The last, which is the principal motive of the play, does not connect and unify the other episodes, but comes in by the way, and is developed in a couple of excellent scenes. As a satiric drama with a personal object, *The Poetaster* has been often overrated — in fact, too much stress can easily be laid upon the personal element in the quarrel.[1] It was a natural phenomenon, the result of the sudden and arrogant intrusion of a new type of play, and that a drama, satirical with a thoroughness unknown since the days of the old Attic comedy. Marston and Dekker assumed to themselves the *rôle* of protagonists against Jonson, but it is clear that behind them stood a surprised and indignant troop of playwrights and actors, and that there rallied to their support the representatives of the other professions which had been assailed — lawyers, soldiers, and perhaps courtiers. The *Apologetic Dialogue* which he added to the play had to be withdrawn; and for a time Jonson deemed it prudent to forgo comedy and try

"If Tragedy have a more kind aspect."

---

[1] Mr Fleay has devoted much inquiry to the identification of individuals, and a full discussion is Roscoe Addison Small's *The Stage Quarrel between Ben Jonson and the so-called Poetasters*, Breslau, 1899. We know so little about the lives and personalities of the authors concerned, that it is difficult either to verify conjectures or to deduce anything of interest or importance from them if correct.

The result was the stately and scholarly *Sejanus His Fall*, produced at the Globe in 1603, and published in 1605. The essentials of tragedy Jonson, in accordance with neo-classic tradition, finds in "truth of argument, dignity of person, gravity and height of elocution, fulness and frequency of sentence." In structure he made no attempt, as Milton did later, to reproduce the Greek model. "Nor is it needful, or almost possible, in these our days, and to such auditors as commonly things are presented, to observe the old state and splendour of dramatic poems with preservation of any popular delight." He follows the line indicated in *The Poetaster*, and puts a chapter of history into dramatic form. Jonson scorned to

"Fight over York and Lancaster's long jars,
And in the tiring-house, bring wounds to scars,"

but there is no essential difference between the structure of *Sejanus* and that of an ordinary "History." The plot is quite as wanting in unity as defined by Aristotle, quite as episodic. It relates the history of the reign of Tiberius from just before the murder of Drusus to the death of Sejanus. For every incident, for every character, for every trait of manners, the poet's authority is given. The spirit of Tacitus and Juvenal breathes from its stately scenes. Perhaps the highest compliment which can be paid to *Sejanus* is, that one can turn from the *Annals* to the play and feel the same emotions. *The Poetaster* and *Sejanus* are the first works which endeavour to reconstruct the life of the past in the manner of later historical novelists. Were Jonson's Roman plays still acted, there would be justification for the antiquarian accuracy somewhat irrelevantly lavished by managers on those of Shakespeare.

With the accession of James began Jonson's work as a prolific and popular writer of learned and fanciful masques and entertainments. This did not, however, interrupt the steady development of his dramatic and comic art. Between 1605 and 1616 the poet produced five comedies and a tragedy, and of the comedies four—*Volpone* acted in 1605, *The Silent Woman* in 1609, *The Alchemist* in 1610, and *Bartholomew Fair* in 1614—are the crown and flower of Jonsonian art. In them the poet achieved at last a complete mastery over comedy as he had himself conceived and planned it. The plot is no longer a mere series of incidents, in the course of which various "humours" are deployed and overthrown, but a curiously and compactly built story, full, from the first line to the last, of the bustle and stress of action. The characters are clearly conceived, and elaborated with fierce energy and an overwhelming accumulation of learned and observant detail. "Shakespeare wanted art," Jonson told Drummond, and one begins to understand his point of view when studying these plays, of which a strenuous, obvious, all-controlling art is the principal feature. Jonson is a savage satirist. Every critic has pointed to the obvious fact that his unremitting satiric intention has destroyed the sympathy necessary to create living and interesting characters. And yet one feels these comedies were not written—like those of Aristophanes or like *The Tale of a Tub* and *Gulliver's Travels*—because Jonson desired to satirise some vice or folly which had moved his spleen. He is a satirist because he has resolved to write satiric comedy. Only perhaps in the character of Zeal-of-the-Land Busy does one seem to see a type that Jonson has met himself and spontaneously detested. The others are the product of a learned and observant mind, and a definite and pedantic theory of comic art.

Volpone, or the Fox, for example, is not a satiric comedy springing directly from the poet's observation of the love of gold and the ways of legacy-hunters in his own day. The root idea—the shameless greed of such people, and the exploitation of this greed by a clever knave—is derived from Petronius Arbiter, and the whole play is a marvellously inventive and artistic elaboration of this idea. From it, with the help of a further hint or two from Petronius and other sources, Jonson has evolved a comedy full of powerfully drawn and impressive characters, striking and ludicrous incidents, learned and poetical sentiment, and breathing such a sincere spirit of scornful indignation as almost to give the impression that he is modelling directly from life. Almost, but not quite—and the final impression is rather of a wonderful *tour de force* than of a really penetrating and effective piece of satire.

The Silent Woman is constructed in a similar

fashion. The idea of an eccentric who shrinks from every noise and yet marries a wife, is derived from Libanius, and expanded with the help of multifarious learning and curious observation into what Mr Swinburne justly calls the "most imperial and elaborate of all farces." And just because it is frankly a farce, and the reader is not called on to look through the play at the object of the satire, has it been so popular. One is left free to enjoy the art—the cleverly invented characters, the cunningly constructed plot, the learned and brilliant dialogue. It is not a faultless art; it is not the art of Shakespeare, or even of Molière; but it none the less arrests and compels our admiration and, in this play certainly, our delighted amusement.

The Silent Woman.

Such as it is, Jonson's art reached its culminating point in *The Alchemist*. The closely woven plot has no excrescences. The characters, without exception, are impressive and delightful satiric types,—Face, shameless and adroit; Subtle, the virtuous fraud; Dol Common, as vigorous, if not as human, as Doll Tearsheet; the sublime Sir Epicure and the inimitable "We of the separation," Tribulation Wholesome and Ananias. The satire here, too, does not seem to fly so far above reality as in *Volpone*. Full of learning as it is, the play smacks of actual observation of the knavish life of low London, the life the poet paints again with coarse gusto in *Bartholomew Fair*. Alchemy and every kind of superstitious trickery abounded. And yet the satire is not ephemeral. Substitute spirit-rapping or palmistry

The Alchemist.

for alchemy, and a telling modern comedy might be modelled on the old. The moral of the whole is the moral of *Reynard*. We are not cheated by the cleverness of knaves, but by our own folly and greed.

In the year following the performance of *The Alchemist* was acted Jonson's second and last tragedy,
Catiline His Conspiracy, in which Cicero and Sallust are treated as Tacitus and Juvenal had been in *Sejanus*, and to my mind the former are dramatically less interesting than the latter. Jonson essayed the chorus in the Senecan style. The effect was not, however, to make the play more lyric or classic. Three years later appeared his last great comedy, *Bartholmew Fair*, stuffed with humours and manners, the coarsest and most rollicking but perhaps the most real in interest and humour of his plays. Rabbi Zeal-of-the-Land Busy completes the study of the Puritan begun in *The Alchemist*. After this play Jonson wrote none that can for a moment compare with these masterpieces. *The Devil is an Ass* (1631) is ingenious in conception, and the satire on projectors vivid and amusing. *The Staple of News* (1631) opens admirably, but tails off into tedious dialogue and tedious morality. *The New Inn* (1631), *The Magnetic Lady* (1640), and *A Tale of a Tub* (1640) all reveal diminishing power, and a Jonsonian comedy demanded Herculean vigour.

Last Plays.

The popularity of that artificial though poetic trifle the Masque was one of the causes of the decline of the drama under James and Charles. On his numerous productions of this kind

Masques.

Jonson lavished his most characteristic gifts—the power of weaving a play around a central idea, stores of accurate learning, fancy, and humour; while his experiments in lyrical measures of various kinds are interesting and frequently delightful, if not always altogether successful. The main end of each masque —the flattery of James and his family—is effected in a surprising variety of ways, and some of the masques are more than ingenious pieces of flattery. The *Masque of Hymen*, for example, is a magnificent piece of symbolic ritual; and some others, such as the *Masque of Queens* and *Pleasure reconciled to Virtue*, suggest that, with more space at his disposal and a worthier audience, Jonson might have elaborated a moral idea with some of the dignity and poetry of *Comus*. But James's courtiers cared more for transformation scenes, music, and dances than for Jonson's learning and morality. The greatest of seventeenth-century masques was an indictment of courtly adulation and sensuality.

The fragment of a pastoral drama which Jonson left behind him in *The Sad Shepherd* is full of feeling and poetry. For more of such work, regular in structure and not devoid of satire, yet at the same time romantic and poetic, one would be willing to forgo some of the strength and ingenuity which in *The Silent Woman* and *The Alchemist* fill us with admiration, yet leave us a little cold and fatigued—

"Non satis est pulchra esse poemata, dulcia sunto."

The very completeness with which Jonson achieved

the task he set before him arouses regret that he allowed his humour, fancy, observation, learning, and constructive power to be directed by so resolute a spirit of pedantry. To "correct" English comedy it was not necessary to deprive it of all interest of story, nor to substitute for often carelessly drawn characters human nature cut in sections and dressed for the microscope. Could Jonson have been content to correct the more glaring faults of popular comedy, making the structure more regular and even, and the characters more consistently typical, while presenting a broad satirical picture of contemporary manners, he would have rendered invaluable service to the English drama. Molière's breadth of vision and deftness of touch were outside Jonson's range; yet he might have created a regular and satirical drama independent of the French, and more interesting and valuable than the superficial and licentious comedy of the Restoration. That he failed to do so is due, however, not only to the pedantic method he adopted. Even in the form it took, Jonson's satirical comedy might have been of greater interest and value, but for the fact that the conditions of English social life prevented his colossal satirical gifts from finding quite adequate themes. In Jonson's greatest comedies — with the exception of *Volpone*—there is a striking disproportion between the elaborateness of the satire and the trifling and ephemeral character of the vices satirised; and one is disposed to explain this, in part at any rate, by the reception given to his first and structur-

Jonson's Art.

ally less perfect comedies, whose range of satire was wider, including courtiers, citizens, lawyers, soldiers, and not exempting individuals. For there was probably more in the famous quarrel of the players than a merely personal matter. The friend to whom *The Poetaster* was dedicated had to undertake for the poet's innocence before "the greatest justice of the Kingdom," and for a time Jonson laid comedy aside. He probably realised that it was unsafe for a player to constitute himself the censor of all classes from courtiers to actors. When he took up comedy again, though he had perfected his constructive art, he either, as in *Volpone*, elaborated his satire on pedantic and unreal lines, or, as in *The Alchemist*, flew at comparatively small game. Only in the Puritans did he find antagonists worthy of his steel whom it was safe to attack, and his satire of them is so trenchant, if, as satire must be, one-sided, that one wishes he had been free to deal faithfully with other classes, and not compelled to waste his powers on pedantic abstractions or on alchemists, "jeerers," news-vendors, and projectors—pigmies whom at the distance of three centuries we can hardly descry. Jonson's touch was too heavy for a task which was within Molière's range and was Addison's proper function—the satire of affectations and minor follies. But had satire been as free for Jonson as it was for Aristophanes or Juvenal, he surely would have been a great and stern censor of the great vices and corruptions of society. As it is, "rare Ben Jonson" is his appropriate epitaph, for there is nothing in the world quite like one of his closely-knit plays, packed with learning, observation, humour, and character.

But though Jonson's influence did not extend to the production of a satiric comedy of manners which will compare with that of Molière, or even with the work of the later essayists and novelists, it did co-operate with other forces to end the fanciful, euphuistic comedy created by Lyly—a comedy in great measure of language, of pun and poetry—of which Shakespeare's early and middle comedy is the flower. Jonson's plays co-operated with the pamphlets of Greene and Dekker to make the comedy of Middleton, Fletcher, and Shirley a superficial and somewhat conventional comedy of manners,—the manners of the gallant, the citizen, and the rogue,—a comedy of humours, and a comedy of more elaborate and lively intrigue.

Jonson's rivals in the famous quarrel referred to above—John Marston and Thomas Dekker—are good types of the journeyman dramatists who catered for the popular taste which it was Jonson's endeavour to reform and elevate. "Nor is the moving of laughter," says Jonson, translating from Heinsius, "always the end of comedy; that is rather a fowling for the people's delight or fooling." This "fowling for the people's delight" is all that the average playwright had in view, and his baits were melodramatic tragedy of crime and vengeance, and loosely constructed comedies of incident, romance, and buffoonery. Shakespeare transformed and glorified the popular type, which Jonson strove to "reform altogether."

Crispinus and Demetrius.

Marston[1] is the more ambitious of the two, but Dekker is the finer genius, poetic and dramatic. Marston affects both tragic gloom and sardonic satire, but in both he is an impostor. His first tragedy, *Antonio and Mellida* (1601, published 1602), is perhaps the most outrageous example of the type of melodrama inaugurated by *The Spanish Tragedy*,—a type which Shakespeare, in the year of Marston's play, transfigured in *Hamlet*. All the machinery of the kind is to be found in Marston's tragedy,—hideous crime, the ghost clamouring for vengeance, the feigned madman awaiting his opportunity. The style is that of Ancient Pistol, and calls aloud for the purging administered by Jonson in *The Poetaster*.

The Malcontent (1604), dedicated to Jonson himself, is a play of much the same sort. The banished Duke, in disguise at the usurper's court, rails at everything, and especially at the shams of court life, in the sardonic vein of Hamlet. The *dénouement* is effected by the favourite device of a play. The style is pruned of some of the worst extravagances of the earlier play, and Marston can write with vigour; but his pretentious satire is as unconvincing as his tragic horrors. *Parasitaster, or the Fawn* (1606), is in the same sardonic style. *The Wonder of Women, or the Tragedy of Sophonisba* (1606), on a favourite subject of Renaissance dramatists, is a flaming melodrama.

---

[1] A collected edition was issued in 1633. *The Works of John Marston*, ed. J. O. Halliwell-Phillipps, 3 vols., 1856. *Do.*, ed. A. H. Bullen, 3 vols., Lond., 1887.

What you Will (1607) and *The Dutch Courtezan* (1605) are Marston's most tolerable comedies, because the least pretentious. The former, a slight farce largely indebted for its plot to Plautus's *Amphitruo*, was probably written shortly after *Cynthia's Revels*. There are allusions to the quarrel of the players. Jonson's arrogant style is parodied; and a couple of characters loosely connected with the plot represent Jonson and Marston. These excrescences do not improve the play, which in itself is a jovial little farce concerned with second marriages and mistaken identities. *The Dutch Courtezan* (1605) is still better. It relates the attempted vengeance of a forsaken mistress. Mr Bullen has, I venture to think, overrated the character of Francheschina, who is drawn crudely and perfunctorily. A finer treatment would have changed the whole tone of the play. But on a quite low level the comedy is good—the story well managed, the characters fairly human and attractive, the style vigorous, and the humour of the by-plot, in which a rascally vintner is befooled, lively and genial though coarse. The best play with which Marston's name is connected, however, is undoubtedly the delightful comedy *Eastward Ho* (1605), in which he collaborated with Jonson and Chapman, and for which they were all three imprisoned. How much he contributed to that amusing picture of citizen types, astute rogues, absurd adventures, and comical repentance, we cannot tell; but the geniality of its humour is, I believe, that of the real Marston, whom Nature never intended for tragedian or satirist. He was a journeyman writer with a vigorous style, and a vein of genuine, though coarse and not very brilliant, wit.

Thomas Dekker[1] was a voluminous composer of plays and pamphlets of the kind well fitted to amuse an audience of London citizens. He was born probably some time before 1577. The first reference to him is by Henslowe in 1597. In 1599 his name is mentioned in connection with no fewer than six plays. His first published works were *The Shoemaker's Holiday, or the Gentle Craft*, and *The Pleasant Comedy of Old Fortunatus*, which appeared in 1600. *Satiromastix* was issued in the following year, and Dekker's greatest play, *The Honest Whore*, in 1604, though the second part was not issued until 1630, and in it Dekker had enjoyed the collaboration of Middleton. In *The Roaring Girl* (1611) Middleton had also a hand; and *The Whore of Babylon* (1607), *Northward Ho* and *Westward Ho* (1607) were composed along with Webster; *A Witch of Edmonton* (1658) with Ford; and *The Virgin Martyr* (1622) with Massinger.

The very names of Dekker's plays indicate the character of the contents. Three strata run through his loosely constructed and carelessly finished dramas. There is abundance of comedy of the popular Elizabethan type—the comedy of the clown, the gallant, the citizen and the citizen's wife, the bawd and the punk. Dekker can be coarse enough, but he does not strike one as coarse in grain. In fact, he is

[1] *The Dramatic Works of Thomas Dekker, &c.*, 4 vols., 1873 (Pearson's reprint). Selected plays in the *Mermaid Series*.

not such a master of vigorous coarse comedy as Middleton. He is on the side of decency and honesty. His citizens' wives in *Northward Ho* and *Westward Ho* vindicate their honour and put to shame their jealous husbands. A careless, kindly gaiety is the best feature of Dekker's comic scenes, which are too often tedious fooling. Such as it is, his humour is nowhere seen to better advantage than in *The Shoemaker's Holiday*, a sunny picture of young love and kindly genial London craftsmen such as Dickens himself might have drawn.

Side by side with this stratum of popular comedy lie, often quite incongruously, scenes of romance and tragedy which reveal a rare and sweet, if not strong or sustained, poetic and dramatic gift. There are touches of exquisite poetry in *Old Fortunatus*, though the treatment as a whole of a poetic theme is lamentably inadequate. But Dekker's dramatic power attained its highest level in those scenes of *The Honest Whore* which portray Bellafront, her father Orlando Friscobaldo, and her betrayer and later spendthrift husband Matheo. These are written with singular vigour and beauty. There are flaws, such as the rhetorical combats between Bellafront and her converter, Hippolito. It is characteristic of Dekker to repeat a device he has once found successful. The characters, moreover, show no marked development. But, on the whole, these scenes deserve the eloquent commendation bestowed on them by Hazlitt. They are like a drawing in which the lines are very few but intensely significant. "It is as if there were some fine art to chisel thought and to embody the inmost movements of the mind in everyday actions and familiar speech." For a little more intercourse with these admirably etched characters we would gladly have spared the tedious humours of the patient man, which fill up the comic scenes. But this blending of the incongruous, this inequality of treatment, is the characteristic of Dekker's work, and indeed of the Elizabethan drama. In lyric sweetness Dekker's songs are not surpassed by those of any writer of his age.

A robuster, if not a finer, genius than Dekker was Thomas Middleton,[1] author of some of the gayest of the comedies of gulling, one or two more romantic and poetic plays, and a couple of tragedies of the grim and brutal type which appealed to the popular taste. He was born probably about 1570, and appears first in Henslowe's diary in the year 1602, collaborating with Munday, Drayton, Dekker, and Webster. *The Old Law* is conjecturally assigned to 1599, but Middleton's first published and an evidently early comedy is *Blurt, Master Constable* (1602). The romantic part is somewhat revolting, and this is not compensated for by the horse-play and bawdry of the comic scenes. Middleton collaborated in many of his plays with Dekker and with William Rowley, author of two independent

Middleton.

---

[1] *The Works of Thomas Middleton, &c.*, ed. Rev. A. Dyce, 5 vols., Lond., 1840. *Do.*, ed. A. H. Bullen, 8 vols., Lond., 1885. Select plays in the *Mermaid Series*, v. introduction by Mr Swinburne, 1887.

comedies of city manners and humours, *A New Wonder* and *A Match at Midnight*. In 1624 his *Game of Chess*, a skit on the proposed Spanish marriage, brought the author and actors into considerable danger.

A Trick to catch the Old One (1608), *The Phœnix* (1607), *Michaelmas Term* (1607), *Your Five Gallants* (lic. 1608), *A Mad World, my Masters!* (1608), and *A Chaste Maid in Cheapside* (1630) are the best of Middleton's farcical comedies. The type is the popular one. The recurrent characters are gay gallants, greedy usurers, citizens and their wives, roarers, bawds, and punks. Every one gulls every one else, and the situations are often highly ludicrous, or must have been so to a not too squeamish taste. Middleton is on the side of youth. Young men induce usurers to compete with one another for the hand of a disguised courtesan, or by ingenious devices rob their old uncles when these refuse to provide for them. Middleton's indelicacy is almost always relieved by real humour. Even *A Chaste Maid in Cheapside* is as amusing as it is outrageous.

In his more romantic plays Middleton betrays the inability which besets all the minor dramatists, to invest a whole play with the poetic charm which illumines portions. What is beautiful and what is repulsive are found side by side. Shakespeare is not exempt from the same fault, but his splendour outshines his spots. In *The Spanish Gipsy* (1653), based on a couple of Cervantes' novels, the scenes of merriment and romance cannot make us forget those of rape and murder; and in *The Old Law* (1656) and *A Fair Quarrel* (1617), scenes and speeches of touching pathos and eloquent morality are surrounded by others of gay but coarse buffoonery.

The scenes in Middleton's tragedy *The Changeling* (1623, published 1653)—in which he collaborated with William Rowley—that lead up to and include the crisis, are some of the most powerful in the tragedy of criminal passion which the Elizabethan drama produced. Beatrice, the heroine, instigated by a sudden passion for Alsemero, bribes De Flores —a poor knight whose love she has hitherto treated with scorn—to murder her betrothed, and discovers too late that she is "the deed's creature," and in the power of a passion more ruthless and masterful than her own. The scene in which this discovery is slowly forced upon her is in its own terrible and brutal way one of the greatest in dramatic literature. Less poetic than Webster's work, it is more intense, every word more entirely relevant. The scenes which follow and the catastrophe are full of the grotesque and ugly details of Massinger's and Ford's tragedy, but the character of De Flores is preserved in sombre consistency throughout.

Women Beware Women (1657) is of the same type, a tragedy of lawless passion and ruthless crime followed by overwhelming vengeance. The catastrophe—attained through the common device of a play within a play—is the most complete holocaust recorded since and including *The Spanish Tragedy*. It has not the same strong central interest as *The*

Changeling, and no character that is not merely repellent. Crime overtaken by vengeance was the receipt for tragedy which the Elizabethans, and not the Elizabethans only, learned from Seneca. There were but few whose instinct guided them as it did Shakespeare, after his first aberrations, to the truth that the tragic hero must have some claim upon our respect and sympathy, a point which Balzac elaborated with acuteness in his criticism of Heinsius' *Herodes Infanticida*.

A more humdrum and prosaic representative of the journeyman dramatist is Thomas Heywood,[1] a voluminous author of plays, poems, pamphlets, and entertainments. Like Dekker, he caters mainly for a citizen audience. He sings the praises of the Lord Mayor and the London 'prentices. His sentiment is kindly, and his morality sound. He dramatises every sort of story, mythological, romantic, historic, and domestic. His histories, *Edward IV.* (1600) and *The Troubles of Queen Elizabeth* (1605), are in the regular chronicle style, and almost pre-Shakespearean in their want of dignity in the serious scenes and the buffoonery of the comic portions. His mythological plays, *The Golden Age*, *The Silver Age*, &c., dramatise simply enough a variety of stories from Ovid. *The Rape of Lucrece* (1608) blends familiar Roman tragedy with outrageous Elizabethan

---

[1] Individual plays were edited by Barron Field and Collier for the old Shakespeare Society. *Heywood's Dramatic Works*, 6 vols., Lond., 1874 (Pearson's reprint). Select plays in the *Mermaid Series*.

farce. One can imagine what Jonson thought of a play on classical history containing such songs as—

"Small coals here!
Thus go the cries in Rome's fair town,
First they go up street, and then they go down;"

and—

"Arise, arise, my Juggy, my Puggy;
Arise! get up, my dear!"

Heywood's most individual plays are the two domestic tragedies, *A Woman killed with Kindness* (1607, mentioned by Henslowe in 1603), and *The English Traveller* (1633). They are in the same key as *Arden of Feversham*, but adultery is not in Heywood's play followed by murder. He tells a story of cruel unfaithfulness and bitter repentance with simplicity and pathos, but with no transfiguring breath of poetry. The style and morality are somewhat humdrum, and the characters a little disposed to whine.

Heywood's romantic comedies, *The Fair Maid of the West, or a Girl worth Gold* (1631), *A Maidenhead Well Lost* (1634), *A Challenge for Beauty* (1636), *Fortune by Land and Sea* (1655), *The Late Lancashire Witches* (1634), and others, describe themselves—stories constructed in the most careless fashion, full of incident by sea and land, patriotic and kindly sentiment, farcical humour, but of the slightest poetic and dramatic interest. His most successful comic type is the careless, shameless, quick-witted knave such as Reignalt in *The English Traveller*.

A far greater poet and dramatist was John Webster.[1]
Of his life we know, as usual, next to nothing. His
name emerges in Henslowe's diary in the
year 1601 as the author of *The Guise, or the
Massacre of Paris*, a play which he claims in a later
dedication, but which is lost. Throughout 1602 he
seems to have collaborated in three or four plays
with Drayton, Dekker, Middleton, and others. In
1604 Marston's *The Malcontent* was produced and
published with additions by Webster. *The White
Devil* appeared in 1612, *The Duchess of Malfi* in
1623, and *The Devil's Law Case* in the same year.
These are probably all the extant plays which were
published during his lifetime. A Roman tragedy,
Appius and Virginia, appeared in 1657, and in
1661 *A Cure for a Cuckold* and *The Thracian
Wonder* were published as by Webster and Rowley.
The serious plot in the former is obviously Webster's
work.

Webster.

Webster's fame rests on two tragedies, *The White
Devil, or Vittoria Corrombona*, and *The Duchess of
Malfi*. They belong to that very distinctive and somewhat melodramatic type of
tragedy which might be called the Senecan-Machia-
vellian. It is Senecan in its sententious morality
and choice of revenge as the leading motive. The
influence of Machiavelli is seen in the principal

*His great
tragedies.*

---

[1] *The Works of John Webster, &c.*, by the Rev. A. C. Dyce,
Lond., 1857; *The Dramatic Works of John Webster*, ed. Wm. Haz-
litt, 4 vols., Lond., 1857; *Webster and Tourneur*, in the *Mermaid
Series*, contains the two tragedies.

characters and sentiments. The chief agents in the history of unnatural crime and bloody vengeance unrolled are politicians of the kind Machiavelli was believed to have idealised. In *The Spanish Tragedy*, the first crude model of this type of tragedy, Jeronimo feigns madness as a disguise in his pursuit of vengeance. A regular part of the machinery became in consequence a real or feigned mad railer at life, and especially court life, and women's vices. Shakespeare's *Richard III.* shows the influence of Kyd's play in an even crude and melodramatic fashion. Richard is the full-blown Machiavellian politician. Margaret of Anjou plays the part of the ghost denouncing vengeance. Clarence's dream, in feeling and versification, recalls Andrea's descent to the lower world, and the balanced stichomuthia of several dialogues is classical. In *Hamlet* the type revived, but, for a modern reader at any rate, the melodramatic interest pales before the psychological and reflective. *Hamlet* has become a problem in character, and the mouthpiece for profound comment, ironic and straightforward, on art and life. Marston's earlier plays are melodramas of this kind. *The Malcontent*, like many other plays of the day, is full of echoes of *Hamlet*. Webster made additions to *The Malcontent*, and was apparently attracted by Marston's combination of tragic gloom and sardonic wit. At the same time, although he alludes to Shakespeare in a rather condescending manner, it is clear from his plays that he was deeply impressed by the pregnant and thrilling phraseology of the great tragedies.

ENGLISH DRAMA. 115

The two plays are thus stories of terrible crimes—sins of lust and hate, and of dire and overwhelming vengeance; and through each runs a vein of bitter comment on princes and women.

Webster's art.

They are studied and elaborate works. Like Jonson, Webster pleads the character of his audience as excuse for not having written a regular tragedy, "observing all the critical laws, as height of style and gravity of person, enriched with the sententious chorus, and, as it were, livening death in the passionate and weighty Nuntius." None the less he had the Senecan model in view. The mocking and bitter comment of Flamineo and Bosola supply the chorus; dumb-show takes the place of the nuntius' relation; and the poet aims at unity and definiteness of plot structure, propriety of character, and height of style.

As regards the plot, indeed, the studied care with which Webster endeavoured to make it include the crime and its punishment has prevented his obtaining the concentration and proportion which give to Shakespeare's plots essential unity. That essential unity is to be sought in the spiritual history of the protagonists. A tragedy achieves artistic unity when every incident is subordinate and auxiliary to the vivid presentation of what these said and did as they passed through some great and fatal crisis. Shakespeare — when not, like lesser men, drawn aside by the temptation to write a taking scene — proportions with wonderful art the degree to which the different characters

Plot.

shall fill the stage and our thoughts. It is those in whose fate we are and must be most deeply interested that are most constantly before us, and with the decision of their fate the play ends. Webster's division of the tragedy into the story of a crime and the story of its avenging has interfered with this concentration and proportioning of the interest. Those for whose fate our feelings are really engaged appear fitfully, and slip from our notice before the play ends. Vittoria is magnificently presented in the opening scenes of *The White Devil*, whispering murder to her lover, baffling her accusers. But thereafter she falls too much into the background, re-emerging in her first splendour only for one moment at the end to cry—

> "My soul, like to a ship in a black storm,
> Is driven I know not whither."

In like manner, after the terrible scenes describing the torture and death of the Duchess of Malfi, the last act drags, beautifully wrought as it is. Our passionate sympathy has attained the highest pitch when her brother's remorse awakens in the words—

> "Cover her face: mine eyes dazzle: she died young."

Shakespeare would have hastened the catastrophe, that all might perish in the same high-wrought moment.

The "propriety" of the characters is as carefully studied by Webster as the structure of the plot.

The "politic" princes and churchmen, the cynical
Characters. bawd and informer driven by poverty
into reckless paths, the courtesan, and the
pure and loving woman, are themselves in every
phrase that falls from their lips. But Webster has
not got much beyond the type, and some of these
types belong only to the stage. The Italian politician may have had his counterpart in real life,
but Webster has not convinced us of it; and his
sardonic and even sentimental villain is somewhat
melodramatic. His women characters are his greatest.
Vittoria is a splendid representative of her class. She
has not the infinite variety and charm of Cleopatra,
but is a more intense and tragic figure. Could the
poet have carried her through the play as Shakespeare does Cleopatra, a centre of ever fresh and
abounding interest, not Shakespeare himself would
have produced a greater character. But Webster
gives us the impression of being able to etch a few
fine poses, rather than to delineate a character who
is alive and interesting in every situation. The
Duchess of Malfi has perhaps more variety than
Vittoria. She combines more qualities, is bold and
timid, loving and proud,—

"Whether the spirit of greatness or of woman
Reign most in her I know not,"—

infinitely pitiful in her death, yet infinitely noble and
queenly. *The White Devil* is a swifter and intenser
play than *The Duchess of Malfi*,—some critics greatly
prefer it,—but the character of the Duchess seems to

me to raise the latter to that higher class of tragedy which represents the fatal conflict of what is noblest in humanity with "inauspicious stars."

It is in his style that the conscious deliberate character of Webster's art is most immediately obvious.

Style. His diction is studiously appropriate, studiously heightened and impassioned. He specially commends the "full and heightened style of Master Chapman," and the influence of Chapman is, I think, observable in the elaborateness and "metaphysical" character of his metaphors. But it was from Shakespeare that he learned the power of thrilling and pregnant figure and phrase. Some of his finest touches are directly traceable to *King Lear* and *Antony and Cleopatra.* But Webster's style is more elaborated than Shakespeare's: it wants the flowing facility of which Jonson complains. Even the most imaginative touches smell a little of the lamp—appear to be laid on from without, although with a fine sense of what is appropriate, rather than to spring spontaneously from the heart of the passion.

A certain grave dignity of style is all that is distinctive in *Appius and Virginia* or in Webster's comedies.

Other Plays. The tragic theme of the former he has treated in a strangely hard and external way. Into the comedies he has put little or none of the sardonic wit which he labours so strenuously in the famous tragedies. Webster has earned his place among the greatest of the Elizabethans by two plays, the theme of which appealed to his genius, at once tragic and melodramatic, and on which he expended

—what the Elizabethans were too sparing of—time and labour.

The two tragedies of Cyril Tourneur [1]—of whose life we know but little—are of the same cast as Marston's and Webster's. They are written to the same didactic receipt—

Tourneur.

"When the bad bleeds then is the tragedy good;"

they reflect in like wise the attraction for the Elizabethan imagination of Italian crime; and they are full like them of echoes from *Hamlet*, to us a problem of character, to the Elizabethans a fascinating melodrama of crime and nemesis.

The Atheist's Tragedy (1611) is a crude picture of the subtle crimes of the "politician" and the nemesis which overtakes him. *The Revenger's Tragedy* (1607) is, despite the earlier date at which it was printed, a maturer play in structure and verse, but it cannot be said with justice that it rises to the level of tragedy. No character detaches himself or herself from the melodramatic and lurid phantasmagoria of lust, murder, and vengeance with the tragic distinctness and beauty of the intense Vittoria, or the nobly pathetic Duchess of Malfi. Yet Mr Courthope is too harsh a critic when he dubs Tourneur bluntly a poetaster. The scenes between Vendice and his mother and sister are not altogether undeserving of Lamb's eloquent eulogy; and through the play are scattered individual "strokes" of nature and poetry, of the kind that are the glory of the Elizabethan drama, which one would

[1] *The Plays and Poems of Cyril Tourneur*, ed. with critical introd. and notes by J. Churton Collins, Lond., 1878.

look in vain for in the tragi-comedy of France or Holland. Such is Castiza's cry when her mother would be her betrayer—

"I cry you mercy! lady, I mistook you;
 Pray, did you see my mother? which way went she?
 Pray God I have not lost her;"—

and Vendice's

"joy's a subtle elf,—
 I think man's happiest when he forgets himself."

The lines in *The Atheist's Tragedy* which describe the drowned soldier will find a place in every anthology gathered from the Elizabethans.

If, as seems to have been the case, Jonson to some extent eclipsed Shakespeare in the eyes of those who affected scholarship and "art," the inheritors of his popularity were undoubtedly Beaumont and Fletcher.[1] They belonged to a higher rank socially than the generality of the dramatists. John Fletcher, the elder, was the son of a president of a Cambridge College who was subsequently Dean of Peterborough, Bishop of Bristol, and Bishop of London. Francis Beaumont's father was a landed proprietor in Leicestershire, and a judge of the

Beaumont and Fletcher.

---

[1] The first folio (containing thirty-four plays and a masque) appeared in 1647, the second (containing fifty-one plays, a masque, and the *Four Plays, or Moral Representations, in one*) in 1679. The commendatory verses prefixed to the first are an eloquent testimony to their popularity. The standard edition is that of Dyce (11 vols.), 1876, now difficult to obtain. New editions by A. H. Bullen, Lond., 1904, and Arnold Glover, Cambridge, 1905, are in course of appearing. Select plays in the *Mermaid Series*. Critical notices are numerous, from Dryden's to Mr Swinburne's (*Studies in Prose and Poetry*). Dr E. Koeppel and others have inquired into sources.

Common Pleas. Fletcher (1579-1625) was educated at Cambridge, but does not seem to have graduated. *The Woman Hater*, formerly attributed to Fletcher, —now generally, on internal evidence alone, to Beaumont, — was published in 1607, and the two friends began to collaborate about this date. *Philaster* (1620) is probably their first joint work. Beaumont had been at Oxford, but only for a short time, being entered a member of the Middle Temple in November 1600. He began as a poet, composing an Ovidian story, *Salmacis and Hermaphroditus* (1602), and he wrote other poems in an extravagantly conceited style. He died in 1616, so that his friend and partner outlived him by nine years. After Beaumont's death, indeed, Fletcher collaborated with other dramatists, especially, it would seem, with Massinger.

The exact manner in which the two dramatists worked together is not discoverable, nor has the work devoted to the problem recently altered the traditional view, which regarded Beaumont as the more careful and correct artist, Fletcher as the more inventive and genial temperament.[1] Differences

Tone of their plays.

---

[1] I have no intention of belittling the interest of the researches of Mr Fleay (*On Metrical Tests as applied to Dramatic Poetry, Part II., Beaumont, Fletcher, and Massinger*, in *Transactions of the Shakespeare Society*, 1874), or of Mr R. Boyle (*Englische Studien*, vols. v. to x., 1882-7). In a fuller history it would be necessary to discuss their conclusions. My position is simply Dr Ward's (who accepts many of their findings), that no important distinction of *ethos* between the two has been revealed. Though, of course, it is of importance to know that it is to Fletcher is chiefly due the licentious use of extra-metrical syllables at the close of the line, which did so much to reduce verse to the level of rhythmical prose. The view that "Beaumont's judgment checked what Fletcher writ" deserves the respect due to an early tradition.

in style and versification are easily detected, but for literary history are less important than the community of spirit which made the work of the two so vivid a reflection of one aspect of the age—of the taste, not of the great body of the English people, but of the exquisites of the court, whose handsome faces and brilliant costumes are preserved for us on the canvasses of Vandyke, and who were soon to be brought into conflict with the sterner temper of the Puritan middle classes. At the same time, they were not above catering for a citizen audience as in *The Knight of the Burning Pestle.*

The plays of Beaumont and Fletcher were enormously popular with the audience whose taste they reflected. Compared with their sparkling "modernity," Shakespeare seemed to Cartwright and to Suckling old-fashioned and coarse; and the opinion of Cartwright and Suckling and Herrick is reiterated by Dryden, after the Restoration had brought back the taste and morality of the court. "Their plays are now," he says, "the most pleasant and frequent entertainments of the stage, two of theirs being acted through the year for one of Shakespeare's or Jonson's. The reason is because there is a certain gaiety in their comedies and pathos in their more serious plays which suits generally with all men's humours." What Dryden indicates is not difficult to find. All the attractive qualities of Beaumont and Fletcher's dramatic work are heightened and obvious—sentiment, eloquence, sweetness of verse, gaiety of dialogue. The best of the more serious

Popularity.

plays, such as *The Maid's Tragedy* (1619), *Philaster* (1620), *A King and No King* (1619), *Thierry and Theodoret* (1621), *The False One* (1647), *Bonduca* (1647), and *The Two Noble Kinsmen* (1634), in which Shakespeare *may* have collaborated, are rich in effective, dramatic, and especially pathetic scenes. The death of Aspatia and Evadne; Arethusa, Philaster, and Bellario in the forest; the discovery of their mutual passion by Arbaces and Panthea; the great interview between Thierry and Ordella before the temple of Diana; the death of Penius; the opening scene of *The Two Noble Kinsmen*, are a few that rise readily to the memory —scenes of heightened pathos, dramatic power, and poetic eloquence.

But the very ease and pleasure with which we recall individual scenes betray the limits of the authors' dramatic range. They stand out like purple patches from the play. It is the scenes we remember, not the characters which they reveal. With Beaumont and Fletcher the last phase of the Elizabethan drama began as unmistakably as its first phase was inaugurated by Marlowe. Sentiment began to take the place of character. The final impression we carry away from a play of Marlowe or Shakespeare or Jonson is of one or two great characters of boundless passion or all-absorbing "humour." The sentiment and poetry are subservient to the presentation of character in action. The most eloquent and moving speeches are not written for the sake of their own beauty, but are the flaming sparks which fly from the contact between the will of steel and the grindstone of

Decadence.

fate. With Beaumont and Fletcher all this is changed. The characters are insubstantial and inconsistent; the most distinctly drawn are the least real. Their heroes, Penius and Caratach and Æcius, are sketched on the old model; but what their creators elaborate with most gusto is not the fierce energy of their conflict with Fate, but the dignified and pathetic eloquence of their resignation. They die to the music of their own virtues, in sentiments so highly strung as to ring false. The best characters in Beaumont and Fletcher's plays are those the very breath of whose life is sentiment. Arethusa and Aspatia, Bellario and Ordella, are charming if ethereal figures. Devoted love and sweet submissiveness flow in golden phrases from their lips. But on the other hand, where energy of will and intensity of passion are most imperatively required, Beaumont and Fletcher appear to me to fall short. Their handling of evil characters and terrible incidents is inferior to that of Webster or Middleton or Ford. Nothing is forbidden to the poet if his treatment be adequate. But he must realise the full significance of what he portrays. Deeds of horror justify their representation by the lurid light which they throw upon the workings of the human heart. Beaumont and Fletcher describe such deeds with a bluntness that is almost levity, or a rhetoric which palls, seldom with any approach to tragic sincerity and power. In Beaumont and Fletcher the sterner notes of the older drama melt into the fluting of love and woe. But how eloquent their pathos is! From no dramatist except Shakespeare could be gathered so many flowers

of poetry in dialogue or soliloquy or song; although
Marlowe and Webster both outsoar them on occasion,
and Dekker's sweetness is purer and more artless, and
in all of these the poetic and dramatic interpenetrate
more closely. Like Webster, they are indebted for
many of their finest phrases to Shakespeare. But,
while Webster remembers the thrilling tragic touches,
the "cover their faces" of *King Lear*, Beaumont and
Fletcher reproduce what is most romantic. Viola's
description of her love in *Twelfth Night* is recalled by
Aspatia's words—

> "Strive to make me look
> Like Sorrow's monument: and the trees about me
> Let them be dry and leafless: let the rocks
> Groan with continual surges: and behind me
> Make all a desolation."

Thinking of Cleopatra, she bids her friends take for
lovers "two dead cold aspics."

> "They cannot flatter nor forswear: one kiss
> Makes a long peace for all."

In comedy Beaumont and Fletcher follow, on the
whole, the beaten track, and describe in flowing verse
and easy dialogue the adventures, serious
Their Comedy. and comic, of lovers. They have some
interesting studies in humours and in the mock heroic
—very slight and hasty when compared with Jonson's
elaborate workmanship. These it is the fashion
now to attribute mainly to Beaumont. Lazarillo, the
gourmet in *The Woman Hater*, Bessus in *A King and
No King*—the merest sketch when compared with

Falstaff or Bobadil—are good examples. But perhaps the most delightful is the light-hearted caroller Merrythought in *The Knight of the Burning Pestle*. Scott was fond of quoting in his *Journals* one of his snatches of song:—

> " I would not be a serving-man
> To carry the cloak bag still;
> Nor would I be a falconer,
> The greedy hawks to fill:
> But I would be in a good house,
> And have a good master too;
> But I would eat and drink of the best,
> And no work would I do."

That he was to some extent the original of Scott's own David Gellatly is, I think, certain. In general, however, it is not the individual characters which are the principal source of interest and amusement in their comedies, but the easily unfolded story, the sparkling careless dialogue with its air of good-breeding, and the distinctness and charm—in spite of serious blots—with which they portrayed the young men and women of their age. Their gaiety is not more hearty or infectious than Middleton's. In fact, the situations and scenes in the comedies of the latter are often more essentially humorous, but Middleton's is almost always a comedy of citizen life and character. Beaumont and Fletcher's, with a gleam of the poetry which illumines Shakespeare's, have also the air of polite society which pervades the later comedy from Etheredge to Congreve. *The Wild-Goose Chase, Rule a Wife and have a Wife, The Little French Lawyer,*

The Spanish Curate, The Scornful Lady, and *Monsieur Thomas* are excellent plays of incident and dialogue. The tone is often licentious, and neither the situations nor the dialogues show much depth of humour or brilliancy of wit if closely scrutinised. But the reader is not tempted to scrutinise them closely. Everything is, as Scott says, set to a good tune. One is borne easily along by the rapid stream of incidents and sparkling, natural conversation.

Of Fletcher's pastoral drama, *The Faithful Shepherdess* (1609-10), it is usual to speak in very high terms, and it has undoubtedly all the beauty of Fletcher's language in description and song. But the soul of the play appears to me cold and even repulsive. Not only are some of the characters vile beyond words, but a frigid sensual conception of love runs through the whole play, marring the intended idealisation of chastity, a theme more congenial to Milton than to Fletcher.

Fletcher's most important colleague after the death of Beaumont, and the principal dramatist of the Twenties and early Thirties, was Philip Massinger.[1] His father was a servant in the household of the Earl of Pembroke. He was at Oxford for a short time, but left abruptly, and came

Massinger.

---

[1] *The Plays of Philip Massinger, with Notes, critical and explanatory,* by W. *Gifford,* 4 vols., Lond., 1805. 2nd ed., 1813. Select plays in the *Mermaid Series. The Political Element in Massinger,* S. R. Gardiner in the *New Shakespeare Society's Transactions,* 1875-6. On Massinger's classical scholarship and his indebtedness to Shakespeare, see Wolfgang von Wurzbach, *Philip Massinger,* Shak. Deutsche Jahrbuch, xxxv-vi.

to London about 1607, where he collaborated with Fletcher, Dekker, Field, and others. In 1622 the *Virgin Martyr* was published as by him and Dekker. From then onward we have a continuous list of plays ascribed to him in the office book of Sir Henry Herbert. At the same time, it is clear from the dedications prefixed to those which he published that his dramatic activity never freed him from poverty. Gifford has conjectured from the tone of some of his plays that he was a Roman Catholic, and others have discovered in his work reflections of the political sentiment of his day.

Dramatically Massinger belongs to the school of Fletcher. He too delineates sentiment rather than character. His heroes and heroines are high-flown sentimentalists. Like Fletcher he is fond of piquant and critical situations, and develops them with abundant rhetoric. In *The Virgin Martyr* and *The Renegado* he has depicted the exalted emotions of the martyr; in *The Unnatural Combat*, more unnatural and ugly passions than even Ford. In the *Duke of Milan* he has traced, following the story of Mariamne, the excesses of uxorious passion. In *The Bondman* he has delineated a lover's transcendent abnegation of self, and in *The Fatal Dowry* a point of honour as exalted as any in a play of Corneille. Massinger's characters are no more real and convincing than Fletcher's, and in wealth of poetic diction he falls far short of him. His style is pure, correct, and dignified, but rhetorical, and verging towards eloquent and rhythmic prose. What distinguishes Massinger, and enlists for him a respect that the bluntness of Fletcher's moral sympathy often forfeits, is the sincere and earnest moral purpose running through his works. He is the most interestingly didactic of the dramatists. Jonson is didactic, because the critics prescribe the inculcation of virtue to the dramatists. But Massinger has a sensitive and eager sympathy with virtue and nobility of character, which breathes through his somewhat hectic characters and scenes of eloquent argument and declamation. He is often strangely licentious in the language he puts into the mouths of all his characters. So in varying degrees is every one of the dramatists, and Beaumont and Fletcher cultivated indecency. But in Massinger this licentiousness has the awkwardness and exaggeration of one who has no interest in, or sympathy with, what he thinks it necessary to introduce. Moreover, he is not saved from awkward exaggeration by a sense of humour. He has little humour and no wit. His lighter comic scenes are inexpressibly tedious, and even disgusting. But, like another and greater sentimentalist, he had the power of grim caricature. Sir Giles Overreach in *A New Way to Pay Old Debts* (1633), and Luke Frugal in *The City Madam* (1632), are almost sublime studies in the manner of Dickens — villains not intelligible but impressive. How strong the didactic impulse was in Massinger is seen if the first of these plays be compared with its original, Middleton's *A Trick to catch the Old One*. What the latter treats in a spirit of pure and reckless gaiety, Massinger converts into grim didactic; and Middleton's two gaily befooled and converted usurers become an inhuman monster, devouring men's lands and prepared to prostitute his daughter's honour for social advancement.

The tendency so obvious in Fletcher and Massinger to diverge from the simple and natural in feeling in search of piquant and morally trying situations and morbid emotions, reaches its extreme in the most characteristic plays of John Ford,[1] whose life coincided in time pretty closely with that of Massinger. His first published work appeared in 1607. He collaborated with various playwrights in plays most of which are lost. His extant plays were produced between 1628 and 1638.

Ford.

Ford was not a professed playwright. He was a lawyer, and apparently had business of some kind. He was thus possibly more free than the average dramatist to follow the bent of his own taste; but there is not, as a fact, any striking difference between his plays and the ordinary fare provided by them. They are highly artificial tragedies of crime and revenge, comedies, and one history, *Perkin Warbeck*. The last is the most natural of his plays, and by no means unpleasing or undignified historic drama. But Ford's reputation, like Webster's, rests on his tragedies about which the most diverse opinions are entertained. The subjects of them are of an intensely painful character

---

[1] *The Works of John Ford, with Notes, critical and explanatory,* by W. *Gifford*, 2 vols., Lond., 1827; revised, with additions and a new introduction, by Dyce, 3 vols., 1869. Select plays in the *Mermaid Series*.

—incest and murder in one, revenge and suicide in another—but well fitted for tragic and poetic handling. Have they been quite adequately handled by Ford? That his plays are not completely successful even Ford's most ardent admirers will admit. The stories are clumsily told; the comic element beneath contempt; all except the principal characters are not only unreal but uninteresting. But what about the central tragic scenes in them? Ford is certainly free from the charge to which Fletcher is liable. There is no levity or callousness in his treatment of things terrible. He is acutely sensitive to the horror and pathos of what he describes. There is no justification, it seems to me, for any adverse judgment on Ford's moral character based on the character of his themes. He is an artist, and handles them with the detached seriousness of the artist. But it is only occasionally that his tragic intensity finds clear and dramatic expression. In *Love's Sacrifice* (1633), which is full of reminiscences of *Othello*, the intention is noble and tragic, but the execution very imperfect; and the same is true, it seems to me, of the more celebrated *Broken Heart* (1633), whose structure is inorganic, beautiful as more than one of the individual scenes is in sentiment and poetry. Only the intense and painful Giovanni and Annabella scenes of *'Tis Pity* (1633) appear to me really dramatic, to portray passion agitating the will and evoking a conflict. There is none of the same dramatic interest in *The Broken Heart*, *The Lover's Melancholy* (1629), *Love's Sacrifice* (1633), and *The Lady's Trial* (1629). The finest scenes in these portray no conflict of passions, no resolution taking shape, but present in a style less rich and fanciful than Fletcher's, less thrilling than Webster's, less declamatory than Massinger's, but with a grave intensity of its own, some fixed phase of a high-flown not to say morbid sentiment. And if the sentiments are unreal the characters are more so. Ford's *dramatis personæ* are not creatures of flesh and blood. The best resemble delicate wax-works, touched with a pale and feverish beauty at times by the intensity of the sentiment which the poet puts into their mouths.

James Shirley[1] (1596-1666), who is generally reckoned the last of the Elizabethans, is a dramatist of lighter build but more varied talent than Ford.

Shirley.

Educated at Merchant Taylor's School and Cambridge, he seems to have turned to play-writing only after he had been in orders, and —on his conversion to Romanism—a schoolmaster. From the year following Fletcher's death to the close of the theatres he was a fertile author of tragedies, comedies, and masques, and a special favourite of the King and Queen. He prepared *The Triumph of Peace*, which was presented at great cost by the Inns of Court on the occasion of Prynne's attack upon the Queen. He visited Dublin at the invitation of the Earl of Kildare, and some of his plays, including the Mystery of *St Patrick for Ireland*, were written for

---

[1] *The Dramatic Works and Poems of James Shirley, with Notes by William Gifford, and additional notes and some account of Shirley and his Writings.* By Alexander Dyce, 6 vols., 1833. Select plays in the *Mermaid Series*.

an Irish theatre. He published poems and printed several of his plays during the years that the theatres were closed, as well as assisting Ogilby in his translations, and died in the year of the great fire.

Shirley's plays include tragedies; comedies of the usual *novella* type, moving between what would most strictly be called tragi-comedy and lighter comedy of manners; and some experiments in the direction of mystery (*St Patrick for Ireland*), morality (*A Contention for Honour and Riches*), and pastoral, his *Arcadia* (1640) being a dramatisation of Sidney's romance.

Shirley's tragedies—of which the best are probably *The Traitor* (1635) and *The Cardinal* (1652)—are of the artificial type of Massinger's and Ford's, but he has neither the moral eloquence of the former nor the intense, if hectic, feeling of the latter. He seems to me a slighter Fletcher, with much of the same ease and naturalness of style, and the same penchant for romantic pathos, and gay, often licentious, comedy of incident and manners. There are scenes and speeches of indubitable pathos and poetry in his tragedies and in the serious scenes of tragi-comedies like *The Wedding* (1629), *The Example* (1637), *The Grateful Servant* (1630), and *The Royal Master* (1638); and Shirley's comedy—of which good examples are *The Witty Fair One* (1632), *The Lady of Pleasure* (1635), and *Hyde Park* (1637)—has the air of good breeding which distinguishes Fletcher's from that of Middleton and Dekker, though to Pepys it appeared sadly old-fashioned.

Of minor men — followers in different ways of

Jonson and Fletcher—Richard Brome, Thomas Randolph, William Cartwright, Jasper Mayne, Henry Glapthorne, Sir John Suckling, and Sir William Davenant, as well as others whom Mr Bullen has rescued from oblivion, it would be impossible in the space at my disposal to attempt distinct characterisation. There are few in which it is not possible to find good things—poetry and humour,—but none are dramatists of real merit, and none struck out any new line. The old themes are repeated in a hackneyed and worn-out style, and in a verse which tends to disappear altogether. The period of buoyant vitality and of development in the Elizabethan drama closed with the death of Fletcher.

CHAPTER IV.

ENGLISH POETRY.[1]

INTRODUCTORY—GEORGE CHAPMAN—THE YOUNGER SPENSERIANS—PROTESTANT AND BOURGEOIS—THE FLETCHERS—BROWNE AND WITHER—QUARLES, MORE, BEAUMONT, ETC.—DRUMMOND AND SIR JOHN BEAUMONT—DONNE AND JONSON—CHARACTERISTICS AND INFLUENCE—CAROLINE COURTLY POETRY, RELIGIOUS AND SECULAR—HERBERT, VAUGHAN, CRASHAW, AND TRAHERNE—CAREW, LOVELACE, SUCKLING, HERRICK—ANDREW MARVELL—MILTON'S LIFE AND EARLY POEMS—POETRY OF THE COMMONWEALTH—WALLER AND DENHAM—DAVENANT AND CHAMBERLAYNE—COWLEY—MILTON'S LATER POEMS—'PARADISE LOST'—'PARADISE REGAINED'—'SAMSON AGONISTES'—CONCLUSION.

SPENSER found no successor able to continue his work of naturalising the Italian romantic epic, that most delightful product of the early Renaissance, into which he breathed the ethical temper of the Reformation — softened by Italian Platonism or neo-Platonism — as well as the spirit of intense

Introduction.

[1] *General Histories.*—It is hardly necessary to enumerate standard works like Saintsbury's *Short History*, &c., and *Elizabethan Literature;* Gosse's *Seventeenth Century Studies*, London, 1874; *Modern English Literature*, London, 1896; and *Jacobean Poets*, London, 1894. More recent are Courthope's *History of English Poetry*, vol. iii., London, 1903, to which I am much indebted though not always in agreement, and though the first sketch of my chapter had been written before the volume appeared; Chambers's *Cyclopædia of*

patriotism which animated Englishmen in the year of the Spanish Armada. To harmonise such diverse elements was a difficult task, and, even before Spenser's

English Literature, ed. David Patrick, Edinburgh, 1901; Jusserand's *Histoire Littéraire du Peuple Anglais*, tom. ii., Paris, 1904; and Barrett Wendell's *The Temper of Seventeenth-Century Literature*, London, 1905. For lives and dates I have followed, generally, the *Dictionary of National Biography*.

Modern Editions.—*Chapman's Works*, London, 1875, vols. ii. and iii., with preface by Mr Swinburne, reprinted separately the same year. *Giles* and *Phineas Fletcher, Sir John Beaumont, Donne, Herbert, Vaughan, Crashaw,* and *Marvell,* were all edited by the late Dr Grosart for the privately published *Fuller's Worthies Library,* 1868, &c. *Giles Fletcher, Herrick,* and some others were issued in the same editor's *Early English Poets,* 1876, &c. Selections from *Phineas Fletcher* are contained in *The Spenser of His Age,* J. R. Tutin, Hull, 1905. *Quarles, Dr Henry More, Dr Joseph Beaumont,* were edited by Grosart in his *Chertsey Worthies Library,* also private. *The Muses Library,* London, 1893, reissued 1903, includes editions of *Drummond,* ed. Wm. C. Ward (who has traced many borrowings); *Donne,* ed. E. K. Chambers (the best text); *Vaughan,* ed. E. K. Chambers; *Carew,* ed. Arthur Vincent; *Herrick,* ed. Alfred Pollard; *Marvell,* ed. G. A. Aitkin; and *Waller,* ed. G. Thorn Drury. *Herbert* has been frequently republished. A good text of the *Temple* is that of Edgar C. S. Gibson in the *Library of Devotion,* London, 1899; *Lovelace* and *Suckling* were edited by W. C. Hazlitt in his *Library of Old Authors,* London, 1856, &c. Lovelace's *Lucasta* has been reproduced in the *Unit Library,* London, 1904. Habington's *Castara* was edited by C. A. Elton, Bristol, n.d. [1812], and by Edward Arber, *English Reprints,* 1869. *Randolph* was edited by W. C. Hazlitt, London, 1875. *Cartwright* and *Davenant* have not been republished complete since *Chalmers' British Poets,* London, 1810. *Denham* was republished with *Waller,* 1857. Chamberlayne's *Pharonnida* has just been reissued in Saintsbury's *Caroline Poets,* Oxford, 1905. Of Milton's poetical works, Masson's, London, 1890, is the last complete one with annotations. Mr Beeching's, Oxford, 1900, has reproduced the original spelling. *Cowley* and *Crashaw* have been edited by A. R. Waller in the *Cambridge English Classics.* Traherne's poems have been published from the MS. by Bertram Dobell, London, 1903.

death, had been rendered impossible by the course of English religious and political history—as impossible as it was after the American war to preserve the early Whig identification of the cause of Britain with the cause of political liberty. Religious persecution made it difficult for the Puritan to identify his zeal for England with his zeal for Protestantism. At the same time, the essentially pagan spirit of the Italian Renaissance was not easily exorcised even by Spenser, and the emancipated artistic enthusiasm which created the Elizabethan drama, poems such as *Hero and Leander* and *Venus and Adonis*, and the sonnets of Shakespeare, was to the stern spirit of Puritanism simply anathema. Before the sixteenth century ended poets were beginning to form different schools, or else the two strains, the secular and the religious, run side by side in a single poet's work without his endeavouring to reconcile them in any way.

This tendency is accentuated in the early seventeenth century. This chapter deals with distinct groups or schools of poets. The patriotic note of Spenser and Shakespeare is heard only from belated Elizabethans as Drayton and Chapman. The Protestant religious poets form a group by themselves; the Catholic Anglicans another. The courtly poets, whether religious or secular, are out of touch with the nation at large, their poetry a delicate exotic. One poet, indeed, emerges with the power that genius gives to harmonise diverse elements. Milton, like Spenser, unites the spirit of the Renaissance with that of the Reformation, and both with patriotism. But he does so only by narrowing though intensifying each, by sacrificing some of the finest elements in the noblest Elizabethan conceptions of beauty, goodness, and country. Milton's ideal of art becomes strictly, even pedantically, classical; his Protestantism is less ethical than Spenser's, and more theological; his patriotism tends to include only those Englishmen who form the chosen people of God.

Of the Elizabethan poets who continued to produce fresh and interesting poetry in the reign of James, *Chapman.* if we set aside Donne and Jonson as the fountain-heads of Jacobean and Caroline poetry, the two most important, Daniel and Drayton, have been included in the volume on *The Later Renaissance*. One veteran and rugged Elizabethan, however, deserves a word as poet as well as dramatist. Chapman's earliest volume of poems, *The Shadow of Night*, containing the pedantic and obscure *Hymnus in Noctem* and *Hymnus in Cynthiam*, appeared in 1594; his *Ovid's Banquet of Sense*—a characteristic contribution to the *Venus and Adonis* class of poem—with *The Amorous Zodiac*—a translation from the French—in 1595; and his completion of Marlowe's *Hero and Leander* in 1598. His great work, the translation of Homer, was begun some time before 1598, when *Seaven Bookes of the Iliades of Homer, Prince of Poets*, appeared with a dedication to the Earl of Essex. The complete *Iliad* appeared in 1611; the complete *Odyssey* in 1614; *The Whole Works of Homer* in 1616. *The Battle of the Frogs* was added later, as well as the *Hymns*.

Chapman comes at the head of a chapter on seventeenth-century poetry as a useful reminder that "fantastic" is not a very distinctive title to apply to the poetry of Donne and his followers,—that if conceit and far-fetched similitudes are a sign of decadence, then Elizabethan poetry was born decadent, for from first to last it is, in Arnold's phrase, "steeped in humours and fantasticality up to its very lips." Whether we consider Chapman's original poems or his translations, his obscure, pedantic, harsh, yet always ardent and fitfully splendid hymns and complimentary verses, or the *Homer* which Keats has immortalised, it would be difficult to conceive a poet who, despite his classics, his eulogies of learning, and his friendship for Jonson, is more essentially "Gothic" as Addison and Thomson used the word. It is a tribute to the genius of Homer that there was so much in the *Iliad* and *Odyssey* which Chapman could translate well, or even greatly. He is at his best, it seems to me, when describing the rush of fighting, and for this, as well as other reasons, his *Iliad* is better than his *Odyssey*; but when full justice has been done to the animation of his style, its entire freedom from otiose filling-out, its not infrequent felicity and splendour of phrase, the last word on the inadequacy of Chapman's colloquialisms and conceits to reproduce the dignity and simplicity of Homer has been spoken by Matthew Arnold.[1]

It is difficult, in the absence of such contemporary evidence as is afforded to-day by critical reviews, to

[1] *On Translating Homer.* Lond., 1861.

date exactly the changes in poetical taste. It seems clear, however, that in the closing years of the sixteenth century there was a reaction against the diffuse, flamboyant, Italianate poetry which Spenser, Sidney, and Lodge had made fashionable,—a reaction which showed itself in the satires of Hall and Marston, but found its fullest expression in the poetry —much of which is satirical—of Donne and of Jonson, who took the place in courtly circles which had been held earlier by Spenser and Sidney. The Spenserians of the early seventeenth century—between whom and Spenser in pastoral poetry Drayton forms an important link—were not courtly poets. Though they look towards the court on occasions, they stand outside its circle. They belong to the Protestant wing of the Anglican Church; and in the somewhat bourgeois and didactic tone of their poetry, their taste for emblems, and the natural, artless tone in which they speak of themselves, resemble the Dutch poets of the same class.

The Spenserians.

The most thorough-going disciples of Spenser among these serious young poets of the reign of James I. were the Cambridge divines and poets Phineas (1582-1648) and Giles (1583-1623) Fletcher, the sons of Giles Fletcher, author of *Licia*, and cousins of the dramatist. They were both Fellows—Phineas of King's, Giles of Trinity College—and both took orders. Giles, after being reader in Greek at Cambridge, became rector of Alderton in Suffolk, and Phineas, after some vicissitudes of fortune, was appointed rector of Hilgay in Norfolk.

In Phineas Fletcher's poetry there were apparently the two distinct strains of which we have spoken above.

Phineas Fletcher. His *Sicelides*, a comedy performed before James in 1614, mingles pastoral love-story with comic scenes not devoid of coarseness; and Grosart conjectured that he was the author of *Britain's Ida* (1627), a frank and voluptuous Ovidian idyll. On the other hand, the Spenserian pastorals and allegories which he published in 1627 and 1633 —describing them as "these raw essays of my very unripe years and almost childhood"—are without exception religious, and so was all his subsequent work in verse and prose. The *Locustæ vel Pietas Jesuitica: The Locusts or Appolyonists* is a strange poem—the first part in Latin, the second in English—describing allegorically the rise of the Jesuits and the Gunpowder Plot. Milton borrowed from it for his allegory of Sin and Death. The *Piscatorie Eclogues* is a fluent imitation of Spenser's pastorals with borrowings from Sannazaro, full of the poet's views and woes. His most ambitious poem, *The Purple Island*, elaborates the suggestion given by Spenser's description of the Castle of Alma (*Faerie Queene*, ii. 8), portraying in a minutely detailed allegory the constitution of man, physical and mental, and enlarging in characteristically theological manner the strife between Temperance and her foes into the Christian warfare between Voletta (the will) and Satan.

This is the way in which his seventeenth-century followers dealt with Spenser's great poem. They cared nothing for his romance—whose influence was not to be felt till much later—everything for the didactic allegory. Fletcher's pastoral openings to each canto are delightful; his style is lucid, nervous, and flowing; the personifications are clever and occasionally effective; but the soul of the reader faints under the strain of such sustained and relentless allegory. There is no escape, as in the *Faerie Queene*, to realms of pure romance, and it is with a sense of profound relief that one hears King James blow his trumpet and summon Christ to the rescue of the hard-pressed Will.

Giles Fletcher was happier in his choice of subject than his brother, and his temperament was more lyrical and mystical. His *Christ's Victorie and Triumph, in Heaven and Earth, over and after Death* (1610), an allegoric, narrative, lyrical rhapsody on the Atonement, Temptation, Crucifixion, and Resurrection, is an interesting link between Spenser's and Milton's religious poetry. The form and language are Spenserian—allegorical, diffuse, and flamboyant,—but the subject is, like Milton's, theological. The more ethical aspect of Protestantism, presented in Spenser's *House of Holiness*, yields to the seventeenth-century preoccupation with theology, the divine scheme of salvation wrought out in eternity. Man, with his puny efforts after righteousness, falls into the background.

Giles Fletcher.

Poetically, the resemblance of Fletcher's poem to Spenser's is deliberate, and superficial rather than temperamental. There is a vast difference between the flow and shimmer of the older poet's romantic stanzas and the strenuous, antithetic declamation of the younger. Fletcher is always ardent; his personifications are far more poetic and impressive than his brother's; the descriptive passages have some of the colour and music of his model's; and his lyrical rendering with variations of Tasso's song of the rose is as fine in its different way as Spenser's. But Fletcher's excessive use of antithesis, the bad taste and extravagance of many of the descriptions (for example, of Christ in the canto on the Temptation, where

> "His cheeks as snowie apples sop't in wine,
> Had their red roses quencht with lillies white,
> And like to garden strawberries did shine
> Wash't in a boul of milk")—

these and other features remind a student, more than anything in Donne or his school, of the faults of Italian "secentismo," of the *Adone* and the *Strage degli Innocenti*.

If the younger Spenserians showed no taste for romance, they were enthusiastic and unwearied cultivators of the pastoral. Whatever wider circles may have thought,— and Colonel Prideaux believes the pastoral was not generally popular in England, which is perhaps equally true of that other over-cultivated form, the sonnet,—the poets themselves were never weary of listening to each other while they sang of the joys of country life and the pains of love, or moralised their strain and descanted on virtue and pure religion. Their

Pastorals.

guides were Spenser and Sidney, and more immediately Michael Drayton. Not only is some of the best of Drayton's seventeenth-century work pastoral, but his *Polyolbion* (begun in 1598, and probably well known to his friends before its publication in 1612 and 1622) had excited enthusiasm for English scenery and rivers. If Jacobean pastoral poetry is often tedious and long-winded, if its cultivators produced no such delicate, courtly exotic as the *Aminta*—to which, after all, the later *Comus* is a very satisfactory counter-weight,—yet under Drayton's influence it became more truly natural in sentiment, a more faithful mirror of English scenery, and some of the sweetest versification of this period, when Donne's and Jonson's bold experiments were unsettling English prosody, is to be found in pastorals written north and south of the Tweed.

All these features are discoverable in the poems of William Browne (1590-1645?) of Tavistock in Devonshire—

"Blessed spot,
Whose equal all the world affordeth not."

Educated at Oxford, he became a member of the Inner Temple, where he was the friend of Drayton, Chapman, Jonson, Selden, Wither, and Brooke. The first part of *Britannia's Pastorals* appeared in 1613. In the following year he published some more regular eclogues, *The Shepherd's Pipe*, to which Wither and others contributed. The second part of the longer poem appeared in

Browne.

1616, the whole in 1625. Browne was also the author of a masque, and of sonnets, jocular verses, epigrams, and epitaphs, the last of which include the beautiful

"Underneath this sable hearse,"

which, however, was till recently attributed to Jonson.

Britannia's Pastorals blends all the diverse strains of Elizabethan pastoralism. Descriptions inspired by Sidney's *Arcadia*, Spenser's *Faerie Queene*, and Drayton's *Polyolbion* are combined with moral allegory and satire, in which the influence of Langland as well as contemporaries is traceable, and all these with Ovidian metamorphoses. A story of wooing and adventure, and the changing of nymphs into streams and flowers, runs through the poem; but there are endless digressions to satirise James's neglect of the fleet, to bewail the death of Prince Henry, or to sing the praise of virtue and of poets dead and living. The whole is borne along on a stream of flowing decasyllabics which suggest the music of the pipe, and whose echo is audible in the varied cadences of Keats's *Endymion*, which irritated the ear of *Quarterly* reviewers.

The same high enthusiasm for moral goodness, for nature, and for song, with a more ardent love-strain, uttered in a sweet but shriller music, are the characteristics of all that is best in the poetry of the much too voluble George Wither (1588-1667). A native of Bentworth in Hampshire, for a short

Wither.

time at Magdalen College, Oxford, and subsequently a member of Lincoln's Inn, Wither's first-published work was a contribution to the satire, popular at the end of the sixteenth and beginning of the seventeenth century. His *Abuses Stript and Whipt* are not so formidable as their title, but the 1611 edition was suppressed, and their reissue in 1613 brought him to the Marshalsea prison. Meantime he had published a lament for Prince Henry, and an epithalamium for Princess Elizabeth, full of the naïve conceits with which the minor complimentary poetry of the period abounds, and of the "plain moral speaking" which Lamb admired. In prison he composed *The Shepherd's Hunting*, a series of very personal eclogues published in 1615. These, with *Fidelia* (1617), an "heroical epistle" of over twelve hundred lines, and *Fair Virtue, the Mistress of Philarete* (1617), a sustained and detailed lyrical eulogy of an ideal woman, contain the bulk of his best poetry, though there are some flowers of poetry in his *Emblems,* and the best of his religious verse is contained in the *Hallelujah, or Britain's Second Remembrancer* of 1641.

Wither's pastoral poetry is lyrical in spirit and form, a vehicle for the communication of his personal experiences and enthusiasms. He has a complete mastery of the seven-syllabled trochaic couplet. His style is easy, homely, and diffuse, comparatively little tormented with conceits, and when touched with enthusiasm for love and friendship, nature and song and virtue, is capable of a soaring flight. Of the charms of nature and consolations of song he writes with the gusto of Burns in the verse-epistles. The lines in which he describes how poetry

> "doth tell me where to borrow
> Comfort in the midst of sorrow,
> Makes the desolatest place
> To her presence be a grace:
>
> . . . . .
>
> By the murmur of a spring,
> Or a least bough's rusteling,
>
> . . . . .
>
> She could more infuse in me
> Than all nature's beauties can
> In some other wiser man,"

are quite in the spirit of Burns's

> "The Muse! nae poet ever fand her
> Till by himself he learned to wander
> Adown some trotting burn's meander,
>   And no' think lang,"

and many another passage where the Scotch poet's *joie de vivre* is most pure and delightful. Wither's *Fair Virtue* is an extraordinary rhapsody, but the strangest thing about it is the skill with which the clear high note is sustained without wearying or growing wearied. The *Fidelia* belongs to an artificial kind, and is far too long, but even in it there are balanced, pointed lines, which were certainly known to Pope when he wrote *Eloisa to Abelard*—

> "Banish those thoughts and turn thee to my heart!
> Come once again and be what once thou wert!
> Revive me by those wonted joys repairing
> That am nigh dead with sorrow and despairing!
> So shall the memory of this annoy
> But add more sweetness to my future joy!"

148 EUROPEAN LITERATURE—1600-1660.

Of Wither's later didactic and satirical verse, "pious exercises and political diatribes," which gained him *Basse and Brathwait.* from Milton's schoolmaster, Alexander Gill, the title of "our English Juvenal," it is unnecessary to speak here. Nor can we dwell in detail on the pastorals of other members of the group to which Browne and Wither belonged, or trace the stream of Spenserian allegory as it lost itself in the sand of didactic babble and mysticism. The pastorals of William Basse (1583-1653?), which show the influence of Browne, were published for the first time quite recently; and attention has just been called to the *Shepherd's Tales* (published first in *Nature's Embassie*, 1621, and completed in 1623 and 1626) of the voluminous Richard Brathwait (1588-1673). The hitherto unknown poem which Colonel Prideaux reprints[1] adds to many reminders how smoothly the decasyllabic couplet was written at the close of the sixteenth and opening seventeenth century, how much its increasing irregularity was due to the deliberate innovations of Donne and Jonson.

Of religious and moralising poets whose writing is in the Protestant and homely tone of the Spenserians, though with more of conceit, the *Quarles.* most popular was Francis Quarles (1592-1644), a native of Essex, educated at Cambridge and Lincoln's Inn, who visited Germany as cup-bearer to the unfortunate Princess Elizabeth. He began in 1620 the publication of an endless succession of paraphrases

[1] *Athenæum*, December 30, 1905.

from Scripture—*A Feast of Worms set forth in a Poeme of the History of Jonah, Sions Elegies wept by Jeremie the Prophet, Sions Sonnets sung by Solomon the King*, &c.—and later wrote prose pious manuals, and defended King Charles. His best known work was the pious and "conceited" *Emblems* (1635), verses composed to woodcuts, all of which except those in the first book are taken from the *Pia Desideria* (Antwerp, 1624) of the Jesuit, Herman Hugo.

Both Dr Henry More (1614-1687)—the Cambridge Platonist—and Joseph Beaumont, the mystical friend of Crashaw, employed Spenserian allegory as late as 1648 to set forth their theosophy.

More and Beaumont.

Beaumont's *Psyche, or Love's Mystery* is an allegory of the soul's temptations and deliverances, with an interpolated sketch of Bible history. More even essayed the Spenserian stanza, but it is poetically a very far cry from the *Faerie Queene* to the *Antipsychopannychia*.

Although the Scottish poet, William Drummond of Hawthornden (1585-1649), cannot be classed with the Jacobean Spenserians, nevertheless his indebtedness to both Spenser and Sidney, as well as to the Italian masters of these poets, connects him more closely with them than with Donne and Jonson. Drummond's poetry is Italianate, florid, and fluent, not condensed, abrupt, or metaphysical.

Drummond.

After completing his studies at Edinburgh University, Drummond spent three years (1606-9) in France studying law and poetry, and it was doubtless in these years, and those which he spent subsequently in leisure at Hawthornden, that he acquired the wide knowledge of literature—classical, French, Italian, and Spanish — which colours all his work. His elegy on Prince Henry, *Tears on the Death of Mœliades*, the most poetical elegy in imagery and verse written between the death of Spenser and *Lycidas*, was published in 1613, and his *Poems* followed three years later. They were divided, after the model of Petrarch and his imitators, into those written before and those after the death of his Laura, Miss Cunningham of Barns, and arranged, in still closer accordance with Marino's *Lira* (1602-14), into *Amorous, Funeral, Divine, Pastoral, in Sonnets, Songs, Sextains, Madrigals*. *Forth Feasting* — the title of which is taken from Marino's *Tebro Festante*, but which in its elevated strain recalls the *Pollio* of Virgil — was composed for King James's visit to Edinburgh in 1617. The religious sonnets of his earlier volume were embellished and added to in *Flowers of Sion* (1625), to a second edition of which in 1630 he affixed his eloquent prose meditation, *A Cypress Grove*. Drummond's literary activity was, in his last years, absorbed by political controversy, in which he espoused the royalist cause.

Drummond's poetry is the product of a scholar of refined nature, opulent fancy, and musical ear. His indebtedness to Spenser, Sidney, and Shakespeare for imaginative phrases is palpable, and many of his most charming sonnets and madrigals are no more than translations from Petrarch, Sannazaro, Ronsard, and Marino. To the last he is especially indebted, not only for love-sonnets as "Sleep, silence child, sweet father of soft rest" and "Alexis here she stayed," but for many grave moral and religious sonnets as "Of this fair volume which we world do name," "Run, shepherds, run where Bethlem blest appears," and "Thrice happy he who by some shady grove." Even where he does not translate he imitates Marino in his choice of subject; and the evolution and movement of his sonnets recall the Italian, especially in the effective close, the powerful reflux of the closing triad. Thus the last lines of what is perhaps Drummond's finest sonnet, "The Baptist,"—

> "Who listened to his voice, obeyed his cry?
> Only the echoes which he made relent,
> Rung from their flinty caves, 'Repent! Repent!'"—

are very similar to the close of Marino's pastoral sonnet on Polyphemus' despair—

> "Piu non diss' egli: e'l monte arsiccio e scabro
> Rimbombò d'urli, e'l lido e la campagna
> Tremonne, e l'altro del Tartareo fabro."

But though Drummond, like other sonneteers, translated and imitated, he had, like the best of the Elizabethans, a personality and genius of his own. His sonnets, though deficient in the passion of Sidney's and Shakespeare's, have few rivals in sweetness and musical evolution, and not less harmonious are the songs or *canzoni* in irregular lines. That beginning "Phœbus arise!" in ardour, colour, and music will bear comparison with Spenser. Of the genuineness of the religious and moral feeling which animates the noblest of his sonnets and poems there can be no doubt. Their philosophic profundity has perhaps been exaggerated. It was not a very difficult task for a scholar like Drummond to fill Platonic or neo-Platonic conceptions with orthodox sentiment.

Scholarship, thoughtfulness, and careful workmanship form the link which, in Mr Courthope's view, *Sir John Beaumont.* connect Drummond and Sir John Beaumont (1582-1627), elder brother of the dramatist, and author of the *Metamorphosis of Tobacco*, a humorous didactic and eulogistic poem, *Bosworth Field*, a short narrative poem, and a number of complimentary and sacred verses. Beaumont seems to me much less of a poet than Drummond. His vein is reflective, and often both his sentiment and style would, as Drayton said of Daniel's, fit prose better than verse. His best verses are the sacred. If he writes couplets with some of the regularity and balance of Dryden, he gets as a rule much less into them, and this was the real crux, for it was the endeavour to give a denser intellectual texture to poetry which gave both harshness and obscurity to the verse of the two poets who began the movement that ended with Dryden.

These two poets, the chief shaping influences of Jacobean and Caroline poetry—John Donne (1573-1631) and Ben Jonson (1573?-1637)— *Donne and Jonson.* were not only almost exactly contemporary, but were knit together by many common sympathies. They were both impatient of the diffuse and flamboyant style of the Spenserian and Italianate poets, and willing for the sake of pregnancy and vigour to overlook harshness and obscurity. Both were certainly admirers and imitators of Latin poetry, especially satirical and elegiac, and both cultivated a vein of frank, even cynical and brutal, satire. They were courtly poets, and wrote abundance of high-flown eulogies and occasional verses, very often addressed to the same patrons. Donne's wit was not less courtly than Jonson's, if we remember that the court for which both wrote was James's.

Despite these resemblances, however, Donne and Jonson represent with startling distinctness the two discordant streams of tendency in the first half of the seventeenth century—the mediæval or scholastic reaction on the one hand, the movement towards the rationalism and classicism of the closing century on the other. Jonson is, as the study of his drama has shown, the first of our classical poets. In his poetry we see the elegancies and extravagances of Petrarchian—what Mr Courthope calls Euphuist—wit meeting with and yielding to the simpler and more appropriate sentiments of classical poetry, the dignified and vigorous common-sense which was to be Dryden's ideal of wit. In Donne's poetry revives all that was most subtle and metaphysical in the thought and fancy of the Middle Ages.

The son of rigidly Catholic parents, who on his mother's side connected him with John Heywood of the *Merry Interludes* and Sir Thomas More,

Donne[1] was educated at Oxford, but without gradu-
ating in order to escape the oaths. His
early manhood blended the experiences of
an Elizabethan gallant and sailor-soldier with those of
a theological student and controversialist. His position as a Catholic, excluded thereby from
public life, and at the same time a man of
as ambitious a temperament as Swift's, combined with
what he calls "an immoderate, hydroptic thirst of
learning," involved him early in the thorny subtleties
of Roman-Anglican controversy; while another side
of his nature drew him to court adventure in love
and war. His strange, virile, powerful, often repellent,
Elegies may record details of actual intrigues, as Mr
Gosse supposes. I am more inclined to believe that,
while Donne's stormy career doubtless supplied experiences enough from which to draw generally, the
Elegies are his very characteristic contribution to the
frankly pagan and sensuous poetry of the Nineties,
represented otherwise by *Hero and Leander* and *Venus
and Adonis*. A soldier as well as a lover, Donne was
with Raleigh and Essex at their attack on the Spanish
fleet in Cadiz, and it was during the abortive Islands'
voyage of 1597 that he wrote his vividly etched
studies, *The Storm* and *The Calm*. During some of
these years he visited Italy and Spain, and in Spanish
literature he was deeply read. His appointment as

Donne's Life.

Donne.

[1] *Life and Letters*, by Edmund Gosse, London, 1899. The fullest account, but not without inaccuracies and hazardous conjectures. See Beeching's *Izaak Walton's Life of Donne* in *Religio Laici*, London, 1902. Compare Jessop's *John Donne, sometime Dean of St Paul's*, London, 1897, and article in *D. N. B.*

secretary to Sir Thomas Egerton seemed at last to have opened the door to Donne's ambition, but his elopement with Anne More in 1601 closed it again abruptly, and years of disappointment and suffering, dependence on patrons and free-lance work in controversy, led him inevitably, after some delays, to holy orders in 1615, and a life as severely ascetic and pious as his earlier had been adventurous. But the fame of the eloquent preacher never quite eclipsed that of the poet.

Donne's poems—with the exception of his elegies on Mistress Elizabeth Drury, *The Anatomy of the World*—were not printed until after his death, and it is accordingly difficult to determine their order with accuracy. His *Satires*— the most interesting and, metrically, the most irregular of the late sixteenth-century work of this kind —may date from 1593, but the earliest unmistakable reference is to 1597. To his first years in town belong probably the more frankly sensuous and cynical of the *Elegies* and *Songs and Sonnets*. Those which strike a higher and more Platonic note may have been written after his engagement to Anne More. The satirical *Progress of the Soul* dates from 1601. The courtly and adulatory *Epithalamia*, *Verse-Letters*, *Epicedes and Obsquies*, as well as the *Divine Poems*, were the product of his later and more regular years.

Works.

Amorous and satirical, courtly, pious, these are the successive phases of Donne's life and poetry,—poetry in which the imaginative, emancipated spirit of the Renaissance came into abrupt contact, and blended in the strangest way with the

Genius.

scholastic pedantry and subtlety of the controversial court of James. The temper of Donne's poetry is that of Marlowe's and Shakespeare's. It has the same emancipated ardour and exaltation. Whatever his theme—love, eulogy, or devotion—his imagination, like theirs, takes wing, so soon as it is thrown off, to the highest pitch of hyperbole. What distinguishes him from the great Elizabethans is the prevailing character of his conceits, his "metaphysical wit." To the imaginative temper of Marlowe Donne superadded the subtlety and erudition of a schoolman, and brought to the expression of his intense, audacious passions imagery drawn from an intimate knowledge of mediæval theology and of the science mediæval, but beginning to grow modern, of the seventeenth century.

Johnson's term "metaphysical"—which he derived from Dryden, and by which it is clear from what he *Metaphysical poetry.* says of Waller's "wit" as well as Cowley's he meant simply learned or technical conceits, drawn not from "the superficies of nature" but from the recondite stores of learning—is both more distinctive than any other name which has been suggested—"fantastic" is very far from distinctive—and is historically interesting and accurate. "Concetti metafisici ed ideali" are, according to Fulvio Testi, the distinctive feature of Italian as opposed to classical poetry. The ultimate source of the conceits and artificialities of Renaissance love-poetry is to be found, as Mr Courthope has indicated, in the poetry of the Middle Ages, from the Troubadours onwards.

But it was in Italy, in the "dolce stil nuovo" of Guido Guinicelli and Dante, that the "metaphysical" element first appeared in love-poetry. "Learning," says Adolf Gaspary,[1] "is the distinctive feature of the new school." Writing first in the Troubadour fashion of the Sicilians, it was with the famous canzone "Al cor gentil ripara sempre amore" that Guinicelli began to write in the metaphysical manner. "The change in his poetry took place under the influence of science. Philosophy, which in that age when Thomas Aquinas and Bonaventura were teaching had again come to be regarded with favour, penetrated even into poetry, which drew from it its subject-matter, and even the manner of its exposition." The high-priest of this ideal, metaphysical, abstract love-poetry was Dante. Petrarch brought love-poetry back to closer touch with ordinary human nature. His finer psychology made Petrarch "the first of the moderns"; on the other hand, his subtle and refined compliments contained the germ, and more than the germ, of what in subsequent sonneteers took the place of Dante's philosophy and Petrarch's psychology — a kind of pseudo-metaphysics which elaborated in abstract and hyperbolical fashion every metaphor, natural or traditional to the theme of love. But the sonnet never lost the cast which it acquired from its origin in this combination of high passion and scholastic philosophy—a strain of subtle thought, a readiness to

[1] *History of Early Italian Literature*, transl. H. Oelsner. Bell & Sons. Compare Snell, *The Fourteenth Century*, p. 120 f. For the love-poetry of Guiniccelli and Dante, see Rossetti's *Early Italian Poets*.

admit erudite and technical imagery—even though it be only occasionally that one finds again passionate and profound reflection upon the nature and mystery of love. A sonnet like " Let me not to the marriage of true minds Admit impediment," is not less intense or philosophic in its own way than a canzone of the *Vita Nuova*.[1]

It is this metaphysical, erudite, scholastic strain which Donne, under conditions similar to that in which it first appeared, renewed and heightened. He is hardly less concerned than Dante with the abstract nature of love. The "concetti metafisici ed ideali" of the *Anatomy of the World* are not more metaphysical and hyperbolical—blasphemous, as Jonson bluntly put it—than those of the canzone in the *Vita Nuova*, which tells how the saints in heaven beseech God for the presence of Beatrice—

"My lady is desired in the high heaven."

The central idea of the *Anatomy of the World*, the all-pervading influence of the loved one, is an expansion of one of the conventions of the school of Dante.

But after all there is a vast difference between Donne and Dante. Donne has no consistent metaphysic of love and its place in the upward movement

[1] See Mazzoni, *La Lirica del Cinquecento* in *La Vita Italiana nel Cinquecento*, Milano, 1901 : "Il Petrarca cantando Laura viva aveva accommodato al gusto commune quell' idealismo filosofico onde era assunta alla vita sempiterna dell' arte la Beatrice dantesca, &c." See also Flamini, *Gli Imitatori della Lirica di Dante* in *Studi di Storia Letteraria*, Livorno, 1895.

of the soul to God. He elaborates in many of the
Songs and Sonnets two radically inconsistent ideas, one
the inherent fickleness of woman, the other the mystical identity of the souls of lovers. But often he
simply ransacks his multifarious knowledge to discover
new and startling conceits in which to express his
bizarre and subtle moods. For it is a mistake—
towards which I venture to think Mr Courthope tends
—to let the intellectual and abstract element in
Donne's poetry blind one to the passionate feeling it
expresses. No love-poetry of the closing sixteenth
century has more of the sting of real feeling in it
except Shakespeare's. There is nothing quite like
Donne's love-poems in the language, except, perhaps,
some of Browning's. Passion seems to affect both
poets in the same way, not evoking the usual images,
voluptuous and tender, but quickening the intellect
to intense and rapid trains of thought, and finding
utterance in images, bizarre sometimes and even
repellent, often of penetrating vividness and power.
The opening of one of Donne's songs affects us like
an electric shock, jarring and arresting—

"For God's sake hold your tongue and let me love,"

or—

"I long to talk with some old lover's ghost
Who died before the God of love was born,"

or—

"Twice or thrice had I loved thee
Before I knew thy face or name,
So in a voice, so in a shapeless flame,
Angels affect us oft and worshipped be";

and many of the best, as "The Anniversary," the wonderful "Ecstasy," "The Funeral," "The Relic," "The Prohibition," preserve throughout this potent and unique impressiveness. Donne's *Songs and Sonnets* cannot take a place beside the great love-poetry of Dante, Petrarch, and Shakespeare. There is too large an element in them of mere intellectual subtlety, even freakishness. But his poetry is not to be dismissed as the result of conflicting conceptions of nature clashing in a subtle and bizarre intellect. It has a real imaginative as well as historical value, because it is the unique expression of a unique temperament.

The difference between Donne and Jonson comes out very distinctly if we compare their eulogistic verses. The non-dramatic poetry of Jonson is contained in the *Epigrams* and *Forest*, which he published in 1616, and the posthumous *Underwoods* (1640). A large proportion of it, including the best of the epigrams, consists of eulogistic addresses to patrons and friends. Donne's *Verse-Letters* are of the same kind, and there is abundance of eulogy in his *Epithalamia* and *Epicedes*. It is when he is paying compliments that Donne's mind works most abstractly, and that his subtleties are most purely intellectual. In the verses *To the Countess of Salisbury, August 1614,* beginning "Fair, great and good," he elaborates with the utmost ingenuity the statement that the Countess is superexcellent in a world which has grown utterly corrupt, but he gives no indication of the qualities in which her excellence is shown. He tells the Lady Carey that while others are virtuous in this or that humour —phlegm, blood, melancholy, or choler — she has virtue so entire that it has made even her beauty virtuous, exciting not to passion but to goodness. Jonson's eulogies are in a different strain. He can be fancifully complimentary, but it is in a more Humanist and elegant, a less pedantic style,—witness the beautiful lines to the Countess of Bedford or those to Susan, Countess of Montgomery, or those to Mary Lady Wroth—

> "He that but saw you wear the wheaten hat
> Would call you more than Ceres if not that;
> And drest in shepherd's tire who would not say
> You were the bright Œnone, Flora, or May?"

Delicacy and pathos are blended in his epitaphs. If "Underneath this sable hearse" is not Jonson's, it is quite Jonsonian. But Jonson's most characteristic and classical eulogies are relevant and appropriate appreciations, compliments a man might be proud to receive, because they tell something about him to posterity, couched in a style and verse often obscure and harsh, but often vigorous and felicitous. The very ruggedness of the lines to Chief-Justice Egerton and those to Sir Henry Savile give them an air of burly veracity which is very taking. His eulogy of Shakespeare in the lines prefixed to the First Folio contains juster criticism of Shakespeare's genius and Shakespeare's art than anything he said or wrote in prose. The ease and urbanity of Horace Jonson never attained, but his best eulogies have classical relevancy and restraint.

Jonson's songs, which are scattered through the plays and masques as well as the above-named collections, have not the passion or subtlety of Donne's, nor the careless note of the very finest Elizabethan songs. They are more consciously elaborated even when most simple, but at their best they have a concentrated sweetness, a unique combination of strength and charm which make Jonson's lyrics unmistakable in any anthology. And their range is very remarkable, from the swing and abandon of "Drink to me only with thine eyes," and the elaborate, Comus-like "Slow, slow fresh fount," to the patter verses of the *Gipsies Metamorphosed* and delightful snatches like—

> "Buz, quoth the blue fly,
> Hum, quoth the bee,
> Buz and hum they cry,
> And so do we."

Influence of Donne and Jonson.

The "metaphysical" turn which Donne gave to "wit" is distinctive of English poetry at this period, and it did not tend to the general improvement of poetic style. The earlier Euphuists, Petrarchists, Arcadians, Lyly and Sidney, Marlowe and Shakespeare, had been mainly concerned with style in their quest of conceits and golden phrases. "The uncontented care to write better than one might" had been the chief source of their beauties and their aberrations. The same care, become a craze for novelty, for new and startling conceits, is the characteristic of Italian Marinism, "the craving to improve upon what is incapable of improvement." French "préciosité" has its source in the same concernment with style; but French preciosity is a malady of growth, not of decay, a phase in the movement towards a greater refinement of manners and speech.[1] The "précieux" were concerned with what might *not* be said as well as with what should be said. Still both Marinism and Preciosity were phases in the Renaissance cult of style. "Metaphysical wit" marked the passing of interest in English poetry to some extent from style to content. Donne in his *Verse-Epistles* and *Epicedes* is more intent upon the subtle thought or thoughts he wishes to develop than on their lucid and harmonious expression, though ever and again he flashes into a magnificent phrase; and Donne's followers convey ingenious fancies, often not worth the carriage, in an obscure uncouth style, and in verse grating as "a brazen canstick turned." Nor did Jonson's influence counteract this tendency. Though his thought is more natural than Donne's, he, too, is concerned with what he says quite as much as with how he says it, more intent on vigour and compression than beauty of phrase and musical numbers. The first half of the seventeenth century produced more than one poet of singular interest, poets whose work has a deeper personal note than that of most of the Elizabethans, and in Milton and Herrick two, in different ways, consummate artists, but the general level of poetical expression and verse,

[1] "Il preziosismo è forma di ritenutezza: il marinismo è forma di dissolutezza," says Professor Graf. *Nuova Antologia*, 1° Ottobre 1905. *Il Fenomeno del Secentismo.*

as judged, say, from the eulogistic poetry produced in such abundance, is lower than that which had been reached at the close of the sixteenth century.

What was best done was in lyrical poetry, in which the influence of Donne and Jonson appears both blended and distinct. Donne's closest followers are the devout Anglican poets. They strike the same deep personal note; and the wide range of metaphysical imagery gratified their taste for quaint analogies, for symbols, and for points rhetorically effective rather than purely poetic. The courtiers, too, could turn metaphysical images to their service in compliment and badinage—

> "Ask me no more whither do stray
> The golden atoms of the day,
> For in pure love heaven did prepare
> Those powders to enrich your hair."

But Jonson is their leader in courtly eulogy; a great deal of their imagery is, like his, a blend of Petrarchian and classical; their sentiment, though touched occasionally with the Platonism which the Queen brought over from the Hôtel de Rambouillet, is in general pagan and sensuous rather than Petrarchian or ideal.

This lyrical poetry, grave or gay, pagan or devout, was the product of the halcyon years which preceded *Caroline Court Poetry.* the storm that broke when the Long Parliament met, and it reflects the spirit, not of the nation at large, but of the court of Charles, its gaiety and love-making on the one hand, its concern for Catholic doctrine and decent services on the other, its self-centred indifference to what was happening on the Continent, or what was moving in the heart of the nation. The conflict abroad found no echo in English poetry. Vondel's imagination was agitated by every incident in the Thirty Years' War. Carew, when invited, declines to sing of the death of Gustavus—

> "What though the German drum
> Bellow for freedom and revenge, the noise
> Concerns not us, nor should divert our joys."

Of the disaster that was to overwhelm those joys the poets express no foreboding. Only in *Lycidas* does the trumpet sound a warning note.[1]

Of the religious poets who followed Donne—the preacher as well as the poet—and voice the spirit of Laud's reformation, the most influential and the most sustained artist was George Herbert (1593-1632), whose volume, *The Temple, Sacred Poems and Private Ejaculations* (1633), was published in the same year as the poems of his master and friend were issued posthumously by his son. Like Donne, Herbert, for reasons that were perhaps mingled, had turned from worldly ambition to religion, and found an outlet for his temperament in asceticism and exalted piety. The crisis through which he passed is traceable in his poetry, and lends it a personal note of struggle, disappointment, and consolation which prevent it from degenerating into frigid Anglican didactic. For the general tone is didactic. There is something of the accomplished university orator and the winning parish

Herbert.

---

[1] Much of the poetry written during this period was not collected and published till after 1640.

preacher in Herbert's quaint, carefully elaborated, effective treatment of the various phases of a single theme, the spiritual lessons and experiences of one who found both discipline and consolation in the theology, sacraments, and symbols of the Anglican church. Like Donne, Herbert rejects the pastoral and allegorical conventions of the Spenserians.

> " Who says that fictions only and false hair
>   Become a verse ? Is there no truth in beauty ?
> Is all good structure in a winding stair ?
> May no lines pass except they do their dutie
>   Not to a true but painted chair ?
>
> Is it no verse except enchanted groves
> And sudden arbours shadow coarse-spun lines ?
> Must purling streams refresh a lover's love ?
> Must all be vail'd while he that reads divines,
>   Catching the sense at two removes ?
>
> Shepherds are honest people : let them sing ;
> Riddle who list for me and pull for prime :
> I envy no man's nightingale or spring :
> Nor let them punish me with loss of rhyme,
>   Who plainly say, My God ! My King ! "

Not so subtle and daring as Donne's imagery, Herbert's quaint figures are managed with great rhetorical effectiveness, worked out with an almost Tennysonian lucidity and relevancy, and are often not less beautiful poetically than rhetorically effective, as in, perhaps, the best known of his poems, the lines on *Virtue*, beginning—

> "Sweet day so cool, so calm, so bright ! "

or in the *Church Floor*, with its characteristically quaint and imaginative symbolism—

> "Mark you the floor? that square and speckled stone
> Is Patience:
> And the other black and grave wherewith each one
> Is cheker'd all along
> Humilitie:
> The gentle rising which on either hand
> Leads to the Quire above
> Is Confidence:
> But the sweet cement which in one sure band
> Ties the whole frame is Love
> and Charitie.
> Hither sometimes sinne steals and stains
> The marble's neat and curious veins:
> But all is cleansed when the marble weeps.
> Sometimes Death puffing at the door
> Blows all the dust about the floor:
> But while he thinks to spoil the room he sweeps.
> Blest be the Architect whose art
> Could build so strong in a weak heart."

Herbert's love of symbolism extends to the form of his verses. He has poems in the shape of wings and crosses, and, more happily, writes of *The Trinity* in a verse of three lines, of *Sunday* in one of seven, and describes Aaron's dress in stanzas that swell out and die away like bells.

The influence of Herbert's fine spirit and prevailing though quaint rhetoric is witnessed for by Baxter, and is clear from the work of his two chief followers, greater poets at their best than himself, but less careful workmen—Henry Vaughan (1621-2-1695) and Richard Crashaw (1613-1649). Vaughan was a Welshman of whose life we

Vaughan.

know very little beyond the facts that he was at Jesus College, Oxford, and in his later life became a physician. He was not at first religious, but was apparently converted by reading Herbert's poems. The verses contained in his *Secular Poems* (1646) and *Olor Iscanus* (1651) do not rise much above the level of the amatory and complimentary verses which the young gentlemen of the universities and court produced in too great abundance. Several are merely translations. The lines to the Usk, which give their name to the second collection, have little descriptive or moralising force. His best poetry is his religious, contained in the *Silex Scintillans* (1650-56). He follows Herbert, often closely in choice of theme and imagery, but he is less concerned about Church seasons and services, and he lacks Herbert's sustained pointedness, his effective elaboration of his conceits. Vaughan's fame rests upon poems and passages in which he reveals qualities quite distinct from Herbert's—a delicate, intense feeling for the spiritual affinities of nature unique in the century, an occasional sublimity of imaginative vision to which Herbert never attained. In this last respect some of Vaughan's lines reach the level of the greatest poetry the century produced, as—

> "I saw Eternity the other night
> Like a great ring of pure and endless light,
> All calm as it was bright :
> And round beneath it Time in hours, days, years,
> Driv'n by the spheres
> Like a vast shadow moved ; in which the world
> And all its train were hurled " ;

But it is only on occasions that he approaches this level. Vaughan was a mystic, not as Donne from too intense and subtle reflection, but from visitings of

> "that blessed mood
> In which the burthen of the mystery
> Is lightened";

and under the influence of that mood he apprehended the divine in simpler and more enduring symbols than the correctly Anglican Herbert or the ecstatically Catholic Crashaw—

> "On some gilded cloud or flower
> My gazing soul would dwell an hour,
> And in those weaker glories spy
> Some shadows of eternity."

Crashaw. A more ardent temperament than either Herbert's or Vaughan's, a more soaring and glowing lyrical genius, belonged to Richard Crashaw (1613-1649). The son of a Puritan preacher who denounced the Pope as Antichrist, Crashaw at Cambridge came under the influence of that powerful wave of reaction of which the Laudian movement was only a symptom. His artistic temperament felt the charm of church music and architecture, and his ardent disposition responded, like the Dutch Vondel's, to the Catholic glorification of love as well as faith, the devotion to Christ and the Virgin of the martyr and the saint. He read Italian and Spanish, and was infected by the taste for what one might call the religious confectionery of which Marino's poems are full. His *Epigrammata Sacra* (1634) elaborate with great cleverness and point tender and pious conceits. Of his English poems, the secular *Delights of the Muses* (1648) include experiments in conceit and metrical effect such as *Love's Duel* and *Wishes*, and eulogies in the highly abstract style of Donne's, with less of thought and more of sentiment. But his most characteristic and individual work is the religious poetry contained in the *Steps to the Temple* (1646) written before, and the *Carmen Deo Nostro* (1652) published in Paris after his ardent nature and the failure of Laud's endeavour had driven him to seek shelter in the bosom of the Roman Church, poems on all the favourite subjects of Catholic devotion—the Name of Christ, the Virgin, Mary Magdalene weeping, martyrs, saints, and festivals.

Crashaw's style may have been influenced by Marino as well as Donne. His conceits are frequently of the physical and luscious character, to which the Italian tended always, the English poet never. He translated the first canto of the *Strage degli Innocenti*, frequently intensifying the imaginative effect, at other times making the conceit more pointed and witty, occasionally going further in the direction of confectionery even than Marino. The latter does not describe hell as a "shop of woes," nor say that the Wise Men went—

"Westward to find the world's true Orient";

nor would Marino, I think, speak of the Magdalen's tears as flowing upward to become the cream upon the Milky Way. Marino's early and purer style in religious poetry is better represented by Drummond's sacred sonnets.

But if Crashaw's taste in conceits is at times worse than Marino's, his lyrical inspiration is stronger, his spiritual ecstasies more ardent. There is more of Vondel than Marino in the atmosphere of his religious poetry. The northern temperament vibrates with a fuller music. His hymn, *On the Glorious Assumption*, is written in the same exalted strain as Vondel's dedication of the *Brieven der Heilige Maeghden*, but Vondel's style is simpler and more masculine. Crashaw's fire is too often coloured — "happy fireworks" is the epithet he applies to his beloved Saint Theresa's writings — but its glow is unmistakable, and occasionally, as in the closing lines of *The Flaming Heart*, it is purified by its own ardour.

A devoted Anglican like Herbert and Vaughan, but a bolder quester after the divine as revealed not in Church creeds and symbols but in nature and in the heart of man, was Thomas Traherne (1636-1674), rector of Credinhill in Herefordshire, and chaplain to Sir Orlando Bridgman. In his lifetime Traherne published nothing beyond a contribution, entitled *Roman Forgeries*, to Anglican controversy, and a *Christian Ethics*, which was in the press at the time of his death. It was left to Mr Bertram Dobell in the present century to make public the ardent and mystical poems, which had been preserved in manuscript for more than two centuries, and were on the eve of perishing.

Traherne's poetry glows with an ecstasy as ardent as Crashaw's, but more intellectual and mystical than the Catholic poet's sensuous and coloured strains. Like most mystics, he has but one theme—the history and message of his own enlightenment, and the same is the theme of his prose *Centuries of Meditations*. That enlightenment had its source in the experience which Vaughan recalls with a sigh in *The Retreat*, namely, the ecstatic joys of innocent childhood. But Traherne's joys were intenser than Vaughan's, more akin to the mood of Wordsworth when

> "The earth and every common sight
>   To me did seem
> Apparelled in celestial light,
>   The glory and the freshness of a dream."

And from these experiences Traherne drew a bolder and profounder philosophy than either Vaughan or Wordsworth, which recalls rather the mystical audacity of Blake. "My knowledge," he says, "was divine. I knew by intuition those things which, since my apostacy, I collected again by the highest reason." For Vaughan there is no return to life's early ecstasy in this world; Wordsworth can but be thankful that it has been. But Traherne recovered it through the highest reason, and learned that, as in infancy, earth might be already heaven. What the highest reason taught him was, that the intense joy which the beauty of the created world had given him in youth, and which the world's false hierarchy of values for a time obscured, is the very end and purpose for which the world was created. It is only when God beholds the world reflected in the souls of men, evoking their gratitude and love, that His desire in creating is fulfilled—

> "Our blessedness to see
> Is even to the Deity
> A Beatific vision! He attains
> His ends while we enjoy. In us He reigns."

And again—

> "In them [*i.e.*, human souls] He sees,
> And feels, and smells, and lives;
> To them He all conveys;
> Nay even Himself: He is the End
> To whom in them Himself and all things tend."

The soul whose value is thus final is for Traherne the one great reality; and the mystery of its existence limited to a small body, yet in thought—and what is more real than thought?—embracing the universe, is one on which he dwells in rapt strains. All of Traherne's poetry is the record of these experiences and reasonings. He was an orthodox Anglican, but we hear comparatively little in his poetry of sin and of the death of Christ. Sorrow and the macerating sense of sin are swallowed up in the ecstasy of a soul made one with God by mutual need and love, and tasting already the joys of Paradise.

> "Did my Ambition ever dream
>   Of such a Lord, of such a Love! Did I
>   Expect so sweet a stream
>   As this at any time? Could any eye
>   Believe it? Why all Power
>   Is used here,
> Joys down from Heaven on my head do shower,
> And Jove beyond the fiction doth appear
> Once more in golden rain to come
> To Danaë's pleasing fruitful womb

> His Ganymede ! His Life ! His Joy !
> Or He comes down to me, or takes me up
>   That I might be his boy,
> And fill, and taste, and give and drink the cup;
>   But those tho' great are all
>   Too short and small,
> Too weak and feeble pictures to express
> The true mysterious depths of Blessedness.
> I am His Image and His friend,
> His Son, Bride, Glory, Temple, End."

Such audacious ecstasies transcend the limits of average humanity, which is more at home with the fearful joys of Herbert and Vaughan, or the more sensuous and remote ecstasies of Crashaw, but they are not in Traherne less profoundly religious. As an artist Traherne is not studious of phrase, or conceit, or cadence. He has absolutely none of the merely rhetorical metaphysics of Cowley, from whose Pindarics he may have derived the structure of his more elaborate strains. His poetry is metaphysical because the thought is so; but the expression is perfectly simple and natural, at times too expository and direct, and marred by a frequent use of the expletive "do," but often kindled into felicity by the ecstasy of the poet. Individual poems of striking interest are "Silence," "The Choice," "The Anticipation," "The Circulation," "On News"; but Traherne's excellencies are scattered through all his work.

Herbert and the religious lyrists of the school of Donne voiced the serious spirit of the court party, the Anglicanism of Andrewes and Laud. Herbert, indeed, was hardly less influential than her great preachers and divines in giving to the English Church of the seventeenth century that character which, when she had disappeared from sight, kept her alive in the hearts of many as an ideal of sweet reasonableness and decent order—

> "Beauty in thee takes up her place,
> And dates her letters from thy face."

The more worldly, not to say dissolute, temper of the cavaliers colours, as well as the drama of Fletcher and Shirley, the light lyrics and adulatory eulogies of quite a number of poets about the court or in the universities, imitators in various ways and degrees of Jonson's classical and Donne's scholastic wit.

Of them all, Thomas Carew (1578-1639?), sewer-in-ordinary to Charles, whose favour he seems to have gained more by wit than worth, was, with the exception of Herrick, the most finished artist. His masque, the *Cœlum Britannicum*, an elaborate compliment to the mutual fidelity of Charles and Henrietta Maria, based on Bruno's *Spaccio della Bestia*, was produced in 1633, and his verses were collected and issued posthumously in 1640. He wrote an elegy on Donne—

> "A king that ruled as he thought fit
> The universal monarchy of wit"—

in which he commends the emancipation from convention and imitation which Donne brought to English poetry. There is, however, a good deal that is conventional in Carew's own imagery. He does not altogether, like Donne, eschew the help of Cupid and the gods. Jonson is more directly his master than Donne. Superficial feeling, elegant, occasionally outrageous, conceit, correct expression—natural both in diction and order,—musical verse, these are the characteristics of Carew's work. In songs like "Ask me no more" and "He that loves a coral lip," classical finish and polish of style are given to the high-flown fantastic conceit of the Renaissance.

In the employment of wit for the purpose of gallant, high-flown flattery, no one went further without becoming, like Cleveland, absolutely nauseous than Richard Lovelace (1618-1658), a brilliant courtier, and in the years of trouble and disaster a loyal cavalier. No one makes more frequent or extravagant use of the consuming fire of love, tears that drown, beauty which outshines the sun and out-perfumes the east; nor is this extravagance of conceit redeemed by perfection of workmanship. Nevertheless two of Lovelace's lyrics, quite characteristic in conceit and style, are the brightest gems of cavalier poetry. In "Tell me not, Sweet, I am unkind" and "When Love with unconfined wings," conceit is glorified by becoming the expression of noble and passionate sentiment.

Lovelace.

There is more of spontaneity and of wit, in the modern sense of the term, in the poems of Sir John Suckling (1608-1641) than in either Lovelace or Carew. If the last is the voluptuous and the second the gallant, Suckling is the gay and reckless courtier. His passion for gam-

Suckling.

ing, his lavish equipment of one hundred horse for the abortive Scottish war, are quite in keeping with the tone of his sparkling love-songs. He reproduces some of Donne's more reckless defiances of the conventions in love with less intensity but greater ease and humour. In delightful gaiety no poem could surpass—

> "Out upon it I have loved
> Three whole days together";

and in the incomparable *Ballad upon a Wedding* there is not only gaiety but exquisite description. The poet with whom he suggests comparison is his contemporary Vincent Voiture, neater perhaps and more pointed at his best, but with far less of feeling and imagination.

But of all the poets who may be classed somewhat loosely as court lyrists, the greatest in virtue both of vigour of fancy and perfection of technique is Robert Herrick (1591-1674), one of the "sons of Ben" at Cambridge and London for a few years, who wrote his best poems in what he considered banishment at Deanbourne in Devonshire, where he was rector from 1629 to his death, though ejected during the years of the Commonwealth. Herrick was not of the school of Herbert or Crashaw. His saints were "Saint Ben" and the classic poets to whom he dedicated an enthusiastic strain in the verse entitled "To Live Merrily and to Trust to Good Verses." These are the literary source of his inspiration. Guided by them he found another, when he went to Devonshire, in the superstitions, rites, and customs which still lingered in English country-life. He was the poet of all pretty things, and it is their prettiness which he accentuates and heightens,—flowers, fairies, young girls, rites pagan and Christian, good wine, and good verses. He enumerates them in the opening lines of *Hesperides* (1647), in which he gathered together most of his secular epigrams, songs, and other verses. The spirit of the "pious pieces" which compose *Noble Numbers* is not very different. Herrick does not approach God with the earnest pleading of Herbert, the rapt love of Crashaw, or the mystic awe of Vaughan, but with the artless frankness of a child confessing his naughtiness and asking to escape too severe a penalty.

The technical perfection of Herrick's work within its limited range places him as an artist second to Milton only. Of English poets none seem to inherit so closely, though in very different ways, from the French poets who composed the Pleiad, Milton fulfilling as none of them had been able to do the bolder programme of epic and tragedy and ode, Herrick catching all the pagan grace and fancy of their lighter Anacreontic strains to which he gave certainly no less of classical perfection of style. Had such ease and finish been attained by writers of eulogistic, satiric, and reflective verse in decasyllabic couplets, there would have been little for Dryden and Pope to do in the way of "correcting" English poetry.

A poet whose early and best work, written under the Commonwealth, has the motives and temper of

courtly poetry—qualified by a graver Puritan spirit
—is Andrew Marvell (1621 - 1678), the
son of the clerical headmaster of Hull
Grammar School. Educated at Cambridge — where
he passed through some religious vicissitudes — he
travelled abroad, and on his return became tutor to
Lord Fairfax's daughter (1650 - 52), at Nunappleton
House in Yorkshire. It was here that he wrote,
though they were not published till much later,
lyrical verses which have links with the courtly
poems of Waller, the religious poetry of Vaughan,
and Jonson's Horatian eulogies of great men and
praises of a country life. His political satires were
written later, and are discussed in the next volume.

Marvell.

Marvell's poetry is unequal, but at its best it
bears the mark of a singularly potent and poetic
individuality. No verses are more familiar from
anthologies than his noble Horatian ode on Cromwell, the imaginatively phrased *To His Coy Mistress*,
especially the lines beginning

> "But at my back I always hear
> Time's winged chariot hurrying near";

and the richly descriptive *Upon Appleton House*, *The
Fawn*, and the *Bermudas*. Marvell's treatment of
nature has been compared to Vaughan's. It seems
to me much more entirely descriptive and decorative. He speaks once of "Nature's mystic book,"
but it is in introducing an elaborate compliment to
his pupil as the source of Nature's beauty. That
is not Vaughan's manner

It was in the year following the publication of Donne's *Poems* and Herbert's *Temple*, the year of Crashaw's *Epigrammata* and Carew's *Cœlum Britannicum*, that *Comus* was presented before the Earl of Bridgewater; and its publication with Lawe's music followed in 1637. It was the first indication that, among those who regarded with an ever-increasing hatred the ecclesiastical policy of Laud, and to whom the courtly lyrical and dramatic poetry was as the dissonant music of Comus and his rout, there had been growing up, in the person of the delicate, studious, and carefully educated son of a Puritan scrivener,[1] who had just after seven years' study quitted Cambridge, "church-outed by the prelate," unable to take orders in an Anglican Church reformed by Laud, and was living in bookish seclusion at Horton, a poet after the order of the few greatest the world has produced, a poet who, combining the high seriousness of the Spenserians with the classical culture and regard for form of Jonson, was destined to add to Elizabethan achievement in drama and song equally high achievement in epic, while imparting a new grandeur of diction and evolution to the ode or sustained and elaborate lyric, and making in the drama experiments of singular interest and beauty.

Milton.

[1] David Masson, *Life of Milton in connection with the History of his Times*, London, 1859-80; index, 1894. An invaluable work for the study of Milton and the whole period. Mark Pattison, *Milton*, 1880 (*Men of Letters Series*). Garnett, *Milton*, 1889 (*Great Writers Series*). The most brilliant recent appreciation is that by Professor Raleigh, 1900.

The strength of individuality which marks Milton's work from the very first makes the traces in it of contemporary influence appear superficial, interesting as they are to the literary student. His youthful versions of the Psalms contain reminiscences of his reading in Sylvester, Spenser, Drummond, and other poets who enjoyed Puritan approval, but the rich embroidery of "Let us with a gladsome mind" is already characteristic. The verses *On the Death of a Fair Infant* are a charmingly executed, elegant conceit of the kind Jonson elaborates in some of his eulogies, as the second epigram to *Mary Lady Wroth* or the immediately preceding one to *Susan, Countess of Montgomery*; while the verse, the "Troilus" stanza with a closing Alexandrine, is Spenserian. Milton's early work is not untouched with the frost of conceit, but it is never scholastic and metaphysical conceit—

Influences.

> "That trimming slight
> Which takes our late fantastics with delight."

What is worst and what is best in Donne alike repelled Milton. His occasional conceits are rather of the Marinistic or Petrarchian type. The earth which

> "woos the gentle air
> To hide her guilty front with innocent snow,"

is akin to Théophile's dagger which blushed for its crime. The conceit in the lines *On Shakespeare* is suggested by a sonnet (cxxxi.) of Petrarch.

But conceit is a subordinate element even in

Milton's earliest poetry. The sign-manual of his work are the "poetic diction" and the artistic evolution, and both are in evidence in the noble ode with which, in 1629, he enlarged the compass of English lyrical poetry. The hymn *On the Morning of Christ's Nativity* (which is indebted for suggestions to Tasso's *Canzone Sopra la Cappella del Presepio*), is the most finely evolved ode which English poetry had produced up to that date. It is not more poetic in feeling than the *Epithalamium*, but its thought-scheme is more complete, its *crescendo* and *diminuendo* elaborated with more conscious art. Beginning in a tone of hushed awe, the hymn rises steadily, one bell-like stanza pealing out above another, till the climax is reached in the angels' song, when it slowly subsides through the yet sonorous stanzas on the passing of the idols to the quiet close beloved of Milton. The two lyrical studies in "humours," composed at Horton, *L'Allegro* and *Il Penseroso*, have the same skilful evolution, the same wholeness, and a maturer beauty of style. With *Comus*, composed at the same period, they are the most purely delightful of Milton's poems. Love of nature—none the less genuine because a student's love — reminiscences of Spenser and Shakespeare, Chaucer and Ariosto, pastoral and masque, Greek tragedy and Greek philosophy, mingle in these exquisite poems, written before classical pedantry had a little hardened his conception of style and form, and while he was still happy, unembittered by controversy, or by disappointment public and domestic.

Early Poems.

Comus blends in a result that is altogether individual—a new dramatic kind, as distinct and delightful as the *Aminta*—suggestions derived from many sources, classical drama, Italian pastoral and Jonsonian masque, Fletcher and Shakespeare. But its largest debt is to *A Midsummer Night's Dream*. In that play and *The Tempest* Milton recognised work of Shakespeare's which was *sui generis*, provoking no comparison with "correct" classical tragedy and comedy; and if one work more than another floated in the back of his brain while he wrote *Comus*, it was Shakespeare's play "in the fairy manner." *Comus* also is a tale of a single night's adventure in a wood where there is magic in the air, though by Milton all is given a high and grave moral purpose. Even the style, though rich in classical imagery and literary association, is redolent of Shakespeare and the dramatists as Milton's style never was again.

For with *Lycidas* (1638) emerged the Milton of *Paradise Lost*, classical in his conception of poetic style and form, combatively Puritan in spirit. Johnson's criticism of *Lycidas* as an elegy does not altogether miss the mark. *Lycidas* is no more a moving lament than *Paradise Lost* is a profoundly satisfying religious poem. So far as King is concerned, the poem is a conventional compliment, touched with pathos perhaps only once, in the lines—

> "Ay me! while thee the shores and sounding seas
> Wash far away where'er thy bones are hurled,"

and with pure and high feeling in the heavenly vision of the close. Otherwise the sentiments which interest us are those which the poet utters regarding his own ambitions as a poet or the shortcomings of the Laudian clergy, in the passages where, breaking through the pastoral convention, he speaks in the trumpet-tones of the sonnets, and in the personal accents of a later lyric poetry. Apart from these passages, it is as a work of art that the poem commands admiration—by its marvellous evolution, the beauty of the ever-varying cadences (which were inaudible to Johnson), and the completeness with which the poet has assimilated and reproduced the artificial classical pastoral, as he was later to reproduce the artificial classical epic. There are none of Spenser's naïve, would-be realistic touches—his "cakes and cracknels," "curds and clowted cream" —and the poem gains thereby in harmony of impression.

Milton's visit to Italy, and the encouragement he received from Italian literati and from the aged patron of Tasso and Marino, encouraged him in the plan formed at Horton of writing some great poem that the world should not willingly let die. Italy was the home of the "Heroic Poem" in theory and achievement, and Milton's first dream was apparently to "out-go" Tasso and compose an heroic poem on the subject of King Arthur and his knights. He began, but found the task too difficult; and indeed it is difficult to conceive a satisfactory treatment even by

Italy.

Milton of the Arthurian legend with the machinery and in the style of the classical epic. The mythical character of the story may have repelled the Puritan; and it made the subject unsuitable for the epic according to Tasso's theory. His failure with Arthur, or some other reason, inclined him for a time to the drama, and in 1640-42 he was busy noting possible themes, mainly scriptural but not excluding history, and outlining plays on the subject of the Fall, which contain already all the principal moments of *Paradise Lost*, when he was diverted by what he deemed the more pressing duty of moulding England to a chosen people of God, and emptying the phials of his wrath on those who retarded this consummation. During these years his only poems were the occasional sonnets. Johnson's neo-classical prejudices saw in the sonnet merely an elegant trifle, but Milton was following the greatest of his Italian masters in using the sonnet to utter trumpet-notes on political themes; and the grand style to which he had finally attained in *Lycidas* is as evident as in *Paradise Lost* in these splendid, and in the history of English poetry so inspiring, poems.

Sonnets.

The years of Milton's silence as a poet were years of rapid poetic decadence and transition. How remote Milton's poetry in style and conception was from the fashionable verse of the day it needs only a glance at the volume which contained *Lycidas* to realise. That great poem had

Mid-century Poets.

to keep company with verses in which Joseph Beaumont inquired—

> "Why did perfection seek for parts?
> Why did his nature grace the arts?
> Why strove he both the worlds to know,
> Yet always scorned the world below?
> Why would his brain the centre be
> To learning's circularitie,
> Which, though the vastest arts did fill,
> Would like a point seem little still?"

and Cleveland, the Cavalier satirist, declared that

> "I am no poet here; my pen's the spout
> Where the rain-water of my eyes runs out
> In pity of that name whose fate we see
> Thus copied out in grief's hydrographie."

And this was the general style of eulogistic addresses, satires, and religious verse like that of Benlowes. From such contorted thought, and the uncouth expression and versification which went with it, there were two modes of escape. That which Milton took, the way of genius, was not open to all; the other was to attain, even at the cost of imaginative loss, to a poetry of common-sense and clear, balanced, oratorical expression. In this movement towards a poetry of common-sense, satire of current affairs, and pointed, well-balanced eloquence, all good things, but none of them quite compensating for the finer spirit of poetry which they expelled, the writers whom Dryden singled out as his predecessors were Edmund Waller (1606-1687), Sir John Denham (1615-1669), Sir William Davenant (1605-1668), and Abraham Cowley (1618-1667).

The services of Waller and Denham were in the main metrical. In their poems the decasyllabic couplet regained some of the regularity and balance it had lost in the rugged lines and abrupt enjambments which Donne and Jonson encouraged. This is true at any rate of Waller. Educated at Eton and Cambridge, Waller was elected to Parliament at the age of sixteen; carried off a wealthy city wife in 1631; became after her death an intimate of the circle to which Falkland and Edward Hyde belonged, and the suitor of Lady Dorothy Sidney, the Sacharissa to whom his polished love-verses are addressed. He took an active part in the Long Parliament, following the moderate constitutional line of Hyde, but in the famous plot of 1643 lost his nerve, and behaved in a way which Clarendon has branded. Like others, he later made his peace with Cromwell, and wrote on him the noblest of his poems. Like others, he followed it up with eulogy of Charles restored.

Waller.

"Smooth" is the epithet with which Waller's name is linked, and it is the most obvious feature of all his eulogistic verses and elegant songs, which were written at different times from about 1623 to the end of his long life. He was not the first poet to write smooth and balanced couplets, but he cultivated the art more consciously and conscientiously than any of his predecessors and contemporaries, stimulated, he says,— and there is no reason to doubt his word,—by admiration of the closing couplet in the *ottava rima* of Fairfax's *Tasso*. Waller's smoothness, like Balzac's polished periods, was due in great measure to the comparative emptiness of his poetry. He was eminently well qualified "to carve heads on cherry-stones," and with the exception of a few delightful songs—notably *On a Girdle* and "Go, lovely rose"—and some noble stanzas in the address to Cromwell, it would be difficult to find a thought in his poems fitted to startle or arrest. Dryden's achievement was to give balance and regularity to verse which had the pregnancy and vigour of Jonson's and Donne's.

Denham's "strength" is more dubious than Waller's "sweetness" or "smoothness," and is certainly not of a herculean character. The son of a Lord Chief-Justice of the King's Bench in Ireland, and educated at Oxford, Denham was in close attendance on the King and Queen during the years of trouble; but though made Surveyor of Works after the Restoration, he, like many others, reaped little happiness from his attachment to the House of Stuart. He wrote one worthless play, *The Sophy*. Of his poems the majority are occasional pieces, of which the most celebrated is the descriptive, moralising *Cooper's Hill*. The thoughts are prosaic and commonplace, but they are natural and relevant; and the style has some of the easy, pointed eloquence which was to be cultivated in the next age. Four lines added later have become classic—

> "O could I flow like thee and make thy stream
> My great example as it is my theme!
> Tho' deep yet clear, tho' gentle yet not dull,
> Strong without rage, without o'erflowing full."

They are echoed in one of Wordsworth's earliest characteristic poems, *Remembrance of Collins*—

> " O glide, fair stream! for ever so
> Thy quiet soul on all bestowing,
> Till all our minds for ever flow
> As thy deep waters now are flowing."

There is far more vigour both of thought and expression, in the once popular poetry of Abraham Cowley (1618 - 1667), whom Clarendon accounted Jonson's greatest successor. Drawn to poetry, like many another subsequently, by the *Faerie Queene*, Cowley wrote his *Pyramus and Thisbe* at ten years old, and his *Poetical Blossoms* were published when he was fourteen. At Cambridge he wrote a pastoral drama and a Latin comedy as well as his *Elegy on William Harvey*. Driven from Cambridge, he followed his friend Crashaw to Oxford, where he secured the friendship of Falkland, and was attached to the service of Lord St Albans. He attended on the Queen at Paris, and conducted her correspondence with the King. In 1647 his *Mistress* was published, and in 1656, after his return to England, his *Poems*, which included the *Pindarique Odes* and the fragmentary epic the *Davideis*. He studied medicine, and after the Restoration his chief interests were scientific; he was an original member of the Royal Society. He continued to write verses — including an *Ode to Hobbes*—but his most interesting product were the delightful *Essays*, in which he combined verse and easy, natural prose.

In Cowley's poetry, which enjoyed extraordinary

popularity, one can note very clearly the meeting of stream and sea. His wit is as "metaphysical," as pedantic and fantastic, as Donne's; but he has neither the emancipated imaginative ardour of the Renaissance, nor the devotional and ecstatic tone of the Catholic reaction, but the alert, inquisitive, rational temper of Dryden and the epoch of the Royal Society. When not merely light badinage, his love-verses are frigid and execrable conceits. His *Pindariques* are often bright and vigorous, but are as like Pindar's odes as one of his essays is like the prophecies of Isaiah. His *Davideis*, in which he expands the incidents of David's adventures during Saul's reign by means of dreams and descriptions — just as Saint-Amant was doing in his *Moyse Sauvé*—is written in the pointed and tasteless style of Marino's *Strage degli Innocenti*, and in a less poetic tone. In the pursuit of a point the pious Cowley will deviate into blasphemy, as when he makes the Deity foretell Saul's suicide—

"That hand which now on David's life would prey
Shall then turn just and its own master slay."

What is best in Cowley are poems—like the lines on a retired life, the *Elegy on Harvey*, or the verses on Crashaw's death — in which he is a link between Jonson and Dryden, with less of fancy than the former but greater ease of expression, less sonorous and effective than the latter.

Cowley was not the only poet who essayed the heroic poem under French and Italian influence. Sir William Davenant (1606-1668), the son of a vintner at

Oxford, made Poet-Laureate in 1638, and like Cowley and Denham in the service of the exiled Stuarts, was a prolific dramatist, and wrote one or two delightful songs; but his most ambitious work was a fragment of a romantic epic, *Gondibert*, published in 1650 with an elaborate letter to Hobbes and a reply from that not very romantic philosopher. William Chamberlayne (1619 - 1689), of whom we know very little beyond the fact that he was a physician at Shaftesbury, began about 1642 a long romantic epic, *Pharonnida, an Heroick Poem*, published in 1659. In both of these we see the influence not so much of the Italian romantic epic as of the French heroic romance in prose. The central feature is a love-story, and the supernatural machinery which had been such a feature of the epic has disappeared. Davenant reveals his model when he declares his intention of dividing his poem into books and cantos corresponding to the acts and scenes of a play, for this had been, Baro says, D'Urfé's design in the *Astrée*. Chamberlayne's poem has all the features of the kind—the unknown hero loved at first sight by the princess, whose passion is combated by her sense of what befits her rank, the endless whirl of incidents, and the final "recognition" and marriage. There is little or no dramatic interest in the *Pharonnida*; the style is tortured; and the verse overflows the line and couplet pause till it is hardly verse at all. But there was far more poetry in Chamberlayne than in most of his contemporaries; picturesqueness, pathos, and passion gild his obscure and affected style. But the greatest of heroic poets found his model, not in French epic or long-winded romance, not even in the more justly admired work of Tasso, but went back to the greater epics of Greece and Rome.

When Milton resumed the task which he had laid aside in 1641, the subject of the Fall was his final choice. The subject was to the serious thought of the seventeenth century of central importance in the history of the race, and round it had gathered the most agitating controversies in Protestant and Roman Christendom. In the *Doctrine and Discipline of Divorce* (1642) Milton defined his attitude towards "the Jesuits and that sect among us which is named of Arminius": "Yet considering the perfection wherein man was created and might have stood, no decree necessitating his freewill, but subsequent, though not in time yet in order, to causes which were in his own power: they might perhaps be persuaded to absolve both God and us." Whether this be the strictest Calvinist doctrine or not, it is the justification of "the ways of God to man" which Milton elaborated in *Paradise Lost*.

Paradise Lost.

That his final preference of epic to dramatic form was due to the study of Andreini and Vondel is not proved and not provable. Milton's indebtedness to Vondel (which has been asserted solely on the ground of the resemblance between incidents and expressions) has not been urged or supported by those Dutch critics who have given the

Form.

matter closest attention.[1] They have recognised that, when allowance has been made for the common indebtedness of both to Scripture, to patristic tradition, to the classical and Italian poets, as well as to that early favourite of both, Du Bartas, to say nothing of Grotius, there is not sufficient ground to establish the thesis that one poet actually influenced the other.

[1] Nicholas Beets, *De Paradijsgeschiedenis en de Nederlandsche Dichters, Verscheidenheden*, ii. 58, and J. J. Moolhuizen, *Vondel's Lucifer en Milton's Verloren Paradijs*, 'sGravenhage, 1895, decide against Mr Edmundson's thesis (*Milton and Vondel*, Lond., 1885). The German critic, Rudolf Buddensieg, *Die Grenzboten*, 1887, is more favourable. August Muller, *Ueber Milton's Abhangigkeit von Vondel*, Berlin, 1891, and Gustaaf Zeegers, *Joost van den Vondel*, Antwerpen, 1888, recognise resemblances, but will not go further. I quote these last from Moolhuizen. When Milton borrows from classical or Italian poetry, he makes no disguise of the fact; he was borrowing from what every one recognised to be the great models for imitation, and the resemblance is generally not more interesting than the difference. The alleged borrowings from Vondel seem to me of another kind. Many suggest at once either mere plagiarism or accidental resemblance. More closely examined, many of the resemblances disappear; others are explicable when one remembers "the fewness of the radical positions in Scripture"; the most striking can generally be traced to a common source. How difficult it was *not* to think of the same devices is proved by the fact that in his scheme of a drama, drawn up before 1642, Milton closed the first act with a "Chorus of Angels singing a hymn of Creation." Just so did Vondel close the first act of *Adam in Ballingschap* (1664).

As for Andreini, Belloni (*Il Seicento*, cap. vi.) claims for him pretty much everything which Mr Edmundson attributes to Vondel. That, as Mr Garnet says, Milton got from Andreini the idea of his first sketch of a tragic Morality I am not prepared to deny, but would venture to suggest that Milton *may* have derived his idea of presenting to Adam mute personified abstractions from Du Bartas' *Les Furies* and from the speech of Adam in Grotius' *Adamus Exul*, Act V., beginning

"Hinc pallidorum longa morborum cohors
Turpisque egestas sequitur," &c.

The fact is that by 1641 Milton had outlined very fully in his schemes for a drama the contents of *Paradise Lost*. All the principal moments are present in the sketches which he drew up—the fall of the angels, the creation of the world, the Temptation, and the consequences of the Fall in history. But none of them could be presented on the stage. All were necessarily relegated to choral ode, descriptive speech, or the symbolism of the Morality. Grotius had dramatised the scene of the Temptation, but Milton's sense of dramatic propriety evidently shrank from a scene in which one of the actors was to be a serpent. Consideration of these limitations, as well as of the necessary exclusion of God from all direct participation in the action, is sufficient to explain Milton's preference for the epic form. There is nothing, as Dr Nicholas Beets has pointed out, from which Vondel's *Lucifer* suffers more than from the fact that the action is left entirely to secondary agents. One of the finest "strokes" in Milton's description of the war in heaven is that the ultimate victory over Lucifer belongs to the Son of God alone.

For the artistic ideal which he thus set before him, the harmonious reproduction of the different elements of the Virgilian epic, Milton could have chosen no more appropriate theme, and none better suited to the sublime cast of his own mind. Only with a Scriptural theme, and with none so harmoniously as this central and transcendent one,—in which the human element is so small and of so unique a character,—was it possible,

The epic.

at any rate for a Protestant audience, to introduce the supernatural machinery without incongruity and absurdity. When in Tasso's poem God commissions Gabriel to incite Godfrey to renew the war, it is not the human which is elevated, but the divine which is depressed. *Paradise Lost* is the exception which proves Boileau's rule that the supernatural beings of the Christian religion are not available as epic machinery, for, in *Paradise Lost*, the requisite harmony is secured by raising everything to the level of the superhuman—a level from which it is only "in rare moments of rest and reprieve" that the poet descends.

Yet that even Milton suffered from the seventeenth century's entanglement in the tradition of a conventional epic is hardly to be denied. The greatest fault of *Paradise Lost*, regarded simply as a work of art, is that the interest steadily subsides as the poem proceeds. The first plunge *in medias res* is overwhelming in its grandeur. Than the first book no sublimer poem in its special kind was ever written. We feel that we have travelled a long way from its originality and splendour of invention, when we find ourselves in the middle of Michael's pedantic *résumé* of Old Testament history. The substance of these books was an afterthought. Milton's intention, when he sketched his drama, was to follow Du Bartas and Grotius and adumbrate the consequences of the Fall allegorically. He might have done well to abide by his original intention and make Adam's visions more general and suggestive, less detailed and didactic.

The most serious fault, however, that modern

criticism has found with *Paradise Lost*, concerns it not so much as a poem but as a professedly religious poem. The interest in Milton's *dramatis personæ* is in the inverse ratio of their religious rank. Nothing in his poem is greater than his treatment of the fallen angels. One need only turn to Tasso's and Marino's grotesque infernal conferences to appreciate with gratitude the dignified presentation of Satan and his peers debating of war, or solacing themselves with song and converse high

The religious poem.

"Of fate, free-will, foreknowledge absolute."

Elizabethan tragedy has no more dramatic figure than Satan in these opening scenes, or a situation of sublimer pathos than when he faces his fallen host, and

"Thrice he essayed, and thrice, in spite of scorn,
Tears such as angels weep burst forth."

Satan may be, as Mr Courthope has said, the last great representative of the Macchiavelian politician whom Marlowe and Kyd and Shakespeare brought upon the stage, but there is a pathos in his ruined virtue which none of his prototypes possess. Almost accidentally, moreover, he has acquired some of the heroic resolution of the Calvinistic Hollander who refused to bow before the tyranny of Spain, the pride of those who brought Charles to the scaffold and vindicated that deed to a startled Europe. Vondel saw a resemblance between Lucifer and Cromwell which Milton would not have allowed. But Vondel's sympathies were with kings and magistrates, and what he emphasises is Lucifer's hypocrisy rather than his pride. He is pushed to the front by the discontent of others; he fights for God against God; at the last moment he wavers and almost relents. Milton's Satan is the sole author of the rebellion in heaven and all that follows from it.

Of the other actors, Adam and Eve are certainly not wanting in humanity. They are intensely human; but they hardly attain to the dignity of humanity in its first innocence and independence sufficiently to make them the adequate heroes of this "treurspel aller treurspelen," tragedy of tragedies, as Vondel calls it. It is evident that Milton's whole treatment of Adam and Eve was too deeply coloured by his own sublime egotism, his memory of his own experiences. He was too anxious to inculcate a lesson, and the moral of the story, that it is a man's duty to keep his wife in due subjection, hardly rises to the tragic level, though Eve repentant is one of the gems of the poem.

But it is in the celestial portions of the poem that criticism has found Milton most wanting as a religious poet. This is not the place to discuss Milton's theology. The important thing is not the theology but the impression produced on the imagination. Milton's heaven is not wanting in majesty and splendour. The poet was too deeply read in the Hebrew prophets not to have at his command magnificent images and sublime effects. Still, when we close the poem, we feel acutely that the poet has never caught a glimpse of the Beatific Vision, in which alone could be found the meaning of the great tragedy, and which lesser men than Milton—Giles Fletcher, Crashaw, Vaughan, Vondel—descried at moments. To that vision there is no access "nisi per charitatem," and some want of love was Milton's misfortune. Vondel is a less sublime poet, a far less wonderful artist, than Milton, but there is more of Christian feeling in his description of the cloud of sorrow which veiled the throne of the Godhead when Lucifer rebels than in the fierce derision with which Satan's first movements are noted in Milton's heaven.

But when Milton's limitations have been most fully enumerated, *Paradise Lost* remains one of the world's greatest poems, in invention, imagination, construction, language, and harmony. The sublimity and beauty of the style — a style as individual, as bold in its rejection of precedent, even of English idiom, as in a different way was Carlyle's later prose, —the sustained and majestic rhythm of the verse, never flag from the opening invocation to the quiet and solemn close. If a poet is to be judged, not alone by individual beauties, but by the greatness and completeness of his achievement, Milton's place as the second of English poets is unassailable.

Milton's last works showed no failure of the originality, the power of creating and perfecting new forms, which had signalised his work from the outset. *Paradise Regained* (1671) is not the only short epic on a New Testament subject which the seventeenth century produced, but it is by far the finest. It is not likely that Milton knew

Vondel's *Johannes de Boetgezant*. The resemblances which Mr Edmundson pointed out have their common source in Tasso. It is more probable that he knew the *Strage degli Innocenti* of Marino, and the severity of Milton's style is due possibly both to his sense of what was appropriate to his sacred theme, and to his disgust at the extravagance and "wit" of Marino and Cowley. But already, in *The Reasons of Church Government*, he had contemplated an epic "on the brief model of the Book of Job," and that was undoubtedly the work chiefly in his mind, as he composed his story of the Temptation mainly in dialogue; and if not so elaborate a work as the greater poem, the art of *Paradise Regained* is not less subtle, while its ethical tone is nobler. If Satan in *Paradise Lost* has some of the strength of Puritanism in resistance, it is to *Paradise Regained* one must go to study the source of Puritan strength—the disregard of wealth and glory, the submission of the will to God, and God only.

In *Samson Agonistes* (1671) Milton realised another long-cherished ambition, and reproduced classical tragedy as he had done classical elegy and epic; and, as in these, he assimilated and reproduced the form of Greek tragedy, including the chorus, with a completeness and harmony which no poet of the Renaissance attained, and that, while breathing into it a spirit which is Hebraic rather than Hellenic, and making it the vehicle for the expression of his intensest personal sentiments. In Samson Milton saw himself and the cause for which he fought.

The wheel had come full circle, and the combat to which he sounded the first note of onset in *Lycidas* closed with this fierce cry of anger, and passionate prayer for vengeance. It was not the Stuarts alone who had failed to read aright the lesson of defeat. Puritanism needed, as Mr Trevelyan has said, to go to school with rationalism to reacquire some of the elements of Christianity.

Milton's poetry was the last great expression of two enthusiasms, which had passed away even while he wrote—the artistic enthusiasm of the Renaissance and the spiritual enthusiasm of the Reformation. No poet realised so completely the Renaissance ideal of poetry cast in classical moulds,— carried out so entirely and majestically the programme of the Pleiad. Tasso's poem had been a compromise between classical epic and mediæval romance. Jonson's attempts to reproduce classical forms in the drama appear pedantic and boyish beside Milton's. In general, Renaissance epic and tragedy are lifeless failures. French tragedy, as it finally took form, is a very different thing from Greek tragedy. Milton, and Milton only, succeeded in producing living and beautiful poems in correct classical forms. And into these classic forms he poured the intensest spirit of the Protestant movement. No one carried to bolder logical conclusions the first principle of Protestantism, the interpretation of Scripture by the unfettered individual reason and conscience. The completeness with which he accepted the right of individual interpretation separated him

Conclusion.

from the religious bodies around him, while the rigour with which he still clung to the Bible kept him out of touch with the larger rationalism of the age. There was no room in Milton's later poems for the Platonism of Spenser which lingers in *Comus*. Hellenic thought and Hebraic revelation come into harsh conflict in *Paradise Regained*, when Christ arraigns what Satan has so eloquently and sympathetically described.

Even while Milton wrote, the spiritual atmosphere, religious, political, and artistic, had changed around him. To realise the change, one has only to turn from—

"Of Man's first disobedience and the fruit," &c.,

or—

"Hail Holy Light, Offspring of Heaven," &c.,

to—

"In thriving arts long since had Holland grown,
Crouching at home and cruel when abroad;
Scarce leaving us the means to claim our own;
Our King they courted, and our merchants awed."

The spirit of the age that was past, with its passionate pursuit of high if somewhat narrow ideals, religious, political, and artistic, is not reflected more clearly in Milton's elevated diction, and the imaginative structure of his poems, small and great, than that of the age of reason, toleration, and constitutional discussion is in Dryden's vigorous conversational style, and his alert and acute ratiocination in verse.

CHAPTER V.

ENGLISH PROSE.

"AN IMMODERATE HYDROPTIC THIRST OF LEARNING"—BACON—JONSON. DIVINES—ANGLO-CATHOLIC: ANDREWES—DONNE—JEREMY TAYLOR; PURITAN: ADAMS; LATITUDINARIAN: HALES — CHILLINGWORTH. CONTROVERSIALISTS: HALL — TAYLOR — MILTON. "CHARACTERS": HALL — OVERBURY — EARLE. BURTON — DRUMMOND — BROWNE — URQUHART—FULLER. PHILOSOPHY: HOBBES. HISTORY: CLARENDON. BIOGRAPHY: WALTON.

THE review of English prose [1] in the preceding volume of this series closed with the great name of Hooker.

Hooker. In the *Ecclesiastical Polity*, English prose, though not yet without faults of cumbrousness and diffuseness, for the first time grappled successfully with the task of setting forth in lucid, weighty, and harmonious periods a sustained philosophic argument, and, so doing, established its right to take the place of Latin even for learned purposes,

---

[1] Minto, *A Manual of English Prose Literature*, 3rd ed., Edinburgh, 1886; Saintsbury, *Elizabethan Literature*, 1903, *Short History*, 1898; Craik, *English Prose Selections*, vol. ii., London, 1893; Chambers, *Cyclopædia of English Literature*, ed. David Patrick, Edin., 1901-3.

useful as it might be to retain the latter for works addressed solely to the world of scholars.

The note which Hooker struck, the note of gravity and dignity, remained the dominant one throughout at any rate that portion of the seventeenth century with which this volume deals. Prose, like poetry, felt the strain of the growing seriousness and combativeness of the age, the increasing intellectuality of temper. Pure poetry is somewhat of an exotic in the seventeenth century; even Milton's purest poetry is his earliest. Both poetry and prose are enlisted in the service of religious controversy or the growing interest in science and philosophy. The earlier seventeenth century cannot be called an age of prose, in the sense that its temper is prosaic. It was not, like the next age, suspicious of enthusiasm: enthusiasm was too much the air it breathed. But that enthusiasm was not, as in the years which produced the *Faerie Queene* or Shakespeare's historical plays, the joyous enthusiasm of a nation awakened to a sense of its own greatness and the charm of letters, and not yet profoundly divided against itself. It is inquiring and combative, fanatical sometimes, often satirical and scornful, melancholy, occasionally mystical, hardly, even arrogantly, intellectual. Learning is its idol, "an immoderate hydroptic thirst of learning." The old learning, scholastic and traditional, subtle and argumentative, revives with vigour in the work of the ecclesiastical and theological controversialists at the very time that in the writings of Bacon and Hobbes the new

Learning.

spirit of inquiry, distrustful of enthusiasm and distrustful of tradition, is growing active. Such an age naturally begot a rich and strong but varied prose. To a uniform and perfect medium, like that which Balzac, Descartes, and Pascal evolved in France, it did not attain. Yet the prose of the early seventeenth century has great qualities. It has the freshness of forms which have not yet become stereotyped and conventional. Its writers know how to mingle colloquial vigour with dignified and serious eloquence, racy Saxon with musical Latin polysyllables. In splendour of poetic imagery and harmony, the best prose of Donne and Taylor and Milton and Browne has been only occasionally equalled since. Bacon has hardly a rival in condensed felicity of phrase and wealth of illustration, and Hobbes's prose is as clear, forcible, and formed a style as has ever been used in philosophic exposition. The prose of the seventeenth century is not to be dismissed as unformed by Arnold's comparison of extracts from Chapman and Milton with Dryden's prefaces. Neither Chapman nor Milton is quite a characteristic writer. The seventeenth century is the first great period of modern English prose, while it was forming under classical, but independent of French, influence. The advance which it made after the Restoration in uniformity, elegance, and ease was not made without a corresponding loss in freshness, harmony, dignity, and poetic richness of phraseology.

No better proof of what has been said regarding the subordination of the purely literary to other interests could be found than the work of the great thinker and author who meets us on the threshold of the century. Francis Bacon[1] (1561-1626), whose life and public career need hardly be detailed here, was as careful a student of the art of clear, dignified, and persuasive utterance as of any other of the many fields of inquiry his restless mind surveyed. *The Colours of Good and Evil* (1597)—which, with the first draft of the *Essays*, was his earliest literary publication,— and the *Promus of Formalities and Elegancies*, show, what is equally clear from everything he wrote, how consciously he studied to speak and to write effectively. But it was not for the sake of style that Bacon studied style. He recognised how frequently "the greatest orators, . . . by observing their well-graced forms of speech, lose the volubility of application." He condemned the Ciceronians of the Renaissance, who "began to hunt more after words than matter, and more after the choiceness of the phrase, and the round and clear composition of the sentence, and the sweet falling of the clauses, and the varying and illustration of their works with tropes and figures, than after the weight of matter, worth of subject, soundness of argument, life of invention, and depth of judgment." Style to Bacon is an instrument of power—a means by which to commend his policy

Bacon.

---

[1] *Works*, ed. Spedding, Ellis, and Heath, 14 vols., London, 1857-1874. Life by S. R. Gardiner, *D. of N. B.* Innumerable studies, including *Life and Philosophy*, Nicol, 1890 (*Philosophic Classics*), *Bacon*, Dean Church, 1884 (*Men of Letters*).

to statesmen and sovereigns, his new instrument for unlocking the secrets of nature to scholars at home and abroad.

The earliest of Bacon's papers which have been preserved—*An Advertisement touching the Controversies of the Church* (1589)—has all the characteristics of his later work,—breadth and subtlety of thought, gravity, heightened by the tinge of archaism in the diction, the well-built sentences, now long, now short, as occasion demands, never getting out of hand, the perfectly chosen phrase, the felicitous illustrations and quotations. There is not an "empty" or "idle" word. "His hearers," Jonson tells us, "could not laugh or look aside from him without loss." His readers cannot afford to overlook a word if they would appreciate his argument or do justice to his art as a writer; though they will recognise in it an art that is always conscious of its end and in methods a little over-elaborate. Neither in rhetoric nor diplomacy did Bacon ever recognise, with Pascal, that there is an "esprit de finesse" which can achieve more than studied method, that "la vraie éloquence se moque de l'éloquence." Bacon excites our admiration: he never carries us away.

The Advancement of Learning (1605) is in the same closely reasoned persuasive style, but more elaborate in its rhetoric. The first book is a brilliant popular *Apologia* for learning. After a eulogy of the king, characteristic of the age, but which Bacon alone could have penned, he proceeds to meet the detractors of learning, whether divines or politicians, on their own ground, with arguments consciously adapted to "popular estimation and conceit," expounding texts and meeting text with text, example with example, developing in approved rhetorical style the most telling "topics" his well-stored mind had at command. The analysis that follows, of the errors which have misled learning, is more pregnant with valuable suggestions. But the whole book is confessedly a brilliant and ingenious "concio ad populum." In the second book he addresses himself more seriously to his main task, a review of the existing state of knowledge and its more patent defects, than which, perhaps, nothing he wrote is a more vivid reflection of Bacon's mind — his wide-ranging view (more ample than exact in detail); his fertility of suggestions, often fruitful anticipations, if not seldom fantastic; his exact and discriminating phraseology, and his wealth of felicitous illustration, surprising and illuminating analogies. In science and philosophy Bacon was, indeed, nothing so much as a thrower-out of brilliant and fertile suggestions, and the stater and re-stater in startling and far-shining phrases of one or two central ideas. Of these almost all are foreshadowed in *The Advancement of Learning*. For the actual formulation of a logic of science he did less than Kepler and Galileo, because he knew less of the actual methods of science. The methods which he describes in the *Sylva Sylvarum* (1627), a collection of notes in natural history published posthumously, and in the *New Atlantis* (1627), a brief sketch of an imaginary republic, and the results which he anticipates (transubstantiations of all kinds, including the making of gold), show what a remote glimpse he had caught of the promised land into which Kepler and Gilbert and Galileo were already entered. His notes interest only by their phrasing, as when he concludes that the celestial bodies are made of true fire or flame, which "with them is durable and consistent and in his natural place; but with us is a stranger and momentary and impure: like Vulcan that halted with his fall."

In the *Essays* (1597-1612-1625) Bacon had the advantage of dealing with a subject which he had studied more closely and experimentally than he did physical science. To understand human nature and how to manage it was his constant endeavour, though the motive for which he studied it and sought advancement was leisure, and opportunity for scientific research. The *Essays* are the fullest and finest expression of the practical wisdom he had acquired from study, experience, and meditation. Profound wisdom, and practical shrewdness amounting almost to cunning, are mingled in them with satire and rich meditative eloquence. His master in political philosophy is Machiavelli, the first "to throw aside the fetters of mediævalism and treat politics inductively." The effect is seen in such essays as that on "Of Greatness of Kingdoms and Estates," "Of Simulation and Dissimulation," "Of Great Places," "Of Cunning," "Of Suspicion," and "Of Negotiating." With scientific detachment he notes every means, important or trifling, worthy or ignoble, by which human nature is worked on, power acquired and maintained. There was, undoubtedly, in Bacon a certain degree of moral obliquity as well as weakness. But he was humane, and by no means without ideals. Behind all his worldly ambition and crooked policies lay an ideal enthusiasm for knowledge; and he was acutely sensitive to both moral and religious motives. The tone of the *Essays* is not throughout that of cold scientific analysis. Only one side of his nature is represented by such essays as those named. Those "Of Truth," "Of Death," "Of Unity in Religion," "Of Revenge," "Of Friendship," bear witness to another; while others, such as those "Of Regiment of Health," "Of Plantations," "Of Masks and Triumphs, "Of Gardens," are delightful results of that wide range of interest, of curious inquiry, which is the chief characteristic of Bacon's thought, as felicitous illustration is of his style.

The spirit of the *Essays*, the analytic, unsentimental, though not undignified, somewhat Machiavellian temper, is that in which he composed his *History of Henry VII.* (1622). It is a careful, sympathetic study of a king who played the game of ruling a state with both wisdom and subtlety. Bacon's style is, as befits the form of the work, plainer than in the essays; as pregnant as ever, but less rich in illustration. Yet here, too, he does not disdain a happy figure. "He did make that war rather with an olive-branch than a laurel-branch in his hand." "For his wars were always to him as a mine of treasure of a strange kind of ore: iron at the top and gold and silver at the bottom."

Bacon's *Essays* are not the only literature of the kind which has come down to us from the seventeenth century. Ben Jonson's *Discoveries*,[1] like Bacon's, are collections of notes and aphorisms on various subjects, cohering at times into regular short essays. In the earlier editions of the *Essays*, it must be remembered, the note or aphorism character was more obvious than in the later ones. Jonson's never received the final shaping and polishing which Bacon's passed through.

Jonson.

The essays of each are what might be expected from the character, tastes, and life of the two men. Bacon is the statesman, and inductive student of nature and human nature,—one who has mingled in great affairs, and moved in high circles. His *Essays* are a manual for princes and statesmen. Jonson is the poet and student, poor and a little embittered, looking out on life with a clear and manly gaze, but chiefly interested in letters, and the place assigned to the man of letters. Jonson's morality is robuster than Bacon's, but then he writes from the study, not from the court. His tendency is not towards compliancy, but rather to petulant arrogance. He inveighs against envy and calumny, and pours contempt on courtiers, critics, and bad poets. But it is on literature that he writes most at length,

[1] Ed. F. E. Schelling, Boston, 1892, and in *The Temple Classics*, Lond., 1896. For a criticism see Swinburne's *Study of Ben Jonson*, Lond., 1889.

and what he has to say is altogether excellent—the first really valuable notes on style and composition which we have. Beginning with *De Stylo*, he has a complete essay on what he calls "Eloquentia," which covers prose composition as a whole, especially as supplemented by some notes on epistolary style. Laborious practice and judicious reading are the means of acquiring a good style, which consists, in Swift's phrase, of "proper words in proper places." "Ready writing makes not good writing, but good writing brings on ready writing." Such maxims are an index to Jonson's own practice. We recognise in them the author of the carefully ordered, closely knit, consciously elaborated comedies. He admires in Bacon what it was his own endeavour to attain to; and condemns in Shakespeare a facility he never himself enjoyed.

In many of his critical dogmata, it must be remembered, Jonson is simply reproducing classical and Italian precepts. In his ideal estimate of the poet, the importance he attaches to training (Exercitatio, Imitatio, Lectio) as well as "natural wit," his exaltation of Aristotle ("what other men did by chance or custom, he doth by reason"), his conception of the proper end of comedy, Jonson is the scholar and critic of the Renaissance. But, indeed, the Jonson of the *Discoveries* is throughout the Jonson of the plays and poems. There is the same high and courageous idealism, passing too readily into arrogant self-assertion, the same learning and industry, the same strength and fulness without charm of style.

Jonson has not Bacon's fine rhetoric, his abundant illustrations and images. But his prose is well phrased, and, by its happy mingling of short and long sentences, acquires an easy and dignified movement.

The work which Hooker began, the statement and defence of the Anglican position against Rome on the one hand and Geneva on the other, with a superabundance of learning, and in grave, elaborate, and sonorous style, was continued in the seventeenth century by a series of controversialists and preachers. To Lancelot Andrewes[1] (1555-1626), indeed, the Laudian school looked back with hardly less reverence than to Hooker. A scholar who had mastered fifteen languages, and was familiar with the whole range of patristic theology, he was not only a controversialist able to enter the lists with Bellarmine, but, during the last years of Elizabeth and the first of James, the greatest preacher of his day, "stella predicantium." His method is characteristic both of his age and of the position which he claimed for the Church whose representative he was. In all the preaching of the day the sermon took the form of a minute analysis of the text, word by word, with a view to eliciting its full significance, doctrinal and practical. But to this exposition Andrewes brought, not the narrow, rigid interpretation of orthodox Calvinism, but all the re-

Divines— Andrewes.

---

[1] Sermons (in six vols.) and other works, ed. J. P. Wilson, in *Library of Anglo-Catholic Theology*, Oxford, 1841-54. Study by North in *Classic Preachers of the English Church*, Lond., 1878.

sources of patristic learning, his aim being to elicit what he considers the primitive and catholic significance. Tracking every word to its last lair, it is not strange that in the fashion of the time he often quibbles and plays on it. "If it be not Immanuel, it will be Immanu—hell; . . . if we have Him, and God by Him, we need no more: Immanuel and Immanu—all." A modern reader misses a well-marshalled, lucidly-developed argument. He feels, as in reading the controversial literature of the day, that he cannot get enough away from the parts to survey the whole. Yet Andrewes' sermons have a charm of their own, if one is not too entirely out of sympathy with the thought to care for reading sermons at all. His style is colloquial, even careless, but saturated with biblical and patristic phraseology; and the unction which these phrases had for himself he communicates to his reader, and doubtless did so in a still higher degree to his audience.

John Donne[1] (1573-1631), satirist, amorist, soldier, courtier, and finally (1615) priest and ascetic, the eloquent Dean of St Paul's, was a scholar hardly inferior, in profundity and variety of learning, to Andrewes. "An immoderate hydroptic thirst of learning" had been, he complained, a barrier to his worldly advancement in early life. His transition from the Romanism which he inherited from a distinguished ancestry, to Anglicanism, was dictated per-

Donne.

---

[1] *LXXX. Sermons: Life by Walton*, 1640. *Works*, Alford, 6 vols., London, 1839; text carelessly edited. Studies by Lightfoot in *Classic Preachers*, &c., and Beeching, *Religio Laici*, Lond., 1902.

haps by ambitious motives, but was not effected without a thorough study of the points at issue. He assisted Morton in his controversies with Rome, and his first published work was a learned and acute defence of the royal supremacy, the *Pseudo-Martyr* (1609), a closely reasoned treatise, unadorned with anything of his later eloquence. Accordingly, his method as a preacher does not differ essentially from that of Andrewes. He divides and subdivides his text, and where the question is a refined one of doctrine or conduct, he follows the orthodox scent through a not always lucid labyrinth of fathers and doctors. But his eloquence has a broader sweep than Andrewes. It is less colloquial, less dependent on the unction of scriptural and pious phrases. When he disentangles himself from definitions and controversy to bring home to his hearers a doctrine or an admonition, his style becomes irradiated with the glow of a bizarre and powerful imagination. He has dramatic touches that remind one of Webster, and passages of glowing, sonorous, periodic eloquence not surpassed by Burke. But such passages of pure eloquence are perhaps rare. The scholastic subtlety and learning with which the most impressive passages are generally interwoven, effective in their own day, militate against any wide enjoyment of Donne's intense and imaginative eloquence to-day.

Donne died in 1632, before he had received the bishopric to which he was designated by Laud and Charles. In 1633, the attention of the former, ever on the outlook for talent when conjoined with a conforming spirit, was attracted to a young Cambridge Fellow, who had taken the place of a friend in the pulpit of St Paul's and amazed his hearers by the luxuriant beauty of his eloquence. Jeremy Taylor[1] (1613-1667), as a pure orator, a master of clear, flowing, picturesque, and poetic language, has perhaps no rival except Ruskin. He was only twenty-one when, as Perse Fellow of Gonville and Caius College, he was taken up by Laud and sent to Oxford to study divinity and casuistry. He was made a Fellow of All Souls (1636) and rector of Uppingham (1638), and took part in the controversies of the day, attacking the Roman Catholics in the *Sermon on Gunpowder Treason* (1638), and replying to the Puritans in *Of the Sacred Order of Episcopacy* (1642). In sermons preached at Uppingham, and apparently in conversations with Spencer Compton, Earl of Northampton, he had formed the conception and laid the foundation of his first work of edification, *The Great Exemplar*—a life of Christ arranged and commented on—which was not published till 1649. During the Civil Wars and the first years of the Commonwealth Taylor found a haven in Wales, where he taught in a school, and acted as chaplain to Lord and Lady Carbery, residing in their house, Golden Grove. Here he wrote and published his *Liberty of Prophesying* (1647). Here he delivered the golden and

Jeremy Taylor.

---

[1] *Works*, ed. Heber, 15 vols., Lond., 1820-22; ed. Eden, 10 vols., Lond., 1847-54; Gosse, *Jeremy Taylor*, 1904 (*English Men of Letters*); Tulloch, *Rational Theology*, Lond., 1872; Alfred Barry in *Classic Preachers*, &c.

famous sermons which ultimately made up the *Eniautos* (1655), and here he wrote the works by which he is probably best known to-day, his *Holy Living* (1650) and *Holy Dying* (1651), as well as other more controversial treatises. *A Discourse of Friendship* (1657) was addressed to "the most ingenious and excellent Mrs Katherine Philips," better known as the matchless Orinda. The *Ductor Dubitantium*, on which he spent so much labour, his *magnum opus* in the rather barren field of casuistry, was published in 1660. The last years of the Commonwealth were years of trouble and bereavement, and although the Restoration brought greater temporal prosperity, the hard fate which sent him to struggle with Presbyterians in the north of Ireland prevented that prosperity from spelling happiness and leisure for congenial work. He died in 1667.

It was not an altogether unkind fate which cut short the career that Laud had mapped out for Taylor. His strength did not really lie in the kind of argumentative, doctrinal, controversial preaching of Andrewes and Donne, which he would have had to cultivate as a champion of the Anglican Church. His controversial works are the least interesting of his writings. *The Liberty of Prophesying* is the most valuable because it handles the largest question, and is an expression of temperament, not merely a product of learning. Even so it can easily be overrated. It is a symptom rather than a cause of the growth of liberality in thoughtful minds, which the bitter and endless religious controversies were accelerating. Chillingworth and Hales are more thoroughgoing representatives of the movement, and indeed Jeremy Taylor's thought probably owes a good deal to the former. Neither controversy nor casuistry was the latter's *forte*, but edification, the exposition in eloquence of unsurpassed poetic richness of the beauty of holiness, the folly and misery of sin, the vanity of life, as these appeared to a nature of greater delicacy and purity of feeling than strength and originality of intellect, and endowed with an almost Shakespearean wealth of language. Liberated from the thorns of scholastic theology and patristic quotations, with which the sermons of Andrewes and Donne are beset, Jeremy Taylor is able to develop his own ardent and refined thought in sentences comparatively simple and direct in structure and balance, but matchlessly full in flow, and in imagery shot with all the colours of a poetic imagination. If he quotes, it is not to fix a definition or indicate and refute an error so much as to enrich the setting of his own thought, and the quotation is as often from the poets of Greece and Rome as from the Fathers. No preacher of the day is more golden-mouthed than Jeremy Taylor. If he is not, nevertheless, widely read, it is because of the limitation of his thought and the somewhat Sunday-school character of his ethical teaching. He hardly comes into close enough contact with the realities and conditions of everyday life.

There was no lack of either sermons or treatises on the Puritan side of the controversy which agitated the century. Not many, however, belong to literature. Whoever has turned over the pages of the endless sermons preached by Scottish and other divines before the House of Commons will not find much to reward his search, though he must admire the ingenuity with which the duty of reforming the Church on Presbyterian lines is extracted from the most unlikely texts. A man of very real literary power, however, and a good representative of the strength of Puritanism when directed to moral and not purely ecclesiastical questions, was Thomas Adams[1] (1612-1653), a member of the Calvinist and Puritan wing of the Anglican Church. On matters of Church order his tone is quite moderate. He speaks of "the comely ceremonies" of the Church, and defends public prayer against the over-exaltation of preaching. Indeed he would seem to have been dispossessed by the Commonwealth. To attribute the poverty of his later days to Laud, as the *Dictionary of National Biography* does, hardly fits the dates. We know, indeed, comparatively little of his life. His sphere as a preacher included Bedfordshire, Bucks, and London.

Puritans— Adams.

Adams' strength lies in his vigorous and colloquial yet by no means unlearned denunciation of sin. He comes to much closer quarters with wrong-doing in its concrete manifestations, especially of injustice and oppression, than the refined and ideal Taylor. His style is the best example, till we come to Bunyan, of what could be done in handling effectively and artistically the colloquialism of the pamphlet writers. It is direct, pithy, racy, and full of felicitous, homely metaphors, but without any of the refined beauty of

[1] *Works*, Lond., 1629.

ENGLISH PROSE.

colour or rhythm which shines in Jeremy Taylor's. Yet an analysis of one of his quaintly titled sermons, as *The White Devil or The Hypocrite Uncased*, will yield perhaps more practical suggestion and trenchant exposure of vice than a similar treatment of a discourse preached at Golden Grove.

The Broad Churchmen of the day are most adequately represented by Chillingworth and Hales. In them the growing spirit of moderation and toleration speaks in plain and straightforward language. Their common endeavour is to find a basis of agreement for Christians in such points as are "few and clear." William Chillingworth[1] (1602-1644) was converted to Romanism, and reconverted by his own studies and the arguments of Laud. He summed up his position in *The Religion of the Protestants a Safe Way to Salvation* (1637). In a plain, weighty, nervous style, rising at times to rugged eloquence, he defends the Bible as the sole source of religious knowledge, and the Apostles' Creed as containing all that is necessary to salvation.

Broad Church— Chillingworth.

If Chillingworth was driven into moderation by Romanism, John Hales[2] (1584-1656) was sent in the same direction by Calvinism. He attended the famous Synod of Dort to report the proceedings to the English ambassador. The result of what he saw there of theological intolerance was that he "bid John Calvin good-night,"

Hales.

---

[1] *Works*, 3 vols., 1838. Tulloch, *op. cit.*

[2] *Golden Remains*, ed. (with Life) by Bishop Pearson, 1657; reprinted and enlarged, 1673 and 1688. Tulloch, *op. cit.*

and expressed in the plainest language his contempt for the infallibility of councils and universal belief as a test of truth,—" human authority at the strongest is but weak, but the multitude is the weakest part of human authority"; while in his tract on *Schism and Schismatics*, which was not to the taste of Laud (though Hales's explanations or qualifications were accepted as satisfactory), he was equally blunt as to the authority of the Church, "which is none."

These friends of Lord Falkland were the heralds of later toleration and the appeal to reason and reason only, and their plain clear style was the reflection of their thought. The controversy between Anglicanism and Romanism, appealing not only to Scripture but to history and the Fathers, overshadowed during the whole of James's and the first part of Charles's reign the conflict with Puritanism. That conflict was carried on with other weapons than the pen; and it was not till the Long Parliament met that the Marprelate controversy was renewed in fiercer tones than under Elizabeth, and that the Anglican Church awoke to the fact that her most serious antagonist was not Rome. From the mass of pamphlets which began to pour from the press after 1640, Hall's *Humble Remonstrance in Favour of Episcopacy* (1640) and Jeremy Taylor's *Episcopacy Asserted* (1643) are still known, at any rate, by name; but the most famous are those on which Milton[1] set the

Controversy—Milton.

[1] *Prose Works*, ed. Toland, 1698; rep. 1738 and 1753; ed. Symons, 1806, Fletcher, 1833, Mitford, 1851. St John, 4 vols., Lond., 1848-53. The *Areopagitica* has been frequently edited separately, and the *Tractate of Education* also.

impress of his unique, intense, and exalted personality. The "dread voice," which had spoken already in *Lycidas*, thundered in sublime and truculent periods against Episcopacy in *Of Reformation in England* (1641), *Of Prelatical Episcopacy* (1641), *Animadversions on the Remonstrants' Defence against Smectymnuus* (a scurrilous onslaught upon Hall), the *Reason of Church Government urged against Prelaty* (1644), and an *Apology for Smectymnuus* (1642). The *Reason of Church Government* is brightened by an eloquent *apologia* for entering on controversy, and a discussion of the forms appropriate for a great poem, and of the high function of poetry. The *Apology for Smectymnuus* contains a similar parenthetic defence of his own character, his college career, and his life of studious retirement at Horton— passages in which prose of an exalted beauty that has no parallel outside the prophetic books in the English Bible is found side by side with abuse unmeasured, pedantic, and even petty.

<small>Church Government.</small>

Milton did not long keep in line with his Presbyterian friends. In the *Areopagitica, A Speech for the Liberty of Unlicensed Printing* (1644), the noblest, purest, most restrained and ordered of his prose writings, it is already for him almost "out of controversy that bishops and presbyters are the same to us, both name and thing." And it was not a purely abstract zeal for liberty of thought which evoked his eloquent appeal and aroused his impatience of presbyters, but the desire to speak his mind freely on a subject that touched him closely; for in the same year he issued without licence an enlarged version of his *Doctrine and Discipline of Divorce*, which had appeared in 1642, and he followed it up with two expository and one controversial pamphlet on the same subject. The boldness which the Divorce pamphlets revealed did not forsake Milton as the Rebellion advanced. He identified himself with the extreme wing of the Independents, placed his faith in the strong man Cromwell, and became the champion of regicide in pamphlets, Latin and English. Of the former the most famous was the *Defensio pro Populo Anglicano* (1651) against Claude Somaise or Salmasius, of the latter the *Eikonoklastes* (1649) and *Tenure of Kings and Magistrates* (1649). At the very moment of the Restoration he published his *Ready and Easy Way to Establish a Free Commonwealth* (1660), denouncing servitude to kings and planning government by a perpetual parliament presiding over almost independent county councils.

Divorce.

Regicide.

Through Milton's prose pamphlets runs the same double strain—the classical and the biblical—which blend and conflict in his poetry. On matters of religion and church government he is for the Bible as the sole guide, without respect for tradition or councils, interpreted by the individual reason subject to no authority that has any power beyond instruction, admonition, and reproof. In matters political he can appeal to the Bible also. Kings are unlawful because Christ forbade his followers to exercise lordship; but his ground principle is that of the Levellers, who,

Edwards declared in his *Gangræna* (1646), "go from the laws and constitution of kingdoms, and will be governed by rules according to nature and right reason." To Milton, in like manner, "the law of nature is the only law of laws truly and properly to all mankind fundamental: the beginning and the end of all government: to which no parliament or people that will thoroughly reform but must have recourse." And to the defence of this position, and the denunciation of kings, he brought the temper and the "topics" of classical antiquity, the sentiment which made Hobbes declare, "I think I may truly say, there was never anything so dearly bought as these Western parts have bought the learning of the Greek and Latin tongues."

But Milton was not one of the great thinkers of the century. He had not the philosophic breadth of Hooker, or the penetrating if limited vision of Hobbes. His pamphlets are read not for their political wisdom, or because they represent the feeling of the great mass of Englishmen on either side, but because of the high and confident temper of their faith in freedom and reason, the deep interest of the "autobiographical oases," and the strength and beauty of their prose. Milton's prose is pedantic in structure and frequently scurrilous in phraseology, but it rises to heights English prose has not often attained. His command of word, phrase, and figure, learned and poetical, homely and sublime, is unlimited; and if the rhythm of his sentences is not as regular as Hooker's and Browne's, or so flowing as Taylor's, it has at its best a larger compass, and in none is the poet's fine ear for musical combinations of consonants and vowels so obvious. Rich in prose poetry as English literature is, it has nothing that in sustained elevation of thought and splendour of phrase surpasses *Areopagitica*.

A form of prose literature which touches the sermon literature of the seventeenth century on the one hand and its comedy on the other is the character sketches suggested by the *Characters* of Theophrastus.

Characters. Bishop Hall,[1] the trenchant Anglican preacher and controversialist, who, like Donne, had begun his career as a satirist, was one of the earliest in the field with his *Characters of Virtues and Vices* (1608),—the "penurious book of characters" to which Milton refers contemptuously,—avowedly modelled on the Greek. They are written with the vigour and point, if also with the want of any high distinction, which belong to Hall's work in general. The virtues especially suffer from the abstract handling, which is the weakness of the *Characters* generally. It is only occasionally that they are enlivened by concrete detail or happy image, as when he says of the Good Magistrate, in a figure that recalls Bacon, "Displeasure, Revenge, Recompense stand on both sides the bench, but he scorns to turn his eye towards them, looking only right forward at Equity, which stands full before him." In treating of

Hall.

---

[1] *Works*, ed. Rev. Josiah Pratt, 10 vols., Lond., 1808; Peter Hall, 12 vols., Lond., 1837-39; Rev. Philip Wynter, 10 vols., Oxford, 1863.

the Vices, Hall is the trenchant satirist who wrote *Virgidemiarium*, somewhat subdued. He gets his blows home in a style which is vigorous and effective.

In Sir Thomas Overbury's [1] *Characters* (1614), the type of this particular kind of literature was more definitely fixed than by Hall. Overbury's original *Characters* were added to by various hands, and they became the model of succeeding attempts. To get a witticism into every sentence was the ambition of the writers, and the result is often very strained. But seventeenth-century wit, if it is often fantastical to and beyond the verge of absurdity, passes readily into poetry. Overbury's *Fair and Happy Milkmaid* is quite a little pastoral; and in the *Microcosmographie* (1628) of John Earle [2] (1601 ?- 1665), the friend of Falkland and Clarendon, and Bishop, after the Restoration, of Worcester and of Salisbury, observation, true wit, sense, and feeling are all blended. The tone is infinitely pleasanter than the hard and arrogant satire of Overbury. Their closest parallel in the combination of wit, feeling, and philosophy are the poetic characters, the *Zedeprinten* (1625) of the Dutch poet Huyghens, who strikes at times, however, a higher note. But Earle's characters are sympathetically studied and artistic-

[1] *Works*, ed. (with Life) by Rimbault, Lond., 1856. *Characters* in Morley's *Character Writings of the Seventeenth Century*, Lond., 1891 (*Carisbrooke Library*).

[2] The *Microcosmographie* passed through three editions in 1628. The first edition contained fifty-four characters, the sixth (1635) seventy-eight. The most elaborate edition is that of A. S. West, Lond., 1898. Morley, *op. cit.*

ally drawn. *A Child, A Grave Divine, A Young Raw Preacher, A Discontented Man, A Downright Scholar*, are good examples of his range—poetic, dignified, satiric, and humorous. His *Antiquary*, compared with Scott's Jonathan Oldbuck, shows the limitations of the author's sympathies, and also of the kind. The abstract character at its best will not bear comparison with the concreter creations of the later essay and novel.

Earle.

Analysis of character and criticism of life connect the *Characters* with the pamphlet literature of the later sixteenth century, and with the comedy of Jonson and Middleton. They connect them also with such works as the *Anatomy of Melancholy* (1621) of Robert Burton [1] (1577-1639), whose life was spent in omnivorous reading at Christ Church, Oxford. The novel had not yet appeared to absorb all this critical tendency, which has a much more legitimate outlet in prose than poetry. Accordingly we find it abounding in works that are, or profess to be, scientific, and which show distinctly the influence of the great essayist and informal critic of life Montaigne. A more extraordinary book than the *Anatomy of Melancholy* is hardly to be found. It has a plan, although Sterne learned from it, as well as from Rabelais, the art of digression which he used to such remarkable effect in *Tristram Shandy*. Burton's object is to analyse, describe in its effects, and prescribe

Burton.

---

[1] *Anatomy of Melancholy*, ed. Rev. A. R. Shilleto, with preface by A. H. Bullen, 3 vols., Lond., 1893. Most of the quotations are identified and verified.

for human melancholy. By melancholy he practically means, or comes to mean, unhappiness, discontent. His book is thus a survey, enormously erudite, occasionally eloquent, always shrewd, and quietly humorous, of "the ills that flesh is heir to." Democritus Junior the author calls himself, after the philosopher who, according to tradition, always laughed at the follies and vanities of mankind. In a long ironical and humorous preface, which contains the quintessence of the whole work, he gives some account of himself, and a broad survey of human misery. Thereafter he plunges into a systematic discussion of the causes, symptoms, and cure of melancholy. This is followed by a more particular description of *Love Melancholy* and *Religious Melancholy*. There is a certain parade of anatomy and medicine, but the author takes a wider range than the merely medical. Everything is a cause of melancholy—God, the devil and other evil spirits, magicians and witches, nurses, education, study, &c.; and on each and every one of these sources he dilates with an infinite display of learning—there is not a sentence without a quotation—occasionally passages of real eloquence, and a never-failing undercurrent of irony. In the division entitled *Love of Learning or Overmuch Study, with a Digression of the Misery of Scholars and why the Muses are Melancholy*, he discusses with a gusto, fully appreciated by Dr Johnson, who strikes the same note in *The Vanity of Human Wishes*, the sorrows of scholars, and closes with a vigorous, partly English, partly Latin, denunciation of Simony. He opens the discussion of Love Melancholy, again, with a serious and eloquent eulogy of Charity. Thereafter he proceeds to a discussion of "heroical love," elaborated especially from Latin poets and Italian writers, in a way that is not always edifying, but closes—ironically or seriously, who can say?—with the prescription of a happy marriage as the only cure for the woes of lovers. Burton's style, apart from its excess of quotation, has nothing particularly notable about it. It is simple, straightforward, and can be vigorous, but is not specially distinguished in phrase or rhythm.

Beauty of phrase and musical cadence are the charms which have given enduring life to the musings of an author not more learned than Burton, nor with more claim to be classed among the original thinkers of the century, but possessing in a higher degree the impassioned imagination of the poet. This was Sir Thomas Browne [1] (1605-1682) the antiquarian and philosophic doctor at Norwich. The son of a London merchant, Browne was educated at Oxford, but pursued his medical studies at Montpellier, Padua, and Leyden. He returned to England in 1633, and practised for some time at Halifax in Yorkshire, where, in all probability, he composed the *Religio Medici*, a meditative and eloquent survey of his beliefs and sympathies. The work, circulating in manuscript

Browne.

[1] *Works*, ed. Simon Wilkins, 3 vols., Lond., 1852. *Religio Medici, A Letter to a Friend, Christian Morals*, ed. William Alexander Greenhill, Lond., 1881. *Urn-Burial* and *Garden of Cyrus*, ed. do., and completed by E. H. Marshall, 1896. Pater, *Appreciations*, Lond., 1889. Gosse, *Sir Thomas Browne*, Lond., 1905 (*English Men of Letters*).

was published without authority in 1642, when it elicited a small volume of *Observations upon Religio Medici* (1643) by Sir Kenelm Digby (1603-1665), another enthusiast — as Browne was himself — for strange phenomena and the mysteries of science. The first authorised edition of the *Religio Medici* appeared the same year, when it excited great interest, was translated into Latin, and circulated on the Continent. Meantime Browne had settled at Norwich, where the rest of his life was spent in practice as a physician, and in study scientific and antiquarian. Of his private and family life details are preserved in the *Correspondence*. His most elaborate contribution to science was the *Pseudodoxia Epidemica* (1646), an examination of many accepted beliefs in the sphere of natural science. More occasional productions were the famous *Hydriotaphia: Urn Burial, or A Discourse of the Sepulchral Urns lately found at Norfolk* (1658), *The Garden of Cyrus* (1658), the posthumous *Christian Morals*, and other short tracts.

There is, it seems to me, more truth in Mr Pater's contrast between Browne and Pascal than in Mr Gosse's parallel. Nothing is further from the mind of the author of the *Religio Medici* than any absolute separation of theology from science or philosophy. Theology rests on tradition, philosophy on free inquiry; but Browne is far from making the distinction logical and complete. To his religious beliefs he had obtained by grace certainly, but also by "the law of mine own reason." The "wingy mysteries in divinity and airy subtleties in religion" transcend but do not contradict reason ("they have not only been illustrated but maintained by syllogism and the rule of reason"), and so far from being willing to resign them to theologians while he turns to science, they are his favourite subject of meditation. "'Tis my solitary recreation to pose my apprehension with these involved enigmas and riddles of the Trinity, with Incarnation and Resurrection." And when Browne turns from divinity to philosophy it is not to find, with Descartes and Kepler and Galileo, nature a mechanism, whose laws are to be deduced mathematically, a homeless world from which Pascal fled to the God of Abraham, Isaac, and Jacob, *not* of the philosophers and men of science. In nature Browne finds a second book wherein the hand of God may be traced. "'Beware of Philosophy' is a precept not to be received in too large a sense, for in the mass of nature there is a set of things that carry in their front, though not in capital letters yet in stenography and short characters, something of divinity, which to wiser reasons serve as luminaries in the abyss of knowledge, and to judicious beliefs as scales and roundles to mount the pinnacles and highest pieces of divinity." Browne's science is theological, his deepest interest in final causes. The miracles of religion do not surprise one who knows the marvels of nature and the miracles of his own life. If Browne's *Religio Medici* startled the readers of his day, it was not in virtue of any divorce of reason from faith, but rather of the confident, rationalist though devout tone in which he approached questions religious and philosophical, — that, and the tolerant character of his sympathies. It is not of the sombre Jansenist Pascal that he reminds the reader, but—despite his orthodoxy, his belief in witches, and the imaginative vein in his reflections—of the later optimistic rationalists and their superficial natural religion, of Addison and his planets—

"singing as they shine
'The hand that made us is divine.'

In the *Pseudodoxia Epidemica* Browne discusses at considerable length the sources of error, and includes among them not only Satan but, like Hobbes and Pascal, respect for antiquity, and undue subservience to authority. He is, however, very far from attaining to any clear distinction between the legitimate spheres of tradition and experiment (the borrowings of poets are arraigned alongside the transmission of untested tenets in science), or to any right understanding of the conditions of valid experimental proof. In none of his works is his style more obscured by Latin neologisms.

The crowning example of Browne's meditative, sonorous, imaginative eloquence is the *Hydriotaphia*. Here his antiquarian rather than scientific turn of mind, his imaginative piety, his musical polysyllables and periods, combined to produce a harmonious and impressive whole. He had read of and reflected on the burial customs of different times and nations, their origin and their significance (burying and burning, urns and funeral lamps, rites and beliefs), and each detail had its charm for his, not sombre but meditative, poetical imagination. Vessels, he tells us, containing wines have been found in ancient tombs which if any have tasted they have far exceeded the palates of antiquity, liquors not to be computed by years of annual magistrates, but by great conjunctions and the fatal periods of kingdoms. The draughts of consulary date were but crude unto these, and Opimian wine but in the must unto them." So he muses, most eloquent when the topic is most fanciful. The last chapter of the five is a not always equal but, for him, wonderfully sustained peroration on the vanity of human "inquietude for the diuturnity of our memories," not leading to any Hamlet-like disparagement of life, but to the exaltation of the Christian hope of immortality, "ready to be anything in the ecstacy of being ever, and as content with six foot as the Moles of Adrianus."

The *Garden of Cyrus*, which accompanied the *Hydriotaphia*, is a fantastic trifle, an excursus on the quincunx, a favourite arrangement for plants and trees in old gardens, which Browne, with an extraordinary parade of learning and the mystical ardour of an ancient philosopher dealing with number, finds everywhere, in the macrocosm without and the microcosm within. Of his posthumous works the most characteristic is the *Letter to a Friend*, composed about 1672,—a strange description of the death of a common friend, in which he analyses and comments on every symptom of his last days, with the same parade of erudition and the same studied eloquence as he had bestowed in the *Hydriotaphia* on burial rites and their significance. Nothing is more characteristic of Browne, antiquarian and rhetorician, saved, and at times just saved, from being merely these by being also a humane and Christian moralist. Sense and absurdity, fancy and wisdom, are inextricably blended in all he wrote. The wisdom does not venture outside the beaten track: the fancy is ready at any moment for the most unexpected flights. Browne's eloquence is not, like Pascal's, a wisdom which is eloquence, an eloquence which is wisdom. It is only at times that the thought of one of Browne's paragraphs is as suggestive and illuminating as the phrasing is imaginative, and the cadence musical. Often the thought is purely fanciful, almost freakish, for one must not overlook the vein of humour in Browne. In general, when he is most serious, his subjects are the familiar topics of Christian morality arrayed in new and splendid, if occasionally quaint and overwrought, garb. Browne's prose and Milton's verse are the finest fruits of seventeenth century Latinism. It is difficult to conceive of a purely Teutonic language achieving such at once sonorous and melodious effects as Browne and Milton produced, in different ways, by the admixture of racy English with Latin polysyllables rich in labials and open vowels. In impassioned and sustained eloquence Browne is not the compeer of Hooker, or Donne, or Milton, or Taylor. He is too prone in the midst of a noble flight to check at some passing sparrow of antiquarian fancy. But of prose as an artistic medium no writer of the century had so easy and conscious a mastery, could produce at will such varied and wonderful effects.

Montaigne is doubtless principally responsible for the egotistic, rambling reflections of Burton and Browne. In the still more egotistical and much more eccentric Scotchman, Sir Thomas Urquhart[1] (1611-1660 ?), was found a felicitous translator of the other great French prose author of the sixteenth century. Indeed Urquhart translated Rabelais rather too literally into his own conduct and serious, or professedly serious, writings. Educated at Aberdeen, he spent some years abroad, when apparently he studied the histories of Gargantua and Pantagruel with the same perfervid enthusiasm as Drummond earlier had felt for Petrarch and Marino and Ronsard. On his return, he devoted such time as he could spare from struggles with creditors and the support of the royalist cause (for which he appeared in arms at the Trot of Turriff and the Battle of Worcester) to writings on very miscellaneous subjects, including epigrams and a treatise on trigonometry, but mainly concerned with himself, his pedigree, his learned projects, his persecutions at the hands of his creditors, and the famous exploits of the Scot abroad. His translation of the first two books of Rabelais' work appeared in 1653. The third by Pierre Antoine Motteux was not issued till 1693.

There was certainly a streak of madness in Urquhart, but there was also a strain of genius. His command of language is extraordinary, and shows to advantage

[1] *Life*, written with scholarship and humour by the Rev. John Willcock, Edin., 1899. *Works*, ed. Maitland Club, Edin., 1854. *Rabelais*, ed. Charles Whibley (*Tudor Translations*), Lond., 1900.

ENGLISH PROSE. 235

not only in his Rabelais but when he describes his
own adventures or the life and death of the Admirable
Crichton. This, and his own exuberant imagination,
made him a wonderfully sympathethic and felicitous
translator of Rabelais, though his own extravagance
was not humorous. He writes as an enthusiastic
interpreter of his original, interpolating an explanatory paragraph when he thinks it is required, adding
synonyms, racy colloquialisms or coinages of his own,
and giving his sentences a full and harmonious flow.
For his synonyms he was often indebted to Cotgrave's
rich storehouse of French and English colloquialisms,
A Dictionarie of the French and English Tougues
(1611), and at times he sows them with a somewhat
lavish hand. Still his version is, as Mr Whibley says,
"a translation unique in its kind which has no rival
in profane letters." Nothing can equal the "race" of
his Elizabethan English. Mr Smith's scholarly and
accurate version is invaluable for the student, but, read
closely along with Urquhart, it seems to stand to it a
little as the revised to the authorised English Bible.

Thomas Fuller [1] (1608-1662) merits a place among
the erudite humourists and wits of the century rather
Fuller. than among the more serious and heavy
divines. His *History of the Holy Warre*
(1639) shows, a critic has said, "much reading but
more wit"; and his *Holy and Profane State* (1642),
a series of characters illustrated by historic examples,

[1] Lives of Fuller by Russell (1844), John Eglington Bailey (1874), and
Morris Fuller (1886). No complete modern edition. *Worthies of England*, 3 vols., Lond., 1840. *Collected Sermons*, Bailey, 2 vols., Lond., 1891.

is one of the happiest and most amusing collections of the kind. Whatever Fuller wrote, — history, as the *Church History of Britain* (1655-56); sermons and reflections, as *Good Thoughts in Bad Times* (1645) or *Mixed Reflections in Better Times* (1660); or local description and history, as in the *England's Worthies* (1662),—his genial humour, nimble wit, clear arrangement, and short pithy sentences make his work eminently readable, if never profound. He had the wit's quick eye for superficial resemblances, without either the poet's or the man of science's deeper sense of identity in difference.

In philosophy, history, and biography, three names— Hobbes, Clarendon, and Walton—stand with Bacon's pre-eminent in the century, and a word or two on each must close this sketch of a period filled with writers not easy to classify.

Thomas Hobbes[1] (1588 - 1679) was one of the acutest and most independent minds that the agitations of the century turned to political speculation. At Oxford he distasted the schoolmen, but formed no distinct design of pursuing any new line in speculation and inquiry. His first visit to the Continent with his pupil and patron, Lord William Cavendish, sent him back to his neglected classical studies, to acquire a useful

Hobbes.

---

[1] *Works*, ed. Sir W. Molesworth, 16 vols., Lond., 1839-46. *Hobbes*, by the late Professor Croom Robertson, Edin., 1886 (*Philosophic Classics*), and by the late Mr Leslie Stephen, London, 1904 (*Men of Letters*). See also T. H. Green, *Lectures on the Principles of Political Obligation*, Lond., 1895. The *Leviathan* has been reproduced in the *Cambridge Classics*, 1904.

Latin style, and translate Thucydides into clear, strong English. It was the reading of *Euclid*, and a second tour in 1634 with the son of his former pupil, that brought him into contact with the scientific thought of the Continent, opened his eyes to the charm of the deductive method of mathematics, and gave him the conception of a work on body, human nature, and the body politic. The first sketch was contained in the originally entitled *Elements of Law*, consisting of two parts, *Human Nature* and *De Corpore Politico*, which circulated in manuscript. The latter was further elaborated in the *De Cive*, published at Paris in 1642 and 1647. Finally, the sketch of human nature, and the more fully elaborated political doctrine, were combined in the English *Leviathan, or the Matter, Form, and Power of a Commonwealth, Ecclesiastical and Civil*, which appeared in London in 1651. Hobbes' later Latin treatises, and his unfortunate excursions into mathematics, need not be enumerated. He composed verse translations of the *Iliad* and *Odyssey*, and in the dialogue *Behemoth* (1679) described the origin and progress of the Civil War from his own absolutist and Erastian point of view.

Hobbes was the friend and occasional secretary of Bacon; but the method he pursued in his treatises was not the inductive one, but the deductive method of Descartes, extolled by Pascal in the *De l'Esprit Géométrique*. His theory of the Commonwealth, its origin, and the absolute character of the sovereign, are presented as a deduction from the description or definition of human nature which he gives in the first book, as that itself is from the materialistic principle that sense and appetite are ultimately movement. The strength and clearness of Hobbes' reasoning follow from his method; while its weaknesses illustrate the difficulties which beset the method when applied to subjects whose definitions are not so simple and arbitrary as those of geometry. Hobbes' conclusions follow from his principles; but these are incomplete, or fictions, or ambiguous terms. The materialistic account of human nature which he gives in the first book is acute and suggestive, but necessarily superficial and inadequate. The state of nature and the contract from which civil society originates are fictions; and the effectiveness of the contract depends upon an ambiguity in his use of the word "right." Equivalent to "might" in the state of nature, when all men are equal and life "nasty, brutish, and short," it becomes in the sovereign, the Leviathan whom men, guided by the law of nature, establish by covenant among themselves, a "right" that Hobbes would have to be independent both of the sovereign's power to enforce it and the subject's contented acquiescence. It is clear that no covenant could establish such a right unless those who formed it had already in a state of nature a conception of right different from might,—a conception of right which implies already the mutual recognition of each other's claims. But overlook Hobbes' fallacy, and all that he says of sovereignty in the second book, and in the third (where he disputes the Church's claim

to an "imperium in imperio," and gives to the
sovereign the sole right of determining men's
opinions, at least as shown in outward action)
follows by a clear and invincible logic. He saw,
with the clear vision of an acute rather than comprehensive mind, a vision sharpened by the anxiety
of a timid temperament living in troubled times,
certain aspects of human nature and civil society.
He saw how deeply the competitive instinct enters
into man's intellectual and moral constitution; how
much positive right depends on might; and he saw
these truths so clearly that he ignored others which
modify and complicate them. And Hobbes' style
is the image of his thought, lucid, precise, ordered,
—no prose of the century is more so,—but wanting in
nuances and harmonies; not so complex ever as Descartes', but a little hard, and wearing after a time;
never irradiated with poetry like Bacon's, though he
has some of his command of felicitous figure and
aphorism; with none of the delicacy, swiftness, and
eloquence of Pascal's.

A century so erudite as the seventeenth was not
neglectful of history, and the number of works coming under this head is large. Bacon and Raleigh,
Daniel and Speed, Drummond and Lord Herbert of
Cherbury (poet also and philosopher), Knollys (first
historian of the Turks) and Heylin (*History of the
Reformation*, 1640), Fuller (whose work has been
mentioned) and Thomas May, who wrote from the
opposite point of view from Clarendon his *History
of the Parliament of England which began November*

1640, are all writers whose work would demand consideration in a fuller history of the thought and learning of the period than this volume pretends to be. One work, however, stands pre-eminent in virtue of its literary and personal interest.

Edward Hyde, Lord Clarendon [1] (1608-1674), was a principal actor in the great events which he chronicled, and intimate with the characters whose portraits he limned "with such natural and lively touches." Such conversance with men and affairs he pronounced, in reviewing D'Avila and other predecessors, essential to the

History— Clarendon.

[1] The History was begun at Scilly in 1646, and continued in Jersey down to the end of what is now the seventh book (1647-48). In his second exile he began to write his life, trusting to his memory and unaided by papers, and by 1670 had brought it down to the Restoration. On recovering his papers he completed the *History of the Rebellion* by incorporating excerpts from the *Life* into the narrative composed in Jersey, and by completing this from the *Life* with additions. The composite character of the work is shown very clearly in the edition of W. Dunn Macray, Oxford, 1888, and Professor Firth has pointed out in a couple of articles in the *English Historical Review*, 1905, how much the accuracy of the work varies according as Clarendon was writing from memory or was aided by documents. From a literary point of view, also, he has shown there are differences between the earlier and later work. In the parts taken from the *Life* there are numerous French terms and phrases, and all the portraits, except those of Falkland, Pym, and Hampden, are additions to the original narrative. In its final form, accordingly, those features were emphasised which connect the history with the famous memoirs of the seventeenth century, rather than with the work of later historians who discover the source of the rebellion less in the character of individual statesmen, than in causes more general and deep-seated.

Clarendon's other works were essays, controversial writings, a *History of the Civil War in Ireland*, and *Contemplations on the Psalms*.

historian. Whether for strictly scientific history it is such an advantage may be questioned, but it certainly lends to an historian's work a personal note and an interest in individual men which heightens the human and literary value. A poignant personal note runs through all Clarendon's great work, begun in Jersey (1646-48) with the treble purpose of providing an historical narrative, guidance for the future, and a vindication of the king, and completed twenty years later with the additional purpose of defending his own career and conduct. Though it did not seem so to Sir Edmund Verney, Clarendon's position was a harder one than that of those whose judgment was on one side while their loyalty and gratitude forced them to espouse the other, for the issue was to Clarendon, as to Falkland, more complex. A constitutionalist and a loyal Churchman, he had to choose between a king whose unconstitutional conduct he had condemned and resisted, and a parliament whose love for the constitution was never so strong as their hatred of bishops. He chose his part: he gave the king, when his violence had left him isolated, a policy and party; and he wrote an account of the war, its causes and leading actors, which remained the accepted one until modified and corrected by the researches of the historians of the later nineteenth century.

Clarendon's reverence for law, "that great and admirable mystery," was inspired not a little by the study of Hooker, and his style perhaps owed something to the same influence. His sentences are cast in the same long and complex mould, tending at times to unwieldiness and even confusion. But the short, clipped style of later historians is not in the long-run less wearisome, and Clarendon's prose has the virtues as well as the faults of its age — dignity, feeling, pregnancy, felicitous phrase and figure. His portraits, whether of friend or foe, if not, as Evelyn said to Pepys, "without the least ingredient of passion or tincture of revenge," are works of art, — full, significant, and suggestive of more than is always said. Charles's weaknesses disengage themselves unmistakably from the eulogy in which they are conveyed, and the picture of the "brave bad man" Cromwell, read fully and dispassionately, is still one of the finest tributes to that great but confessedly complex character.

In an age that was so addicted to the study and portrayal of character, in drama, history, essay, or epigram, it would have been strange if biography had not been cultivated, even though the time had not yet come for ponderous reminiscences and collections of letters. Jonson and Clarendon etched their own portraits; Milton found it difficult to keep himself out of anything he wrote; and Lord Herbert of Cherbury[1] and Hobbes[2] indulged themselves in more detailed autobiography. The puritan Mrs Hutcheson[3] and the cavalier Duchess of Newcastle[3] heralded, in very different ways, that

Biography— Walton.

[1] *Autobiography* (pr. 1764).

[2] *Vita carmine expressa a seipso* (1681).

[3] *Memoirs* of her husband's life pub. 1806, ed. C. H. Firth, Lond., 1885. The Duchess's autobiography (1656) and life of her husband (1667), whom she portrays in the elevated style of seventeenth century romance, have been edited by Prof. Firth, 1886.

form of biography from which a later age has perhaps suffered too much; but it was of divines especially that biographies were written. Christopher Wordsworth's collection [1] runs to four volumes, and of them all—and few are destitute of interest—the most delightful are those of Isaac Walton [2] (1593-1683), who wrote short biographies of Donne, Wotton, Hooker, Herbert, and Sanderson. A peculiar and ineffable charm breathes from the works of Walton, their gentle and pious spirit, their natural and felicitous style, careless in structure but never obscure. *The Complete Angler* (1653-76) is itself a character-sketch as well as a treatise on the mysteries of an art; and in his five lives he is less concerned about accurate details than about all that illustrates the goodness, learning, and devotion of his subjects. Complexity he does not care for. Donne's early life is hastened over, and there was more in Herbert than Walton saw; but the side he chooses to elaborate is presented with extraordinary distinctness and charm.

[1] *Ecclesiastical Biography of England to 1688*, 4 vols., Lond., 1839.
[2] Of the *Compleat Angler* there are over 120 editions. Those of the Lives are also numerous—*e.g.*, by A. H. Bullen, with W. Dowling's Life, Lond., 1884, with preface by Vernon Blackburn, Lond., 1895. *The Temple Classics*, 1898.

CHAPTER VI.

FRENCH VERSE AND PROSE.[1]

WANING OF THE PLEIAD. MALHERBE—PURITY AND CORRECTNESS—VERSE. DISCIPLES—MAYNARD—RACAN. SOCIAL FORCES—HÔTEL DE RAMBOUILLET—ACADEMY. INDEPENDENTS—THÉOPHILE DE VIAU—SAINT-AMANT—MLLE. DE GOURNAY AND MATHURIN RÉGNIER. VINCENT VOITURE. HEROIC POEMS. PROSE-ROMANCES—D'URFÉ—'L'ASTRÉE'; CAMUS — EXEMPLARY TALES; HEROIC ROMANCE — GOMBAULD'S 'ENDYMION'—GOMBERVILLE'S 'POLEXANDRE'—LA CALPRENÈDE—ELIMINATION OF THE MARVELLOUS—ROMANTIC HISTORY—MADELEINE DE SCUDÉRY—CULMINATION OF "PRÉCIOSITÉ"—BOILEAU'S DIALOGUE 'LES HÉROS DE ROMAN.' REALISM AND BURLESQUE IN ROMANCE —SOREL — 'LE BERGER EXTRAVAGANT' — 'FRANCION' — LANNEL—CYRANO—SCARRON. SHAPERS OF MODERN FRENCH PROSE—BALZAC AND THE CULT OF STYLE; DESCARTES—RATIONALISM AND LUCIDITY; —PASCAL—THE WAY OF THE INTELLECT AND THE WAY OF THE HEART. THE 'MEMOIRS'—DE RETZ AND LA ROCHEFOUCAULD—PHILOSOPHY OF THE 'FRONDE'—'LES MAXIMES.'

THE poets of the Pleiad attempted more than they were able to achieve. The ambitious programme of Du Bellay issued in no great and permanent result. There was no Pindar and no

Waning of the Pleiad.

---

[1] Petit de Julleville, *Histoire de la Langue et de la Littérature française des Origines à 1900*, Paris, 1896-1900; Lanson, *Histoire de la Littérature française*, Paris, 1896; Nisard, *Histoire de la Littérature française*, Paris, 1844; Saintsbury, *A Short History of French Literature*, Lond., 1898; Dowden, *A History of French Literature*, Lond., 1897; F. Brunetière, *Manuel de la Litt. franç.*, Paris, 1898;

Virgil in their ranks, no Petrarch and no Milton. The fame even of the great Ronsard was to be shortlived. In spite of the vigorous protests of a Régnier and a Mademoiselle de Gournay, it melted before the scornful glance of Malherbe, "le grammairien en lunettes et en cheveux gris"; and even now that time has redressed the injustice of the seventeenth century, he survives, not as the rival of Pindar and Virgil, but as the writer of some charming sonnets and songs, the poet of "Mignonne, allons voir si la rose." And it is by poems in the same vein that every one of the band is represented in such a collection as Crépet's. They breathed an Italian gravity and sweetness into French poetry which was not without its effect on the work even of their immediate successors; but they produced no poetry of such great and shining merits as to justify to these successors the violence they did in more than one way to the genius of the language and to the French love of sense, logic, and order.

Both these principles found in François Malherbe (1555-1628), the son of a Norman "conseiller," an ardent and even fanatical adherent and champion. Of his life little need be said

Malherbe.

Lotheissen, *Geschichte der französischen Litteratur im XVIIten Jahrhundert*, Wien, 1877, 2nd ed. 1897; Sainte-Beuve, *Tableau de la Poésie française et du Théâtre français au XVIe Siècle*, the *Port Royal* passim, and essays in the *Causeries de Lundi*, &c.; Théophile Gautier, *Les Grotesques;* Faguet, *Dix-Septième Siècle, Études Littéraires*, Paris, 1893; Brunetière, *Études Critiques*, &c., the series of monographs, *Les Grands Écrivains français*, Paris. Selections from the poets with introductory notices in Crepet, *Les Poètes français*, Paris, 1861.

here. He served under Henri d'Angoulême. His merits as a poet were made known to Henri IV. by Cardinal du Périer, on the death of whose daughter Malherbe had written the most beautiful, in its dignified pathos, of all his poems; and from 1605 to his death he was laureate—and no poet was ever more essentially and entirely a laureate poet—to Henri, to Marie de Médicis, to Richelieu, and to Louis XIII.

Malherbe's earliest work was probably Ronsardist in character, but he soon discovered, like Pope, that his way to fame lay through "correctness," and no poet ever became a more thorough-going disciple and prophet of that useful if limited doctrine. The "poetic" which he taught, mainly through his criticism of Desportes [1] (on whose work he made a close-running "commentaire"), and which he practised in his slowly elaborated Odes, was in part the protest of one imbued with a passionate jealousy for his native tongue, her idiom and nuances, against the innovations and licences of the Pleiad. Du Bellay and Ronsard had dreamed of creating

Purity.

---

[1] The annotated copy of the *Œuvres de Philippe Desportes*, Paris, 1600, passed into Balzac's hands, who in a letter to Conrart (1653) describes the characters of the "commentaire": "Je vous dirai . . . que j'ai ici un exemplaire de ses œuvres marqué de la main de feu M. de Malherbe et corrigé d'une terrible manière. Toutes les marges sont bordées de ses observations critiques." Ferdinand Brunot, in *La Doctrine de Malherbe*, Paris, 1891, has extracted from Malherbe's comment his views on poetry, style, and correct idiom. See also *Malherbe*, by the Duc de Broglie (*Les Grands Écrivains de la France*), and the *Œuvres Complètes de Malherbe*, par M. L. Lalanne (*Les Grands Écrivains de la France*, 6 vols.), Paris, 1862-69.

a poetic style distinct in diction and idiom from the language of every day. Malherbe bluntly declared that for poetry, as for prose, the only rule was "proper words in proper places," and that the arbiter of propriety was usage. The "'crocheteurs du port au Foin' were," he said, "his masters in language." Racan reports the saying and Régnier ridicules the doctrine; but both in practice and theory Malherbe admitted the restraining principle of elegance. It was not the usage of the street but of the court which was his norm. Many of Malherbe's other rules, especially his prosody, are an expression of that spirit of order which was soon to become dominant in France, and which already took the form of reverence for rule as rule, which is its greatest vice — the introduction into literary art of the spirit of social etiquette.

To recommend his reforms Malherbe's poetry had, besides correctness, as its most positive excellence, a rich and sonorous versification. The famous lines in the *Consolation à Monsieur du Périer sur la Mort de sa Fille*—

Verse.

"Et, rose, elle a vécu ce que vivent les roses,
L'espace d'un matin"—

are the most poetical Malherbe ever wrote. The thought even of his finest laureate poems is commonplace if quite appropriate so far as it goes. One feels that each ode was probably drafted in prose before being elaborated in sonorous verse; for the splendour of the verse is the redeeming virtue of his work. He invented no new stanzas, but selected and embellished those of the Pleiad which were best suited to his oratorical style. But whether the stanza be a long one made up of octosyllabics, or a shorter one in Alexandrines, Malherbe's verse at its best has a pomp and clangour which it would be difficult to surpass. The ode *Pour le Roi*, written on the Rochelle expedition, is perhaps the finest example of the "grand vers"—

> " Je suis vaincu du temps ; je cède à ses outrages ;
> Mon esprit seulement, exempt de sa rigueur,
> A de quoi témoigner en ses derniers ouvrages
> Sa première vigueur."

In the same strain, and with equal dignity, he writes in what is his favourite ode stanza :—

> " Apollon à portes ouvertes
> Laisse indifféremment cueillir
> Les belles feuilles toujours vertes
> Qui gardent les noms de vieillir ;
> Mais l'art d'en faire les couronnes
> N'est pas su de toutes personnes ;
> Et trois ou quatre seulement,
> Au nombre desquels on me range,
> Peuvent donner une louange
> Qui demeure éternellement."

Malherbe was not the immediate founder of any important school of poetry. Of his "sons," as Jonson would have called them—the young poets who gathered around him to receive his lectures on good French and permissible rhymes— the most important, François Maynard[1] (1582-1646)

Maynard and Racan.

[1] *Œuvres Poétiques*, ed. Gaston Garrisson, 2 vols., Paris, 1885.

and Honorat de Bueil, Seigneur de Racan[1] (1589-1670), are but minor bards. Maynard, who in his earliest volume had followed in the footsteps of the Pleiad and composed Italianate *Amours*, *Élégies*, *Pastorales*, and *Vers Spirituels*, became the most faithful disciple and follower of his master in theory and practice. He insisted that the sense in every line should be complete, a rule fatal to lyrical inspiration, and his odes are strings of well-hammered commonplaces. He cultivated, besides the sonnet, the rondeau and the epigram. On his epigrams he rather plumed himself, but Malherbe declared that they wanted point. *La Belle Vieille* is perhaps the only poem he wrote in which there is a spark of passion. Racan was a careless writer, but with more of grace and charm than Maynard. He paraphrased the psalms in a variety of metres. There are touches of beautiful description in *Les Bergeries*, of which we shall have to speak again, and he composed some delightful odes in the lighter Epicurean vein of Horace. The best is probably the *Stances* beginning "Tircis, il faut penser à faire la retraite," which, like Jonson's *To Sir Robert Wroth*, are a happy echo of Horace's "Beatus ille." His more ambitious odes are mere imitations of Malherbe's. Other disciples of Malherbe are little more than names.

The fact is, the influence of Malherbe's reform was not fully felt at once. It acted perhaps immediately

[1] *Œuvres Complètes, &c.*, ed. Tenant de Latour (*Bibliothèque Elzevirienne*), Paris, 1857.

in a negative way, helping with other influences to extinguish the lyric spirit that had inspired the poetry of the Pleiad, despite its pedantries and extravagances. But his creed of purity, correctness, dignity, and harmony did not receive whole-hearted allegiance until, from the ferment of the first half of the century, the classical ideal took shape in the work of Corneille and the poets and dramatists who belong to the next volume of this series. It was opposed from two sides. Mademoiselle de Gournay, the devoted friend and editor of Montaigne, and the vigorous and poetic satirist Mathurin Régnier, who has been discussed by Mr Hannay,[1] denounced him vigorously from the standpoint of the Pleiad. Malherbe's doctrine and practice consisted, they declared, in

Classicism retarded and advanced.

"proser de la rime, et rimer de la prose."

On the other hand, even in the circles which accepted Malherbe's condemnation of the Pleiad, the influence of Marie de Médicis and the prevalent admiration of Tasso, Guarini, Marino, and Italian poetry and criticism generally, made fashionable a taste for conceit and confectionery alien to the purer style of Malherbe.

Nevertheless, the influences which were to bring in time the triumph of classicism were either actually at work or rapidly taking shape. First and foremost of these is the social. The close of the civil wars made Paris the centre of a dis-

[1] *Later Renaissance*, pp. 308, 309.

tinguished and brilliant society, in which poets and men of letters began for the first time to move, not in the feudal position of dependants on some great noble, as even Ronsard had done, but on a footing of equality. If rationalism, which was growing and was soon to take definite shape in the work of Descartes, may be described as the formal cause of the classical literature of the age of Louis XIV., the influence of polite society was the efficient, supplying the power which subordinated the individual, and imposed the rules of order, clearness, and dignity with all the rigour of social etiquette.

The opening of the seventeenth century is accordingly hardly less distinctly marked as an epoch by the arrival in Paris of Malherbe (1605), by the publication of D'Urfé's *L'Astrée* (1605), or the definitive establishment of Valleran de Léconte's company at the Hôtel de Bourgogne (1607), than by the rebuilding of the Hôtel Rambouillet (1607). Catherine de Vivonne, the daughter of a French ambassador at the Papal court and his Italian wife Julia Savelli, had, when little more than twelve, married Charles d'Angennes, Marquis de Rambouillet. Her sensitive and refined nature was repelled by the licentious morals and camp manners of the court of Henri IV., and after the birth of her eldest daughter, the celebrated Julie, she withdrew from court, rebuilt the Palais Pisani as the Hôtel Rambouillet in a style which revolutionised domestic architecture, and drew around her all

The Hôtel.

who were most eminent in rank, in power, and in intellect; enlisting them in the common cause of decency, refinement, and dignity.[1]

[1] The authority of polite society in letters and taste was recognised later in a peculiarly formal and French manner by the institution of the *Académie Française*. This famous institution originated in some meetings of literary and learned men at the house of Conrart (1603-1675), the first secretary to the Academy, who, though well read in Spanish and Italian, was ignorant of Greek and Latin. The group included Jean Chapelain (1595-1674), the most authoritative critic though the most unfortunate poet of the first half of the century, who did more than any one else to make observation of the Unities a law for French tragedy, but was also one of the last to read and confess his enjoyment of the mediæval romances, and withal a *précieux* of the *précieux* in his poetic diction and pedantic gallantry. Others were Antoine Godeau (1605-1672), a prolific poet, amorous, and later religious; Jean de Gombauld (1599 ?-1666), also a minor poet; Desmarets de Saint-Sorlin, dramatist, and one of Richelieu's most trusted coadjutors; and the Abbé de Boisrobert, also a dramatist and friend of Richelieu. It was at the suggestion of Boisrobert that the informal gathering was made by the great Minister the nucleus of the authorised Academy, March 1634. Among those whom they added to their number were Maynard, Saint-Amant, Racan, Balzac, Benserade, and Voiture.

The aim of the Academy was that which had guided Malherbe in his criticism and composition, to promote purity, dignity, and elegance—the aspects of strength and beauty which polite society approves—in French prose and verse. Usage in word and idiom was to be settled; and eloquence was to be heightened and refined, not, as Du Bellay and Ronsard had prescribed, by enriching the language with borrowings and coinages, but by distinguishing between expressions which are dignified and elegant and those which have contracted meanness "by passing through the mouths of the vulgar." A Dictionary, a Rhetoric, a Poetic were mooted, but of these only the first, and that on a smaller scale than had been planned, was published, and not until 1693. The first occasion on which the Academy asserted its authority was when, at the dictation of Richelieu, Chapelain arraigned the "correctness" of the first great French classical tragedy, the *Cid* (*Sentiments de l'Académie sur le Cid*).

The heroic and the elegant were the cult of the Hôtel, and of the society which it represented and reformed. The heroic spirit of the early century, its idealisation of freedom regarded not as licence but as the power of the will to rise superior to passion and circumstances, is expressed most perfectly in Descartes' *Traité des Passions* and Corneille's great tragedies. It was in the pursuit of elegance that the influence of a now decadent Italy —of Guarini and Marino, as well as the Spanish Guevara — made itself felt, and set the stamp of "préciosité" on conversation and literature. In France, as in England, as in Italy, as in Spain, poetry, lyric and dramatic, was infected by the passion for conceits — not the metaphysical scholastic conceits with which Donne lightened and darkened English poetry, but the Marinistic conceit, super-refined, super-elegant, super-absurd refinements of compliment and flattery. But what was a symptom of decadence in Italian poetry was in French literature—like euphuism at an earlier stage in English—a symptom of a higher concern about style. The preciousness which Molière finally laughed out of fashion had by that time done its work in helping to refine and elevate the language of conversation and literature. Many of the phrases, it has often been pointed out, which Somaise collected in his *Dictionnaire des Précieuses* (1660), are simply felicitous and elegant expressions which have become part and parcel of literary French.

Among the poets most enamoured of conceit are

some in whom lingered the fancy, picturesqueness, and lyrical inspiration which Malherbe banished from French poetry. Théophile de Viau [1] (1591-1626), whose philosophic "libertinism" connects him with an older generation, has many conceits besides the famous dagger which blushed for its crime, and generally they are poetical as well as precious.

Théophile.

> "Si tu mouilles tes doigts d'ivoire
> Dans le cristal de ce ruisseau,
> Le Dieu qui loge dans cette eau
> Aimera s'il en ose boire"

comes from a poem, *La Solitude*, full of feeling and fancy and music, and Théophile can, at his best, build verses with the skill of Malherbe. But he is very unequal, and his odes to great men are as vapid and wearisome as the majority of such pieces at the time.

There is something of the same fancy and picturesqueness, mingled with tasteless conceits, in the earliest work — *La Solitude* and *Le Contemplateur* — of Saint-Amant [2] (1594-1661), famous for his debaucheries, who visited England in 1643 with the Comte d'Harcourt, and wrote in *l'Albion: caprice héroï-comique*, a not very flattering account of her people, and their troubles. Saint-Amant's most characteristic work, however, is his detailed, realistic, Dutch-like pictures of convivial and tavern life, as the *Cabarets*, *Le Poète crotté*, *Fromage*, *Gazette du Pont-Neuf*, and his experiments

Saint-Amant.

[1] *Œuvres Complètes*, ed. M. Alleaume, 2 vols., Paris, 1855-6.
[2] *Œuvres Complètes*, par M. Ch. L. Livet, Paris, 1855. (*Bibl. Elz.*)

in mock-heroic suggested by Tassoni's poem. In this rather tedious kind the best work was done by Paul Scarron, whose *Typhon* and *Virgile travesti* are still known.

The representative poet of elegant conceit and badinage, the cleverest writer of "vers de société,"
Voiture. was Vincent Voiture[1] (1598-1648). The son of a wine-merchant in Amiens, who was also a money-lender, young Voiture, introduced to Paris society under the protection of the Comte d'Avaux and Cardinal de la Valette, became by his wit and literary facility the darling of the Hôtel. In the service of Gaston d'Orléans he saw campaigning, and visited Spain and the Low Countries, and Richelieu sent him as far as Rome; but he remained always a child of Paris. He was not professedly a poet or a man of letters, but simply an "honnête homme," who wrote occasional verses and letters to his friends and patrons. In short, he employed talents that might have done greater work to make himself the most amusing member of the society in which he moved. To amuse and to pay compliments is the sole aim of his poems as of his letters. How coarse the badinage could be which the refined Hôtel enjoyed may be seen from the wickedly witty stanzas to a lady who had the misfortune to be overturned in a carriage. His complimentary verses are very high-flown, and abound in the conventional mythology which Théophile deprecated, but they are kept from being

[1] *Œuvres*, nouvelle édition, par Amedée Roux, Paris, 1858.

frigid by the vein of humour which pervades them. Voiture can mingle flattery and badinage with the most airy playfulness—

> " Julie a l'esprit et les yeux
> Plus brillant et plus radieux,
>   Landrirette,
> Que l'astre du jour et midi,
>   Landriry.
>
> Elle a tout en perfection,
> Hors qu'elle a trop d'aversion,
>   Landrirette,
> Pour les amants *et les souris*,
>   Landriry."

It is in this airy spirit that he composed most of his rondeaux — a form which had been too much neglected after Marot by the serious poets of the Pleiad. The famous *Ma foi* is a good example, and so is *Un buveur d'eau;* but in *Dans la prison* he strikes a more serious note, and in *En bon Français* he uses the form to attack Godeau with vivacity and point. Of his sonnets, the best known is the "Il faut finir mes jours en l'amour d'Uranie," over the respective merits of which and of the sonnet in octosyllables, *Job,* of Isaac Benserade (1612-1694), the graceful poet of the king's "ballets mythologiques," a lively discussion went on for some time in the circle of the Hôtel. His verse-epistles are easy, natural, and gay. The most philosophic and felicitous is that to the Prince of Condé "sur son retour d'Allemagne" on the vanity of posthumous fame. "Préciosité' or Marinism found in the verse of Voiture its best escape from frigidity and tediousness in the confessedly humorous extravagance of social compliment and badinage: unredeemed by the salt of wit, it soon cloyed and disgusted. But the decay of the lyric spirit, of which "préciosité" and the measured eloquence of Malherbe were both alike symptoms, proved complete. Artificiality was expelled from French poetry not by the reawakening of a purer and deeper poetic inspiration, but by the growing respect for good sense, logic, and order, and the consequent development in the drama of a style lucid and rhetorical rather than picturesque and lyrical. Of this style the great perfecter and master in the first half of the century was Pierre Corneille, of whose dramatic work we shall speak at length in the next chapter. Corneille's non-dramatic verse consists of a complete paraphrase of the *De Imitatione Christi*, which he composed during the years that he had abandoned the stage, similar paraphrases of other hymns and religious poems, and some occasional verses. The sonorous eloquence of Corneille's poetry is not in harmony with the deep and quiet inwardness of the *Imitation*, and he gives too often merely a flamboyant paraphrase. But when the poet's imagination is moved, Corneille's verse, as in the drama, has an incomparable *élan*, an elevation of soul as well as style and rhythm, which raises it far above the level of Malherbe's—

"Parle, parle, Seigneur, ton serviteur écoute ;
Je dis ton serviteur, car enfin je le suis ;
Je le suis, je veux l'être, et marcher dans ta route
　　Et les jours et les nuits.

*　　*　　.　　.　　.　　*　　*

R

> Parle donc, ô mon Dieu ! ton serviteur fidèle,
> Pour écouter ta voix, réunit tous ses sens,
> Et trouve les douceurs de la vie éternelle
> En ses divins accents.
>
> Parle pour consoler mon âme inquiétée ;
> Parle pour la conduire à quelque amendement ;
> Parle, afin que ta gloire ainsi plus exaltée,
> Croisse eternellement."

Corneille's occasional verses have the inequality of all his poetry. His compliments are dull and awkward when he has not his heart in what he says. But if that is touched, the *fierté cornélienne* at once gives them, not the sublimity of Milton's great references to his blindness and his perils, but a stateliness and arrogance that is singularly impressive in its way. Such are the lines *Au Roi* on the performance of his tragedies, which are spoiled only by the last line; and such also are the famous *Stances à la Marquise*, in which he bids her remember that old though he be, it is to his love she will owe her celebrity in years to come,—

> "Chez cette race nouvelle
> Où j'aurai quelque crédit,
> Vous ne passerez pas pour belle
> Qu'autant que je l'aurai dit.
>
> Pensez-y, belle Marquise ;
> Quoiqu'un grison fasse effroi,
> Il vaut bien qu'on le courtise
> Quand il est fait comme moi."

A strange phenomenon in the decadence of the deeper poetic spirit, which had animated the sixteenth-century poets down to d'Aubigné and was still active in England and Holland, is the appearance of quite a number of elaborate epics — poems that of all others demand the greatest intensity of imagination to vivify and sustain. Lemoyne's *Saint Louis* (1651-53), Scudéry's *Alaric* (1654), the notorious *La Pucelle* of Chapelain (1656), Saint-Amant's *Moyse Sauvé* (1653), and Godeau's *Saint Paul* (1654), are only some of the epics in from fifteen to forty-two cantos, on subjects heroic and sacred, which appeared during the first half of the century. The explanation is to be found partly in the taste for the heroic, which was one aspect of the movement to elevate and refine social taste, — an aspect most perfectly reflected in the work of "le grand Corneille,"—in great measure in the enthusiasm felt for the "heroic poem" of Italian literature and critical theory. It was a natural mistake to think that a better knowledge of poetic theory should produce better poetry, and the "rules" which critics and scholars had deduced from Aristotle, regarded as the mouthpiece of reason, were taken very seriously indeed. When this critical spirit came in contact with genius, as in the shaping of Milton's *Paradise Lost* and Corneille's tragedies, the result was interesting in the highest degree, whatever view we may take as to its influence on the final outcome. When the genius was wanting, the result is merely pedantic and tedious. The "correct" epics of the Renaissance are, with the exception of Milton's, more dead than the "correct" Senecan tragedies. Of those mentioned, the *Saint Louis* of the Jesuit Lemoyne—

The Heroic Poem.

who was, Boileau declared, too much of a poet to speak ill of, to much of a madman to praise—is the best, flamboyant but imaginative in its descriptions, and sonorous in versification.

The ideals of refined gallantry, of exquisite heroism, which ruled in the Hôtel de Rambouillet and penetrated polite society, are most fully portrayed in the long prose romances,[1] pastoral and heroic, whose period of growth and efflorescence is just the sixty years with which this volume deals. The earliest of these, the famous pastoral romance *L'Astrée* of Honoré d'Urfé, the first part of which appeared in 1607, was, indeed, one of the main sources of these ideals, shaping as it did the life and spirit of the Hôtel.

Honoré d'Urfé (1568-1625), brought up in Forez, on the banks of the "belle et agréable rivière de Lignon," which he has made the scene of his romance, had an eventful career. At the age of twelve or thirteen he became, at his parents' instance, a knight of Malta and took vows. He was educated by the Jesuits at Tournon, and was

D'Urfé.

[1] To the histories and essays cited above add Koerting's *Geschichte des französischen Romans im XVII^{ten} Jahrhundert*, Oppeln u. Leipzig, 1891, on which the following paragraphs are mainly based. The literary sources of the seventeenth century heroic romance Koerting finds in the *Amadis*, the Greek romances, and the pastoral literature of Italy and France. The social and personal factors, however, are of the greatest importance. See some lectures on *Le Roman français au XVIIe Siècle*, by Professor Abel Lefranc, reported in the *Revue des Cours et Conférences* for 1904-5. Koerting gives exhaustive analyses of the chief romances which are difficult of access. A slighter work is Le Breton's *Le Roman, &c.*, Paris, 1890.

well versed in philosophy, mathematics, and languages, including Italian, Spanish, and German. Tradition says that in boyhood he formed an attachment for the fair Diane de Châteaumorand — the original of the shepherdess Astrée — who about 1574 became the wife of his brother Anne. The marriage was annulled by the Pope in 1598. D'Urfé was released from his vows in the following year, and in 1600 the two were wedded. It has been customary of late to distrust the story of an early attachment, and to assert that after their marriage they lived apart from one another; but the researches of Abbé Reure have shown that the latter statement is not true, and there is no inherent probability in the hypothesis that an affection had sprung up between the two in the earlier years of her nominal marriage. D'Urfé's pastoral poem, the *Sirène*, and the *Astrée* were both coloured by his own experience.

The part which d'Urfé took in the wars of the League procured him more than one imprisonment, and compelled him to spend most of his later years at the court of Savoy, a rendezvous of all the most celebrated Italian poets. He himself wrote an epic on the fortunes of the House of Savoy—*La Savoysiade*, of which a fragment was published in 1621,—and his principal work combined Italian and Spanish influences in a way that appealed powerfully to his country and generation. The *Astrée* was one of the sources of the ideal in which Italian refinement and elegance were blended with the heroic French temper of the early seventeenth century.

For the influence of the *Astrée* was in great measure due to the time at which it appeared. As with Lyly's *Euphues,* its dynamic was greater than its intrinsic value. The most widely read romance before the appearance of d'Urfé's work was the *Amadis of Gaul,* the link which connects the heroic romances of the seventeenth century with the otherwise forgotten mediæval epic and romance. The chivalrous tone of the *Amadis* was fully appreciated by the Hôtel de Rambouillet and Madame de Sévigné; and its popularity was not at once eclipsed by the *Astrée.* But there was nothing in the *Amadis* and its imitations to satisfy that demand for a greater refinement of manners and a more ideal conception of love of which the foundation of the Hôtel was an expression, and it was just this which the *Astrée* supplied.

The chief source of the *Astrée* was the famous pastoral romance of Jorge de Montemayor of which Mr Hannay has given an account; but it is also indebted to the *Aminta,* the *Pastor Fido,* and other Italian pastoral dramas; while the general plan of the work and the chivalrous episodes which d'Urfé, like Sidney, interweaves with the pastoral, derive from the *Amadis.* The main story of Celadon and Astrée—their love, their misunderstanding and separation, his life of seclusion in the forest and service of Astrée in the disguise of a shepherdess, and the heroic achievement which leads to the recognition—is told in flowing and rhythmical prose, interspersed with poems and interrupted by more than thirty other love-stories. The action proceeds with the leisureliness of the sun across an orchard wall. Refined and adoring love is the key-note of the whole, broken only by the lively sallies of the inconstant Hylas, the most brightly drawn character in the romance. As a pastoral, Koerting thinks, the *Astrée* is inferior to the *Diana,* but as a romance superior. The reader's interest is more happily enlisted for the hero and heroine and their fortunes. The secondary characters are better grouped around these. Compared with Sidney's *Arcadia*, the *Astrée* is a more harmonious whole. D'Urfé allowed no interest, whether of chivalrous incident or poetic style, to usurp upon the portrayal of refined, devoted, and elevated love-sentiment. And d'Urfé's love, high-flown as it is, is not so much a mere code of gallantry as it became in his followers and in the tragi-comedies, "amour postiche, froid et ridicule," a pretext for absurdly heroic resolutions and refinements of casuistry and eloquence. There is no passion in the love which d'Urfé paints, but there was some degree of beauty in the sentiment, and of elevation in the morality which gained the admiration not only of the Hôtel but of so fine a critic of the heart as Saint Francis of Sales.

The admiration of Saint Francis was shared by his friend and follower, Jean-Pierre Camus (1582-1652), Bishop of Belley, and it was not against the *Astrée* so much as the continuations and imitations of *Amadis de Gaule*, which the *Astrée* superseded, that his moral and religious romances were directed. Nor are they Christian pastorals, as is sometimes said, but rather "novelle" more

Camus.

or less expanded,—exemplary novels, as Cervantes called his,—stories of incidents in real life narrated with a moral purpose, but with very considerable realistic vividness and psychological skill. What he claims as the special merit of his work is their truth, in which respect he contrasts them with "ces Histoires fabuleuses, ces livres d'amour, ces Romans, ces Bergeries, ces Chevaleries et semblables fadaises." The incidents of some, as *La Mémoire de Darie* (1620) or *Diotrèphe, Histoire Valentine* (1624), may have been drawn from actual experience; of others, as *Palombe ou La Femme Honorable* (1624), which was republished in 1853, the source is probably to be discovered in Italian and Spanish "novelle." The last has points of contact with the story of *Romeo and Juliet*.

Neither the religious romance, however, nor the political, of which an example was given in Barclay's Latin *Argenis* (1626), proved in any degree rivals to the romance of love and gallantry.

Heroic Romances.

D'Urfé's successors were Jean-Ogier de Gombauld (1576-1666), Marin le Roy, Sieur de Gomberville (1600-1674), Gautier de Costes, Chevalier de la Calprenède (1609-1663), and Madeleine de Scudéry (1608-1701), as well as many lesser lights such as François de Molière and Pierre de Vaumorière. They did not follow d'Urfé in choosing the pastoral convention to set forth their ideals of heroism and refinement. The *Astrée* was the source of many pastoral and gallant love-plays; but the taste for the heroic and the historic, traceable to political and social conditions perhaps, but also to the admiration of Spanish literature and the study of Plutarch, shaped the romance, as it did tragi-comedy and ultimately tragedy, and the general plan of these endless works traces the heroic adventures of lovers by sea and land—combines, in short, the chivalrous incidents of the *Amadis* with the refined gallantry of the *Astrée* and the Hôtel. Historical epochs and characters are introduced, but the result is the wildest romantic travesty of history. All the heroes of antiquity, the Persian Cyrus and the Roman consul Brutus, the savage Tomyris and the chaste matron Lucretia, are equally gallant and refined, equally familiar with the geography of the "pays de tendre," all equally ready to compose high-flown speeches and madrigals. In these romances, as already in the *Astrée*, an additional interest for curiosity was provided by the introduction of "déguisements," the adumbration in the *dramatis personæ* of contemporary characters. But the persons are so indistinctly and so romantically delineated that this additional interest is for us infinitesimal. The heroic romances are valuable reflections of the ideals and affectations of the day, but they cannot be used to throw light on incidents or characters.

Of the authors mentioned, Gombauld stands somewhat by himself. His *Endymion* (1624) is a pale allegory of his respectful and a little absurd affection for Marie de Médicis. Gomberville's *Polexandre* (1637) is the first example of the seventeenth-century heroic romance proper. The

Gombauld.

Polexandre retains much of the wilder improbabilities of the *Amadis* type, which, with the Greek romances and the fabulous geography still prevalent, was its principal source. The style is swollen and affected. *Cytherée* is even more indebted to the Greek, and equally wild and confused. It was La Calprenède and the Scudérys who gave the heroic romance the form which was most closely in touch with the predilections of the age.

Gomberville.

La Calprenède, a Gascon by birth and temper, and a successful dramatist, in his *Cassandre* (1642-45) and *Cléopâtre* (1647) and *Faramond* (1661) eliminated the supernatural marvels of the *Polexandre*, and interwove his stories of exalted love and heroism with historical names and events. They are endlessly long, one love-story passing into another in the most bewildering fashion, and all of a monotonous sameness; but his episodes are woven, as had never been done before, into a converging series, which ends in not one but a group of happy weddings. Honour and gallantry are the sole motives which in La Calprenède's romances, as in his own and other contemporary tragi-comedies and tragedies, determine the course of history. Occasionally, it has been pointed out, the heroes are involved in something of the same conflict of motives which forms the dramatic centre of Corneille's tragedies, but the conflict is developed on purely conventional and heroic lines.

La Calprenède.

La Calprenède's scheme was followed by the Scudérys, Georges and Madeleine, of whom the latter was the principal partner. In *Ibrahim ou l'Illustre*

Bassa (1641), *Artamène ou le Grand Cyrus* (1649-1653),
and *Clélie ou Histoire Romaine* (1654),
Scudéry.
the heroic, pseudo-historical romances
reached a climax and expired. The cult of precious
sentiment could no further go. Turks, Persians, and
early Romans, who were French statesmen, authors,
and *précieuses* in disguise, palled upon a generation
whose watchword was "good sense," and who were
beginning to prefer Racine to Corneille. Madame de
Sévigné was in 1675 still an enthusiastic reader of La
Calprenède, carried away by the beauty of the sentiments, the violence of the passions, and the success of
the heroes' redoubtable swords; and she shared the
taste with the analytic and cynical La Rochefoucauld.
But her tone is apologetic, and the last word on the
heroic romance was spoken by Boileau. Its further
development in the psychological romances of Marie
de Lafayette belongs to the succeeding volume.

The absurdity of the long-winded love romances,
palpable enough to us,—although the idealisation of
Realistic amorous passion in the novel is, still, more
Romance. widely popular than psychological analysis
and dramatic action, — was also palpable to many
shrewd minds of the generation which produced and
admired these romances. From almost the beginning
of the century a counter-current of realistic and
satirical story, dealing with life as it is, and not as
the Hôtel de Rambouillet loved to imagine it, ran side
by side with the more fashionable stream. Here also
the influence of Spain was dominant. The picaresque
romance, of which a full and trenchant description

has been given by Mr Hannay, is the main source of the French realistic and satiric romances, although the best of the latter excel their originals as paintings of manners and as humorous amusing stories. This does not, of course, apply to the imitation of Cervantes. *Le Berger Extravagant* is the work of an acute and interesting mind, but it will not bear comparison for a moment with *Don Quixote*. The deeper influence of that great work was not felt till a later period.

Setting aside Barclay's Latin *Euphormio* (1603) and D'Aubigné's *Aventures du Baron de Fœneste* (1617-20), which belong in the main to the satirical, fantastic, pedantic literature of the revival of learning, the first sketch of a realistic romance may be found in Théophile de Viau's *Fragments d'une Histoire Comique*, written probably about 1620, which, besides its biographic interest, is a fresh and taking picture, so far as it goes, of young men and their ways in the seventeenth century. But the most elaborate and conscious exponent of realism in opposition to the idealism of the heroic and pastoral romances was Charles Sorel (1599-1674), the author of the *Histoire Comique de Francion*[1] (1622, greatly enlarged in 1646), *Le Berger Extravagant* (1627), and *Polyandre* (1648).

Of Sorel's life we know next to nothing, though Guy Patin has left an interesting description of the "short, fat man with long nose and short-sighted eyes." His earliest work was a conventional love romance, *L'Orphise de Chrysante* (1616), and some

Sorel.

[1] *Nouvelle édition, &c., par Em. Colombey*, Paris, 1858.

shorter *novelle* in the same vein; but, thereafter, he became as thorough-going a champion, in theory and practice, of realism in fiction as any Zola of to-day. "L'histoire, véritable ou feinte, doit représenter au plus près du naturel; autrement c'est une fable qui ne sert qu'à entretenir les enfans au coin du feu, non pas les esprits mûrs." That is the doctrine in the rigid application of which Sorel condemns all romances from the *Iliad* to Sidney's *Arcadia* and d'Urfé's *Astrée*.

This ridicule of romance is the sole purpose of *Le Berger Extravagant*, which was intended to be the *Don Quixote* of the pastoral. There is much that is clever and amusing in its fantastic absurdities, but Sorel failed altogether to appreciate the noble art by which Cervantes preserves our respect and affection for the knight in his absurdities and misfortunes. Lysis, the hero of Sorel's romance, the son of a Paris shopkeeper, who has crazed his brains by reading pastorals, has no quality that claims esteem or interest.

In *Francion* Sorel conducts the picaresque hero, whose life he details from childhood, through an endless series of adventures, which afford an opportunity for the satiric portrayal of different classes—courtiers, pedants, peasants, Paris rogues, lawyers, and men of letters. We owe to Sorel a striking picture of the darker side of literary life in the seventeenth century, such as his great successor Smollett and many others were to give of the same life a century later. "Déguisements" were a feature of the realistic as of the romantic novel, and Malherbe, Balzac, Racan, and other authors are adumbrated in different persons who come under the author's lash. In *Polyandre*, which remained unfinished, he began with the same realistic and satiric purpose a picture of middle-class life, a forerunner of Furetière's *Roman Bourgeois*.

The principal fault of Sorel's, as of wellnigh all these realistic novels, is that they want the romance interest entirely. The incidents may amuse, the pictures of manners and the satire instruct, but the pleasure proper of the novel is not given unless the centre of our interest be the character and fortunes of the hero and those with whom his fate is involved. The pastoral and heroic romances, despite their absurdities, succeeded in arousing suspense in their readers. This is the chief advance that d'Urfé's made on earlier pastoral romances; and there can be no doubt that lady readers at any rate followed the fortunes of Oroondate, of the illustrious Bassa, and of Cyrus with the same acute sympathy as a later generation felt for Pamela and Clarissa. No realistic romance of the seventeenth century, excepting *Don Quixote* and, perhaps, *Le Roman Comique*, has a hero for whose fate we care two straws.

We cannot do more than mention Lannel's *Roman Satyrique* (1624), whose chief interest was its *personages déguisés*; the striking *La Chrysolite ou le Secret des Romans* (1627) of André Mareschal, entitled by Koerting the first French psychological romance, which describes with unusual power a series of incidents, and traces these to their source in the character of the *dramatis personæ*; or the *Page disgracié* (1619, pub. 1640), an interesting autobiographical fragment by the dramatist Tristan l'Hermite. Especially original and interesting are the fantastic romances of Cyrano de Bergerac (1619-1655), collected as the *Histoire Comique des États et Empires de la Lune*. Cyrano's discoveries in the moon and the sun, suggested by Lucian and others, including a couple of English writers of the century, have had many sequels down to the days of Jules Verne and Mr Wells. But the most popular realistic romance of the period was the *Roman Comique* (1651) of Paul Scarron[1] (1610-1660), famous as the husband of Madame de Maintenon, for the physical sufferings he endured with courage and gaiety, and as the author of the *Virgile Travesti* and some comedies in the same burlesque vein. Scarron's romance, suggested by a Spanish one, and containing several interpolated stories translated from that language, was left unfinished. It owes its popularity to the delightful gaiety with which the story is told,—if Sorel makes one think of Smollett, Scarron has a touch of Fielding, —the distinctness and interest of the characters, and also to the fact that the author succeeds to some extent in enlisting our sympathies for his hero, the wandering actor Le Destin. His story is doubtless of a kind more proper to the heroic than the realistic romance; but it may be questioned whether some degree of idealism, some heightening of the principal characters, is not essential to the success as romance even of the most realistic story.

[1] *Le Roman comique, &c., nouvelle édition, &c., par Victor Fournel*, Paris, 1857.

The first fifty years of the seventeenth century witnessed the formation and one might almost say the stereotyping of French prose as it has been spoken and written ever since. "The fifteenth and sixteenth centuries," says M. Faguet, "had prose writers and poets of genius writing in a fluctuating language, which they created as they used, which was not yet fixed and destined to remain the common patrimony of succeeding generations. The language as it can be spoken, and should be written, has for two and a half centuries been that which appears with the *Cid* for poetry, with the *Provinciales* for prose." We cannot here do more than endeavour to describe the ideals which directed the efforts of the three great shapers of perhaps the most perfect medium for the lucid communication of thought which has been formed since the age of Plato and Demosthenes.

Prose style.

The Malherbe of French prose was Jean-Louis Guez de Balzac[1] (1597-1664), the "Grand Epistolier de France." He visited Holland as a young man with Théophile, and wrote a *Discours politique sur l'état des provinces unies*, the liberal sentiment of which he repudiated later, and he spent a couple of years at Rome as agent for the Cardinal de la Valette. Thereafter he withdrew from public life, settled at his country-seat on the Charente, and spent his life in elaborating

Balzac.

---

[1] *Les Œuvres de M. de Balzac* (2 tom.), Paris, 1665. Difficult to procure. Additional letters were edited by Tamizey de Larroque, Paris, 1835.

and polishing his letters and occasional treatises, political, religious, and critical, of which the most ambitious were *Le Prince* (1632) and the *Socrate Chrestien* (1652). His letters had begun to attract attention as early as 1618, and they were the admiration of the Hôtel Rambouillet long before the author was introduced there. The first collection appeared in 1624.

Balzac was as devoted to style for its own sake as Malherbe, and had the same narrow oratorical ideal of correctness, the same devotion to order, dignity, and sonorous rhythm. "Ce n'est pas assez," he says in the *Socrate Chrestien*, "de savoir la Théologie: il faut encore savoir écrire, qui est une seconde science." It was to this "seconde science" that Balzac dedicated his life as steadily as did Descartes to the rational explanation of the universe; and the result was that in his letters and dissertations French oratorical prose attained almost at once to formal perfection of structure and rhythm. It owed this development in some measure to the very barrenness of Balzac's thought. It is well for a writer to have something to say, but for one whose chief function is to attune his medium it is also well not to have too much. Balzac could hardly have made his periods so uniformly musical if he had been striving to utter the thoughts of Montaigne or Descartes. But by Montaigne Balzac's work would have been described as "Lettres vuides et descharnées qui ne se soustiennient que par un délicat chois de mots entassez et rengez à une juste cadence." He excelled in just those

things which the former detested in letter-writing,
—"une belle enfileure de paroles courtoises," "à bienvienner, à prendre congé, à remercier, à saluer, à presenter mon service et tels compliments verbeux des lois ceremonieuses de nostre civilité."

Balzac's dissertations are strings of sonorously elaborated commonplaces. The one theme on which he writes with freshness and with his eye on the object is literature. He was not such an educated critic as the dry and pedantic Chapelain; but in his letter to Scudéry on the *Cid*, in his criticism of Heinsius's *Herodes Infanticida*, and in his remarks on paraphrasing and the sublime simplicity of the Old Testament, he is sound in principle, while in more than one place he writes imaginative and eloquent appreciations. The following sentences on Saint Chrysostom might almost have been written by Sainte-Beuve of Saint François de Sales: "Avec un commentaire de deux syllabes, avec un petit mot qui tempère la rigueur des choses, avec une particule de charité, qui adoucit les menaces de la justice, il défriche les plus dures et les plus sauvages expressions. Il console et rassure les esprits que le texte de Saint Paul avait effrayés. Partout où il passe il laisse des traces de blancheur et une impression de lumière."

Balzac is essentially the man of letters, the prose artist and nothing more. The second great shaper of classical French prose was more interested in the lucid and logical exposition of his thought than in the cadence of his

Descartes.

periods. The life and work of René Descartes[1] (1596-1650) belong more properly to the history of philosophy than of literature. Educated by the Jesuits, he served as a volunteer under Maurice of Nassau and the Duke of Bavaria. It was when in winter quarters in Germany that he conceived his "method," and tested it by elaborating the application of algebra to geometry. He visited Switzerland and Italy, and returned to Paris in 1625, where he spent two years hidden from his friends, immersed in study and reflection. In 1629 he migrated to Holland, which became his headquarters until 1649, when he accepted the invitation of the Queen of Sweden and removed to Stockholm, where he died in the following year. The famous *Discours de la Méthode* was published at Leyden in 1637. A great part of his subsequent writing consisted of replies to objections and learned correspondence. The *Traité des Passions*, written for Princess Elizabeth of the Palatinate in 1649, was published in 1650.

Descartes is the greatest and completest representative of the rationalism which was the chief though not the sole factor in the formation of classical literature in France. He did on a larger scale and in the region of philosophy the work of selection and ordering which Malherbe and

Rationalism.

---

[1] *Opera Omnia*, Amst., 1670-83. *Œuvres Complètes, &c.*, ed. Victor Cousin, 11 vols., Paris, 1824-26. *Œuvres inédites, &c.*, ed. Foucher de Careil, Paris, 1859-60. *Œuvres, &c.*, ed. C. Adam et P. Tannery, 1897, in progress. A centenary edition.

For studies, see bibliographical note in Petit de Julleville, vol. iv., and Histories of Philosophy generally.

Balzac were doing for style in verse and prose. The famous method of the *Discours,* the cultivation of doubt not for its own sake but that from it may emerge the "clear and distinct" first principles of a rational system of knowledge, stands in the same relation to the eclectic and sceptical thought of Montaigne as Malherbe's and Balzac's ideal of style to that writer's rhetorical canon, "c'est aux paroles à servir et à suivre et que le Gascon y arrive si le François n'y peut aller." The attempt has even been made to represent the classical ideal as the æsthetic expression of the Cartesian philosophy, but as M. Lanson justly says, Cartesian æsthetic would reduce art to science, identifying beauty with truth. Rational and ordered truth is an important constituent of the classical ideal in French literature and criticism, but it is not the whole of that ideal, which includes the dignity and elegance that mark it as the product of a polite and cultured society nourished on the literature of antiquity. Descartes' own style has little emotional quality. It is clear, precise, and occasionally felicitous in figure, but the sentences are long and weighted with subordinate clauses,—the adequate reflection of the author's methodical comprehensive thought and purely intellectual purpose. He had not Balzac's desire to rouse admiration, and the only persuasion he sought was intellectual conviction, so that there is no place in his style for elaborate colour or cadence.

It was the wish to gain the heart and the will as well as the understanding which gave to Pascal's style a more shining clearness than Descartes' in dealing with equally abstract themes, a higher eloquence than Balzac's, and a suppleness and variety which no French prose had obtained previously and in which it has remained unsurpassed. Blaise Pascal's [1] (1623-1662) life, and its intimate connection with his writings, have been made the subject of many critical investigations, and eloquently summarised by Chateaubriand. The early development of his mathematical genius, and his researches and discoveries in mathematics and physics; his conversion and that of his family, under the influence of the Jansenist Guillebert, curé of Rouville, in 1646; his "worldly period," in which he opposed the pious desire of his sister to enter Port Royal, and turned from the study of geometry to the study of men, under the guidance of de Méré and Miton as well as Montaigne; his passionate return to religion and settlement at Port Royal in 1653; the composition and publication of the *Lettres Provinciales* (1656), begun as a defence of Arnauld but

Pascal.

---

[1] Innumerable editions of the *Provinciales*, *e.g.*, Havet, Paris, 1885. Fauchère in the *Grands Écrivains de la France*, 2 vols., Paris. Of the *Pensées*, the first that went back to the manuscript was that of Faugère in 1844, which was succeeded eight years later by Havet's, with an elaborate commentary. The last is that by Brunschvieg in the *Grands Écrivains de la France*, Paris, 1905. There is a smaller one by the same editor of the *Pensées et Opuscules*, Paris, 1900, with full connecting biography and comment. Sainte-Beuve's *Port-Royal* is a fascinating study of the religious *milieu* in which Pascal's thought took shape, and of Pascal himself. Another invaluable study is by Boutroux (*Grands Écrivains français*), and one by Sully Prudhomme has just appeared.

passing after the third letter into an ironical and overwhelming exposure of the casuistry of the Jesuits; his last years of illness, during which were composed the *Pensées*, notes for a great defence of Christianity, — these are the principal moments, and they need not be more than recalled here. Besides some scientific letters, only the *Lettres Provinciales* were published in his lifetime. The *Pensées* were arranged and issued by Port Royal in 1670.

Pascal reflected as carefully as Bacon on the art of persuasion, and neither the method which he pursued in the *Lettres Provinciales* nor that which he adumbrated in the *Pensées* was attained by haphazard. He was at one with Montaigne in his scorn of eloquence cultivated for its own sake,—eloquence such as Balzac's, "qui nous destourne à soy,"—and in his love of a style which is "la peinture de la pensée." "Quand on voit le style naturel," says Pascal, "on est tout étonné et ravi car on s'attendait de voir un auteur et on trouve un homme." Where he parts company with Montaigne is in the importance he attaches to order, as necessary to the definite purpose which inspired all he wrote, as the former's style—"desreglée, descousu, et hardy"—was in harmony with his detached and sceptical survey of life. To Pascal a new disposition of the matter made the matter new; and as to the best disposition Pascal was at one with Descartes. The ideal order is the order of demonstration which geometry follows. But few men are guided by the understanding; and the premises for many of our conclusions are too subtle and complex to be isolated and fixed in definitions. To judge aright of many things in life we require "finesse," "l'esprit de justesse," tact, and to persuade we require to possess the art of pleasing. "L'art de persuader consiste en celui d'agréer plutôt qu'en celui de convaincre, tant les hommes se gouvernent plus par caprice que par raison." The heart is reached by another way than the mind: "Jésus Christ, Saint Paul ont l'ordre de la charité, non de l'esprit; car ils voulaient échauffer, non instruire." Thus eloquence excluded for its own sake returns as a legitimate instrument with which to awaken the love of God and the hatred of evil. And Pascal's eloquence is unsurpassed. The shining clearness, the unerring dialectic, the humour, the irony, the grave expostulation of the *Lettres Provinciales*, are unequalled in literature since the Platonic dialogues; and fragmentary as the *Pensées* are, the style, as the subject permits, is in parts even more vibrating and imaginative. The description of man, a nothing between two infinites; of his pursuit of diversion to escape from himself; the image of the reed that thinks, have the force and beauty of the finest passages of the *Republic*. In Plato's and Pascal's eloquence there is no shadow of the rhetoric "qui nous destourne à soy." In Pascal's hands French prose became a medium of such lucidity and precision, such delicacy and resource, that to a foreigner it seems as though it were almost impossible for a Frenchman to write obscurely.

The egotism of French aristocratic society, vividly reflected in all the literature of this period, the "Moi! et c'est assez" which Corneille's tragedies exalt, but which was to Pascal hateful ("Le Moi est haïssable"), the proof of man's corruption, the source of his miseries, of the contradiction which makes him, in order to gratify self, seek in endless diversion an escape from self,—nowhere is this so nakedly painted as in the Memoirs of the early seventeenth century, especially those which describe the confused, frivolous, and criminal intrigues and wars of the Fronde. "Tous les hommes se haïssent naturellement l'un l'autre," says the sombre Jansenist, like the English materialist Hobbes; and certainly patriotism, loyalty, and fidelity were unknown to the princes, cardinals, generals, and great ladies who struggled with Mazarin, and with one another, for power, money, and privilege. There was no lack of intrigue and self-seeking among the courtiers who gathered round Charles at Oxford. "It cannot be imagined," says Clarendon, "into how many several shapes men's indispositions were put, and the many artifices which were used to get honours, offices, preferments, and the waywardness and perverseness which attended the being disappointed of their own hopes." But when all that a cynical critic can say has been said of cavalier dissoluteness and intrigues, and of the negotiations of the Scotch and of the Army with Charles, there remains a vast moral difference between the war of principles in England—principles on which, in the last resort, neither Charles nor the

Presbyterians nor the Army would yield—and the tragi-comedy of the Fronde, when the only persons whom self-interest made loyal to France were the Austrian Queen Mother and the Italian Minister.

The difference is felt acutely when one turns from Clarendon's dignified and moving narrative, or Cromwell's turgid but earnest letters, to the most brilliant of the many memoirs of these years—those of the libertine, ambitious, intriguing, demagogic Cardinal de Retz, and the more impersonal narrative of the equally egotistic and intriguing, but more reflective, critical Hamlet-like Duc de la Rochefoucauld.

The *Mémoires* of Jean-François-Paul de Gondy, Cardinal de Retz (1613-1679), are not to be trusted with regard to anything which it was for his interest to falsify; but they give, nevertheless, a vivid picture of events and actors, and of his own character and motives. A libertine who entered the Church to secure his family rights in the Archbishopric of Paris, a turbulent and ambitious temperament, a restless and intriguing mind, a born demagogue, De Retz's life was one long conflict for power, for the office of first minister, which he never attained. His style reflects his lucid, unquiet mind. It is not classical French prose. It wants the delicacy, the studied ease and grace of the writers whose style was moulded by the *Provinciales* and by the salons. But it is vigorous, coloured, and pointed. His narrative is vivid; his expositions of policy lucid and comprehensive; his character-sketches discriminating and piquant masterpieces.

De Retz.

Among the actors in the first Fronde whom De Retz portrays is François VI., Duc de la Rochefoucauld (1613-1689). "Il y a eu du je ne sais quoi en M. de la Rochefoucauld. . . . Il a toujours eu une irrésolution habituelle; mais je ne sais même à quoi attributer cette irrésolution. . . . Il n'a jamais été guerrier, quoiqu'il fut très soldat. Il n'a jamais été par lui-même bon courtisan, quoiqu'il ait eu toujours bonne intention de l'être. Il n'a jamais été bon homme de parti, quoique toute sa vie il y ait été engagé." "Cet air de honte et de timidité que vous lui voyez dans la vie civile s'était tourné, dans les affaires, en air d'apologie." Not less an egotist than De Retz or more averse to intrigue, La Rochefoucauld was less the man of action and of will. Vanity and passion, rather than ambition for power, involved him in the intrigues and crimes of the Fronde. He was under the influence of women. And when his hopes were shattered, he did not spend his last days like De Retz in trying to find new methods, but digested his disappointment in a philosophy of human nature.

La Rochefoucauld's *Mémoires* are written in the third person, in a colder and more detached tone than De Retz's, and in a more elaborately elegant and balanced style. His portraits are drawn with vivacity, and show as might be expected subtlety and insight. But La Rochefoucauld did a greater service for posterity than write a history of the Fronde. He crystallised the impressions which the experience of those years had left on his mind in a small collection of *Maximes* (1665-1678) which sombre wisdom and perfection of form have made a classic.

The difference between the English and the French wars is not more clearly seen from a comparison of the memoirs than from a study of the philosophic sediment which these wars left behind them in the literature of either country. The most direct effect of the English rebellion and revolution is seen in the political speculations of Hobbes and Locke; and in the cult of moderation in feeling, especially religious and moral feeling, of which the chief spokesman is Addison. Addison's sweet reasonableness is not quite the same thing as Boileau's good sense, for there is in it less of clear reason and more of feeling,—feeling which in Steele has already in it the germ of sensibility. The effect of the French wars is not seen in works on political theory. A war in which no principles were involved created no theoretical problems. Nor did it awaken humanitarian sentiment. That came later, and came from England. The fruit of the Fronde was a clearer insight into human nature, and a somewhat sombre philosophy, a philosophy which detected in every virtue the alloy of self-interest.

Les Maximes.

This philosophy, which runs through the work of some of the greatest writers of the period treated in the following volume of this series, is presented in its quintessence in the *Maximes* of La Rochefoucauld. "Les vertus se perdent dans l'intérêt, comme les fleuves se perdent dans la mer." That is the first principle from which his maxims are deduced, and it is a principle so universal that it is difficult to draw any deduction from it which experience of life and one's own heart will not verify. And La Rochefoucauld's aphorisms have been brought to the test of experience, the experience of reflection and observation. They are models of wit as Johnson defined it, not "what oft was thought," for the shock they give proves that they are not mere platitudes, but "that which though not obvious is upon its first production acknowledged to be just."

In style La Rochefoucauld's ideal is that of Balzac and the *Précieuses*. He cultivated the art of writing as "une seconde science." The *Maximes* were as regards their form a product of the salons, which after the Fronde took the place of the Hôtel de Rambouillet. Each salon cultivated some special form—letters, madrigals, portraits. At that of Madame de Sablé, which La Rochefoucauld frequented, the fashion was maxims, and it was under the influence of the critical spirit which was at work in society that he chiselled, polished, and pointed his aphorisms. In La Rochefoucauld's prose "préciosité," of which there is just a trace in some of the *Maximes*, passed into the perfection of classical prose, the right word in the right place, and no word that is unnecessary.

CHAPTER VII.

FRENCH DRAMA.[1]

THE FORMATION OF FRENCH TRAGEDY AND COMEDY—SIXTEENTH-CENTURY DRAMA — LARIVEY AND MONTCHRESTIEN — THE POPULAR DRAMA— EXPERIMENTS IN THE PROVINCES—HARDY AND VALLERAN LECOMTE —HARDY'S TRAGEDIES, TRAGI-COMEDIES, PASTORALS, AND MYTHO- LOGICAL PLAYS — BEGINNING OF POLITE DRAMA — THÉOPHILE AND RACAN—INFLUENCE OF ITALIAN PASTORAL, AND OF SPANISH TRAGI- COMEDY—MAIRET—THE UNITIES—'SOPHONISBE' AND THE REVIVAL OF TRAGEDY — CORNEILLE — 'MÉLITE' AND THE DEVELOPMENT OF COMEDY — EARLY PLAYS — THE 'CID' AND THE FLOWERING OF TRAGEDY — BATTLE OF THE 'CID' — TRIUMPH OF THE UNITIES— CORNEILLE'S GREAT TRAGEDIES—'LE MENTEUR'—COMEDY UNDER SPANISH INFLUENCE — CORNEILLE'S LAST PLAYS — RELATION OF FRENCH TRAGEDY OF CORNEILLE AND RACINE TO GREEK TRAGEDY AND TO ROMANTIC TRAGI-COMEDY—ROTROU—BURLESQUE COMEDY— 'LES VISIONNAIRES.'

THE early decades of the seventeenth century are not less of an epoch in the history of French drama than *Sources of* of French prose and verse. The classical *French Tragedy.* tragedy of Jodelle and Garnier is a very different thing from the classical tragedy of Corneille and Racine, and the explanation of the difference is

---

[1] The sketch given of the rise of the drama is based mainly on the work of Eugène Rigal, who has cleared up many obscurities and corrected errors in his *Alexandre Hardy et le théâtre français à la fin du XVIᵉ et au commencement du XVIIᵉ Siècle*, Paris, 1889 ; *Le Théâtre*

to be found in the history of the phases through which French drama passed between the opening of the century and the appearance of the *Cid*. Differently as the elements were ultimately blended, the French drama, like the English, was the outcome of an amalgamation of the classical drama of the Renaissance and plays which were directly descended from the mediæval drama. The man who brought together the different seeds and began the fertilisation of the French stage was Alexandre Hardy.

The older academic drama had not quite come to an end when the sixteenth century closed. Larivey was yet to write the last of his comedies, based on Latin and Italian models. Of those who were still writing classical tragedies, the most interesting was Montchrestien. Antoine de Montchrestien[1] (1575-1621), whose adventures and stirring career closed at the stake, was the author of six tragedies on classical, historical, and Scriptural themes—*Hector, La Reine d'Écosse, La Carthaginoise, Les Lacènes, David, Aman*—in the usual Senecan style with long, often eloquent speeches and meditative musical choruses. There is no pretence of action, of developing a story from the interaction of characters

Montchrestien.

---

au XVIIe Siècle avant Corneille, in Petit de Julleville, tom. iv., 1897; and *Le Théâtre français avant la période classique*, Paris, 1901. For other histories, see note to previous chapter, and add the *Histoire du Théâtre Français*, by the Frères Parfaict, Paris, 1745; L. Petit de Julleville, *Le Théâtre en France*, Paris, 1889.

[1] *Les Tragédies de M.*, ed. Petit de Julleville, Paris, 1891 (*Bibliothèque Elzevirienne*). See Lanson's *Hommes et Livres, Études Morales et Littéraires*, Paris, 1895.

and circumstances. A few situations in a familiar story are presented in a statuesque manner—a long monologue, or a dialogue which is simply an interchange of balanced "sentences," very different from the rapid play of Corneille's dialogue instinct with purpose and passion. At the end of each scene the chorus deploys in grave and harmonious stanzas its reflections on the fleetingness of life, the inexorableness of fate, the beauty and dignity of virtue,—

> "Si tu n'aperçois rien d'éternelle durée,
>   Et si tout ce grand Tout n'attend que le trépas,
> Suis toujours la vertu seule au monde assurée
> Qui nous fait vivre au Ciel en mourant ici-bas.
> O l'honneur immortel des âmes généreuses,
>   Fort bien considéré vous avez eu raison
> De rendre vos esprits en vos mains valeureuses,
>   Pour sortir par la mort d'une double prison."

These plays, it is clear, were never written for the popular stage at all. Their observance—vague as it often is—of the Unities of place and time implies as much, for the conventions of the popular theatre included a permissible duration of the action from the creation to the Day of Judgment, as well as the simultaneous representation of different places—what Corneille calls "ce horrible derèglement qui mettait Paris, Rome, et Constantinople sur le même théâtre"—and that not successively and ideally, as on the English stage described by Sidney, but at one and the same time with distinct decorations. The Senecan tragedies might be performed at schools and colleges—to add to the sufferings of the much-enduring students of those days, who greatly preferred farce. Often they must have been written only for readers. Their sole merit was as literature. The beautiful choruses—of Garnier especially — were universally admired, and were imitated in England by Daniel, in Holland by Hooft.

The popular stage had still to be content with the moribund mediæval drama. The performance of sacred mysteries had been forbidden in Paris in 1548, but they seem to have lingered under other names; and there were still the "histoires" and "romans," the "moralités," tending to become more concrete and secular, as well as the ever-popular farces. The general trend of this decaying mediæval drama, wherever it was not displaced by classical tragedy and comedy, was towards simply dramatised stories—drawn from the *novelle* and other sources—in which the story interest is paramount. In Spain, where classical dramatic influence was most successfully resisted, this interest of story subordinated in the work of Lope de Vega almost every other consideration. In England Marlowe, the other university wits to a less degree, and Shakespeare pre-eminently, in virtue of their genius, but not uninfluenced by Seneca, superinduced upon this interest of story vivid dramatic portrayal of character and poetic beauty. Alexandre Hardy[1] was neither a Lope de Vega nor a Christopher Marlowe, yet the work he did was of the

Popular Drama.

---

[1] *Le Théâtre d'Alexandre Hardy*, Erster Neudruck, &c., von E. Stengel, 5 vols., Marburg, 1883-84. The most exhaustive critical study is that by Rigal cited above.

same kind at a much lower level. He disengaged
French drama from the last remnants of Mystery and
didactic Morality; he taught it to present a story,
tragic or romantic, in a condensed and telling form;
and he made a beginning, though a crude and imperfect
one, with the delineation of character and passion.
Or if we look at his work from another point of view,
and compare it with the academic instead of the
popular drama, we may justly say that, while infinitely
inferior to Garnier's as poetry, Hardy's plays have
what these elegiac and lyrical performances have not
—that action which is the soul of a living drama.

We know, unfortunately, very little of Hardy's life
and education. He was certainly not illiterate, as
Sainte-Beuve seems to suggest. He was

Alexandre Hardy.

probably as well educated as Marlowe,
possibly rather better than Shakespeare, if by education we understand academic training. He was
acquainted with the classics as well as with the contemporary literature of Spain and Italy, and in his
poetic theories and licences of diction shows himself
an enthusiastic admirer of Ronsard and his school.
All that we know of his career is that about 1593
he became journeyman playwright, or *poète à gages*,
to a wandering troupe of players under a certain
Valleran Lecomte. The *Confrérie de la Passion* had
the monopoly of dramatic entertainments in Paris, and
by the end of the sixteenth century their performances had sunk to the lowest level of illiteracy. The
future of the French stage depended not on them but
on the efforts of the wandering troupes of professional

actors who made a precarious existence in the provinces, and, like their English contemporaries, sometimes travelled as far as the Low Countries and Denmark. Compelled to interest and amuse, these companies were driven to add to their *répertoire* something besides the outworn moralities, histories, romances, and farces. Valleran Lecomte seems to have experimented with the academic tragedies of Jodelle, de la Taille, and Garnier. In Hardy, however, Lecomte found some one who supplied exactly what he was feeling his way towards,—a dramatist who could produce tragedies not unlike those of Garnier, but with more of movement, and without wearisome monologues and choral odes; who could, in short, dramatise with the utmost rapidity stories of every and any sort drawn from all the most popular reading of the day. Encouraged by such an acquisition, Lecomte rented the Hôtel de Bourgogne in 1599 from the Confrérie, who were beginning to realise their inability to cope with the superior attractions which Italian and provincial companies brought to Paris from time to time in spite of their protests. After some interruptions, and notwithstanding trouble with the Confrérie, and with occasional rivals, which cannot be detailed here, Valleran's company settled at the Hôtel under the name of the King's comedians, and was until 1629 the only company performing regularly in Paris. During these years Hardy was the mainstay of the company, and almost the sole French dramatist of importance. He poured forth plays with the utmost profusion—the number has been put as high as eight hundred; and the variety of their kinds—tragedies, tragi-comedies, pastorals, and mythological plays—shows clearly what was the chief aim of the author, to provide fresh and novel entertainments for a popular audience.

Hardy's earliest efforts were probably "romances" like *Théagène et Chariclée* on the one hand, and tragedies such as *Didon, Mariamne, Panthée, Mort d'Achille, Coriolan* on the other. The

Tragedies.

first, which runs on through several "journées," is closely related to the later mediæval "romans," but shows the influence of the classical school in its less naïve structure and style, and in the introduction of lengthy monologues and colloquies. In the tragedies Hardy's relation to the academic dramatists is very clear. Their works are obviously his inspiration and to some extent his model; but writing for the popular stage, Hardy's main interest is not in "sentences" and rhetoric, but in the conduct of the story. Whatever delays the progress of the action—such as choral odes and lengthy dreams or descriptions—is either dropped or abbreviated. With an art which is by no means subtle or varied, but is effective as far as it goes, Hardy presents the story in its principal moments, in the person of the chief characters, and in speeches and colloquies which are not mere exercises in rhetoric, but portray motive and carry forward the action. The character-drawing is, like the plot-structure, simple and crude, but not ineffective. Decisive resolutions are abruptly formed, and critical actions rapidly developed; but the ruling motives are presented distinctly if without any shading, and are at times dignified and impressive—more impressive in their crude truthfulness than the high-flown gallantry which is the sole motive at work in the tragi-comedies of most of Hardy's successors.

The damning fault of Hardy's tragedies, as of all his work, is the execrable style. He claimed to be
Style. a disciple of Ronsard, and permitted himself all the licences which the latter demanded for poetic diction. But Hardy was not, like Ronsard, a poet. He was an improviser without taste. His style is painfully obscure, abounding in ellipses, inversions, archaisms, and coinages. It is ungrammatical and undistinguished, and at the same time affected and bombastic.

Hardy's tragedies were not the most immediately popular and influential part of his work, but they
The Classic Tradition. preserved and handed on to later writers, as Mairet, Tristan, and Corneille, the main features of the tragic tradition established by Jodelle and his followers. These features are the historical subject, the grave and heightened style, and the concentrated action. Though Hardy allows himself the complete liberty, as regards the imaginary place and duration of the action, which was traditional on the popular stage, he dramatises in his tragedies not a whole story but a final crisis. In *Coriolan*, for example, which, like Shakespeare's play, is based on Plutarch, Hardy begins with the banishment of Coriolanus and his interview with Aufidius. Thereafter Hardy selects for presentation much the same

scenes as Shakespeare. He has not succeeded, however, in presenting the crisis — the conflict between outraged pride and filial affection — with the logical precision and eloquent fulness with which Corneille would have handled the theme. The French drama had to travel a long way and through a variety of experiments before it attained the shining summit of the *Cid*.

The main road through which it was to travel was indicated by Hardy not in the tragedies, but the tragi-comedies based on Spanish and other "novelle," and the closely related pastorals inspired by the *Aminta* and the *Pastor Fido*. The former are, as has been said, the characteristic story-plays of the Renaissance in all countries where the romantic or mediæval type of drama was not entirely superseded by the classical. Spain, France, England, and Holland all produced them in abundance.[1] There is no evidence that Hardy's were modelled on the plays of Lope de Vega. They are drawn from the same source as those of the English and Dutch dramatists

Tragi-comedies.

---

[1] Even in Italy, where the influence of classical tragedy and comedy predominated (see *The Earlier Renaissance*, pp. 323-334), there were composed, besides the imitations of Plautus and Terence, a number of *novelle* or adventure comedies. Such were the comedies of Araldo, J. Nardi, B. Accolti, &c., most of the comedies of the *Accademici Intronati* of Siena, and of the more famous Giovanni Battista della Porta. The plots of many of the French tragi-comedies of this period were borrowed from them, as well as from Spanish sources. See A. S. Stiefel, *Unbekannte italienische Quellen Jean de Rotrous*, 1891, contributed to the *Zeitschrift für französische Sprache*, 1879, where the same writer has continued his investigations of the debt of French comedy to Italian.

—contemporary " novelle," or stories of a similar character from classical sources. The universal theme is the adventures of lovers. In *Felismène* he dramatises the story from Montemayor's *Diana*, which Shakespeare used for the *Two Gentlemen of Verona*. *La Force du Sang* and *La Belle Égyptienne* are versions of stories by Cervantes, which Middleton has woven together in *The Spanish Gypsy*.

There is not much to be said critically of Hardy's tragi-comedies. There is less character-drawing than in the tragedies. They have none of the brilliant complication and dialogue of the Spanish, nor of the exquisite poetry of the English. If the serious scenes are not inferior to those of Rodenburg and Brederoo, there are none of the vigorous comic scenes, vivid pictures of popular life in Amsterdam, with which the latter brightened his dull love-stories. Hardy never ventures outside the four corners of the story he is dramatising to draw from real life, polite or vulgar. The pastorals differ from the tragi-comedies only in the conventional setting. They are stories of the cross-wooing of shepherds and shepherdesses, the wantonness of satyrs, the avarice of parents, and the dark oracles of gods. To indicate their more poetic and unreal character, Hardy uses an octosyllabic line instead of Alexandrines; but he was quite unable to give them the charm of sentiment and poetry which distinguished their Italian originals, and alone could give life to these forerunners of opera and its banalities.

Five of Hardy's plays on mythological subjects—

Procris, Alceste, Ariadne, Le Ravissement de Proserpine, and *La Gigantomachie*—stand somewhat by themselves. These mythological subjects attracted dramatists in all countries at the Renaissance, but not generally with much result. The *Alceste* is a very free adaptation of Euripides, in which the character of Admetus is well sustained. The *Ariadne*, based on Ovid, is much inferior to Thomas Corneille's later play on the same subject.

To 1617 Hardy reigned without a rival. Indeed, until 1625 there was no sign of any general awakening of interest in the drama in that polite world which had begun to rule the destinies of French literature. The rise of new fashions in poetic style in the "correctness" of Malherbe and the elegant conceits of Marino's admirers; the efflorescence of a new prose in the splendid and polished periods of Balzac; the refinement of conversation; the interest in pastoral and polite romance awakened by d'Urfé's *Astrée*—these were sufficient to absorb attention. The theatre was neglected as barbarous. It was not till 1634 that Corneille could boast that it had superseded the romances in public interest.

Hardy's followers.

The movement which led to that culmination began in 1617 with the publication of Théophile de Viau's *Amours Tragiques de Pyrame et Thisbé*, a tragedy, but in the spirit of Hardy's tragi-comedies, whose high-flown sentiment and Marinistic elegances of style fascinated the polite world. The purer taste of a later age ridiculed the dagger which

Théophile and Racan.

blushed for its crimes, but Théophile's style is not all "points." The prophetic dream of Thisbe's mother is eloquently and dramatically described. About two years later Racan appealed to the prevalent taste for pastoral kindled by *L'Astrée*, and the enthusiasm for Italian literature, with his *Arthénice*, recast later as *Les Bergeries*. Racan's play has all the dramatic vapidness of the *genre*, but is the first French play with anything of the poetic beauty of its models, the *Aminta* and the *Pastor Fido*. It contains some delicious description in musical and flowing verses—

> "Aussitôt qu'il fit jour, j'y menais mes brebis :
> À peine du sommet je voyais la première
> Descendre dans ces prés qui bornent la rivière,
> Que j'entendis au loin sa musette et sa voix,
> Qui troublaient doucement le silence des bois ;
> Quelle timide joie entra dans ma pensée !"

Crude plays to amuse the Paris public, which still formed the bulk of the audience, continued to be produced for many years; but the movement which Théophile[1] and Racan[1] thus inaugurated gradually developed, bringing the drama more and more within the range of polite interest, and involving it thereby in the general development of French literature. The immediate consequence was not, of course, the emergence of tragedy and comedy of the classical type. The taste of the day was for romance full of high-flown polite sentiment and elegant writing. To this taste the drama had to minister.

The flourishing of Tragi-comedy.

---

[1] *Œuvres, &c.*, see notes, pp. 249, 254.

Tragedy remained for some years where Hardy had left it. Comedy was tentatively experimented in. Up to 1634, when Mairet's *Sophonisbe* was produced, the popular, almost the universal, type of play produced was the tragi-comedy, abounding in incident, romantic in sentiment, and generally not a little high-flown and super-elegant in style. The pastorals, which were especially admired in cultured circles, and about which literary discussion of the Unities chiefly gathered at first, were only a particular species of the general type. The great sources of inspiration were Italy and especially Spain. The plays of Lope de Vega and other Spanish dramatists were closely translated or freely adapted. The same was done with Italian *novella* comedies; and the Italian pastorals remained the unapproached models of all French plays of the kind. To give any detailed account of the authors of these plays is impossible in our space. Jean de Mairet, Jean de Rotrou, Balthasar Baro, La Calprenède, Georges de Scudéry, Tristan l'Hermite, Pierre du Ryer, all are at work from 1625 or 1628 onwards, and Corneille himself appears in 1629. We must confine ourselves to tracing the process by which, from tragi-comedy and its unreal world of romance, there emerged tragedy portraying the deepest passions of the human heart, and comedy reflecting the manners of actual life. In this connection the names of first importance are Jean de Mairet, and the great Corneille himself. Rotrou is intrinsically, doubtless, a worthier second to Corneille than Mairet, but Rotrou's genius was romantic. No one followed his Spanish masters with more gusto, or recalls some of the Elizabethans more vividly. It was only under Corneille's influence that Rotrou essayed tragedy. Though he is a less great and less interesting writer, Mairet is the more important historically, because in tragedy his relation to Corneille resembles in some degree that of Marlowe to Shakespeare.

Born in Besançon in 1604, educated in Paris, Mairet[1] was only sixteen when in 1625 he produced his first tragi-comedy *Chriséide et Arimande*, based on an incident in the *Astrée*. It is not a good play,— Mairet himself called it "un péché de ma jeunesse,"—but it was successful, and gained him the patronage of the Duc de Montmorency, which he enjoyed till the death of the latter in 1638. *Sylvie* appeared in 1626, and was an immense success. In 1629 he wrote *Silvanire*, an essay in more correct Italianate pastoral, which was published in 1631 in elaborate form, and with a preface on the Unities which has generally been taken to mark an epoch in the history of French dramatic theory and practice. *Les Galanteries du Duc d'Ossone*, a rather coarse experiment in comedy, followed in 1632, and *Sophonisbe*, the herald of the new tragedy, in 1634. The *Cid* eclipsed Mairet's star, greatly to his own chagrin. While Corneille effected the triumph of tragedy, Mairet slipped back to tragi-comedies. Alike as a dramatist and a poet he was outshone, and his

[1] No modern collected edition. *Silvanire*, ed. R. Otto, Bamberg, 1890, with a full and interesting preface on the history of the Unities. *Sophonisbe*, ed. K. Vollmöller, Heilbronn, 1888.

later plays, though enumerated in histories, are never read. He did not die till 1686.

Of the plays mentioned, those important for the history of the drama are *Sylvie, Silvanire,* and *Sophonisbe.*

Sylvie. The first is a pastoral tragi-comedy of unusual interest, both of story and character; and the style, though full of affectations,— there is a dagger here too, "qui va rougir de ton ingratitude,"—and, as in all Mairet's work, unequal, is vigorous and poetic. It is the story of a prince wooing a shepherdess, of the scruples of her father and match-making eagerness of her mother, and of the magic employed by the king to punish the lovers and prevent the marriage. The wooing scenes are natural and affecting; and in those between the parents there is just a touch of the homely realism and humour with which the English and Dutch dramatists invest such scenes, but which was alien to the polite spirit that was more and more to dominate French drama. The play, in short, has all the story interest of tragicomedy, with scenes that border on pure tragedy on the one hand and on comedy on the other. *Silvanire* is much more conventional, and, in consequence, uninteresting. Its importance centres in the introduction on the Unities.

The Unities of Place and Time as well as of Subject, imported from Italy in the sixteenth century by

The Unities. critics and academic dramatists, were unknown to the popular and living drama. They revived about this time as a subject of critical discussion in literary and polite circles where both Italian literature and Italian criticism were in high esteem. The superiority of the *Aminta* and the *Pastor Fido* was ascribed to their adoption, just as Sidney found a proof of the barbarity of English plays in their neglect, and Jonson followed suit even in the face of Shakespeare's achievement. The universal learned tradition of the Renaissance identified dramatic "art" with obedience to the principles extracted from Aristotle by the critics, of whom none stood in higher esteem at this time than Scaliger and Heinsius. Mairet was invited by the Comte de Cramail and the Cardinal de la Vallette to write a "correct" pastoral on Italian lines, and the outcome was *Silvanire*, the recast of a play in blank verse written by d'Urfé at the request of Marie de Médicis. *Silvanire* was published in elaborate form, with the famous critical preface, but the play was a failure and the question was not decided. François Ogier had, in 1628, attacked the doctrine vigorously in a preface to *Tyr et Sidon*, a long and irregular play by Jean de Schelandre; and in the years which immediately followed much was written for and against, the opponents having by no means the worst of the argument. There was, in fact, no inner justification for the Unities in either the pastoral or the tragicomedy. The interest of the latter consists in variety of incident, and the happy emergence of the lovers from a series of trials and mishaps which could only with the utmost improbability be packed into the course of a single day. The dramatic crisis of the pastoral is too slight to make the question of time one of any importance. It was somewhat different with tragedy, in which the French tradition, even as preserved by Hardy, was in favour of a short concentrated action, the dramatisation not of a whole story but a single crisis. To such a type of play, an approximation, at any rate, to a strict unity of time and place might lend intensity and *éclat*. The rigid enforcement of the rules—to which Corneille bowed his head somewhat unwillingly—was a triumph of pedantry, and of the spirit of social etiquette, which enforces its rules with a rigour compared with which religious, moral, and artistic laws operate uncertainly; but this triumph was possible only because in the *Cid* and its successors Corneille evolved a type of tragic action to which a rapid evolution is essential.

After *Silvanire*, Mairet experimented in comedy—which was still represented on the stage only by popular farces, the descendants of the mediæval farces modified by the influence of the Italian *commedia dell' arte* with its stock characters; and in *Virginie*, which has nothing to do with the daughter of Virginius and victim of Appius Claudius, he produced a melodramatic tragicomedy in accordance with the rule of twenty-four hours. Then in 1634, realising possibly the need, for the observance of the Unities, of an appropriate crisis, he turned abruptly to tragedy, which had been for many years neglected, and wrote *Sophonisbe*, the first regular play which in any degree justifies its regularity. The unity of place is not interpreted rigidly, but the time of action is

Sophonisbe.

twenty-four hours, beginning one day and ending the next, the bridal night intervening. The action of the first three acts — the defeat of Syphax, followed by the marriage of his wife Sophonisba to the victorious Massanissa—is got into the twenty-four hours only at the expense of improbability, and that of the kind that jars upon our feelings; but the fourth and fifth acts contain just the kind of incident which Corneille was to make the typical plot of tragedy—a rapid, because intense, conflict between the passion of Massanissa and Roman policy embodied in Scipio. Mairet is not capable of the splendid and sustained eloquence with which Corneille, in his best days, would have elaborated the situation; but even Corneille did not disdain, when he wrote *Horace*, to borrow from the dying speech of Sophonisba.

With *Sophonisbe* Mairet's work culminated. His later plays need not detain us. The further development of comedy, the final crystallisation of classical French tragedy, and the purification and heightening of dramatic style were the work of a young dramatist who had begun to write some five years earlier, and who, after experiments by no means devoid of interest in the direction of comedy, received from Mairet's *Sophonisbe* an impetus which, after a little preliminary stumbling, carried him into the path that he and French tragedy were to follow henceforward.

Pierre Corneille[1] (1606-1684) was, like Malherbe, a

---

[1] *Œuvres*, ed. M. Marty-Laveaux, 12 vols., Paris, 1862-68 (*Grands Écrivains de la France*). Felix Hémon, *Le Théâtre de Corneille*, 4 vols., Paris, 1887. Studies in the histories and by the writers

Norman, the son of an *avocat* holding an official position in Rouen. He was educated by the Jesuits, showing a taste for Latin verses, adopted the profession of his father, and held and discharged the duties of certain offices until as late as 1650. The labours and ambitions of the poet did not exclude those of the citizen and family man. During the years in which his finest and most original work was done he was a magistrate in Rouen, visiting Paris at intervals to arrange for the production of his plays, and to mingle, a little awkwardly, and not with all the dignity of his own heroes, in the literary and polite circles of Richelieu and the Hôtel de Rambouillet.

Corneille.

Rouen was frequently visited by the travelling companies of actors, of whose importance we have already spoken. For one of these, originally the *Comédiens du Prince d'Orange*, under Guillaume Desgilberts, Sieur de Mondory, Corneille wrote his first play, *Mélite*; and with it the company opened in Paris (1629) a career of successful rivalry to the *Comédiens du Roi*, which after some trouble, due to the privileges of the older company, culminated in the opening, in 1634, of the

Mélite.

---

mentioned in opening bibliographical notes. A complete bibliography of the editions, translations, and criticisms of Corneille was issued by M. Émile Picot, *Bibliographie Cornélienne*, 1876. Voltaire's notes on Corneille are piquant and characteristic. Guizot, *Corneille et son Temps*, Paris, 1842 (first ed. 1813), is a notable work. Since the publication of Petit de Julleville's *Histoire Générale*, in which the article on Corneille is by M. Jules Lemaitre, has appeared M. Lanson's *Corneille*, Paris, 1898 (*Les Grands Écrivains français*).

Théâtre du Marais, the second theatre in Paris. Whether Corneille's play was, as tradition says, suggested by an incident in his own earliest love affair, is a matter of small importance. What is important is that in it Corneille struck out, almost unaided, a new and interesting line. He knew nothing apparently of the academic comedy of Larivey, for he tells us he had never heard of the Unities: "Je n'avais pour guide qu'un peu de sens commun avec les exemples de feu Hardy." He preserves the conventional plot of the tragi-comedies of pastoral,—*Mélite* has been called "a pastoral without shepherds,"—but instead of unreal shepherds and romantic princes he endeavoured to draw gentlemen and ladies from real life. It is the first essay in polite realistic comedy,—for the *Duc d'Ossone* is merely a farcical and indecent extravaganza.

The success of *Mélite* brought Corneille to Paris, where he heard for the first time of the rule of twenty-four hours. It was the only rule talked of at that time, he tells us—a proof that the revived interest in the Unities came mainly from the study of Italian pastoral plays. To fall in with the fashion Corneille wrote *Clitandre* (1630-32), a crude and thorough-going tragi-comedy, the absurdity of whose incidents is only heightened by their compression into twenty-four hours. He then returned to the kind of comedy he had sketched in *Mélite*, and *La Veuve* (1634), *La Galerie du Palais* (1634), *La Suivante* (1634 ?), *La Place Royale* (1635), and *L'Illusion* (1636), in themselves, and in the suc-

Comedies.

cessive changes introduced into the texts, show the
steady and determined effort of the author to reproduce the manners and conversation of the polite world.
In *La Galerie* and *La Place Royale* the scene is laid
in a recognisable part of Paris, and we see and
hear gentlemen and ladies, valets and lady's-maids,
"cheapening" and gossipping at the milliner's and
bookseller's. This is the chief merit of the plays. The
plots are improbable, the wit not very striking, and
the characters shadowy. The two last are the best in
virtue of their "humours" and raillery. Alidor in
La Place Royale is an original and thoroughly Corneillian figure. He loves and is loved, but rebels against
the tyranny of his own passion,—

> "Comptes-tu mon esprit entre les ordinaires ?
> Penses-tu qu'il s'arrête aux sentiments vulgaires ?
> Les règles que je suis ont un air tout divers ;
> Je veux la liberté dans le milieu des fers.
> Il ne faut point servir d'objet qui nous possède ;
> Il ne faut point nourrir d'amour qui ne nous cède :
> Je le hais s'il me force ; et quand j'aime, je veux
> Que de ma volonté dépendent tous mes vœux :
> Que mon feu m'obéisse, au lieu de me contraindre ;
> Que je puisse à mon gré l'enflammer et l'éteindre,
> Et, toujours en état de disposer de moi
> Donner, quand il me plaît, et retirer ma foi."

This combination of arrogance and subtlety reappears in all Corneille's great characters. In
L'Illusion Clindor is an excellently drawn type of the
Spanish picaresque hero. Matamore, the Gascon captain, is less amusing than interesting as a herald of
Corneille's tragic eloquence. Corneille was to do finer

work in comedy than any of these early plays, but his first and most signal triumph was to be in tragedy.

Mairet's *Sophonisbe* made tragedy the fashion immediately. Scudéry's *La Mort de César* and *Didon*, Mairet's *Marc Antoine,* Benserade's *Cléopâtre,* the *Mithridate* of La Calprenède, and Corneille's *Médée* are not all that appeared in 1635.

Tragedy.

The common features of these tragedies are the historic subject, and the elevated declamatory style. The influence of Seneca and even of the Greek tragedies is obvious; but there is no return to the elegiac and lyrical Senecan tragedy of Montchrestien and Garnier. The interest of plot, of incident, and generally of love—the love of the romances and tragicomedies—is retained. Corneille's idea of improving upon the *Medea* of Seneca is to complicate the intrigue. Rotrou, in his version of the same author's *Hercules Furens*, gives Iolé a lover to whom she is constant. There is more of character-drawing than in the tragicomedies, attention being more fixed on the central persons. But this dramatic interest proper is still uncertain. There is no clear conception of the nature of a tragic conflict, of an action in which incident and eloquence alike are of interest only as they help to render intelligible and impressive the conflict of the soul. Corneille's *Médée* is an accumulation of horrors. There is no conflict in the soul of Medea—only a wild fury; and most of the finer touches, including the famous "Moi! et c'est assez," are Seneca's.

This was in 1635. At the end of the following year

appeared *Le Cid;* and French tragedy emerged from the confused scaffolding which had concealed and prepared its growth in clear and majestic proportions. Almost as by an accident Corneille had divined the right way, seen whither the centre of the interest must be transferred to produce great serious drama. From a Spanish play crowded with incongruous incident he constructed a tragedy, in which all the interest of suspense that the most skilfully woven tragi-comedy could evoke is sustained and intensified, not by elaborate intrigue and surprising recognitions, but by a moral dilemma, a conflict of the soul. What the *élite* of Paris crowded Mondory's theatre and waited breathless to see was not what would happen next, but what Rodrigue and Chimène would do. When Rodrigue entered Chimène's chamber to offer himself to her vengeance, "il s'élevait un certain frémissement dans l'assemblée, qui marquait une curiosité merveilleuse, et un redoublement d'attention pour ce qu'ils avaient à se dire dans un état si pitoyable." And the eloquence with which the play shines is subordinated to the same end. It does not deploy itself in irrelevant moral, and political "sentences." The description of Rodrigue's defeat of the Moors is in the approved classical style of the *nuntius*. The actors were not willing to forgo these oratorical opportunities. But otherwise the finest speeches exist not for their own sake, but to portray with subtlety and animation the war of motives, the conflict in Rodrigue and Chimène—less relevantly in the Infanta—between honour and passion.

It is an intellectual rather than a purely emotional conflict, and this was to be the case in all Corneille's plays. From the first we are conscious of missing the indubitable accents of the heart, the "nature" of Shakespeare or Racine. When Chimène finds herself first alone after her father's death, it is no outcry of filial anguish that we hear, but the subtle dialectic of a case of conscience,—

> "Ma passion s'oppose à mon ressentiment;
> Dedans mon ennemi je trouve mon amant;
> Et je sens qu'en dépit de toute ma colère
> Rodrigue dans mon cœur combat encore mon père:
> Il l'attaque, il le presse, il cède, il se defend
> Tantôt fort, tantôt faible, et tantôt triomphant;
> Mais en ce dûr combat de colère et de flamme,
> Il déchire mon cœur sans partager mon âme:
> Et quoique mon amour ait sur moi de pouvoir,
> Je ne consulte point pour suivre mon devoir.
> Je cours sans balancer où mon honneur m'oblige.
> Rodrigue m'est bien cher, son intérêt m'afflige;
> Mon cœur prend son parti; mais malgré son effort
> Je sais ce que je suis, et que mon père est mort."

The will at war with, but triumphant over, every opposition, was, now and henceforth, for Corneille the centre of dramatic interest, the subject of his greatest achievements, and the source of his farthest aberrations from nature and truth.[1]

---

[1] Corneille's idealisation of the will—which is also Descartes' in the *Traité des Passions*—has been traced by M. Lanson and other French critics to the influence on French character of the civil wars. This theory, however, hardly allows for the fact that the phenomenon is not confined to France. Corneille's and Descartes' "volonté" is the Italian *virtù*; and the hero with indomitable will had already appeared on the Elizabethan stage, and was to reappear in Milton's

The brilliant success of *Le Cid* evoked the fierce jealousy of Corneille's fellow-dramatists,[1] and led to a pamphlet warfare in which Mairet and Georges de Scudéry (1601 - 1667) — the brother of Madeleine and a prolific writer of high-flown tragi-comedies — took the lead. There were the usual accusations of plagiarism—all the dramatists of the day were in greater or less measure indebted to the Spanish playwrights—but the important question raised was that of the Unities. Corneille had in fact evolved the type of tragedy for which a close approximation to the unities of time and place—in the skilful hands of Racine their complete acceptance—had internal justification. He had adhered, at the expense of some improbability, to the twenty-four hours (Rodrigue's defeat of the Moors occurs in the night between the first and second days), but he had not maintained a pedantic fixity of scene. Scudéry,

The Quarrel over the Cid.

epics and tragedy. It was an aristocratic ideal heightened by the emancipation of the Renaissance and the study of Seneca, and intensified by religious and political warfare. What was new and striking in Corneille was the union of this will with the argumentative subtlety of a Norman *avocat* and a pupil of the Jesuits. Characteristically the ideal is not found in the Dutch literature sketched in an earlier chapter. Yet no one could accuse the Dutch of the War of Independence of weakness of will. But the source of that strength was not aristocratic egotism and pride. It was duty ; and duty—obedience to God and loyalty to country—is the ideal of Hooft and Vondel, of Huyghens and Cats.

[1] Like Jonson with his prologues and epilogues, Corneille intensified this ill-will by the arrogant self-laudation of the lines entitled *Excuse à Ariste*, published shortly after the *Cid*, where he declares, "Je ne dois qu'à moi seul toute ma renommée." Armande Gaste, *La Querelle du Cid*, Paris, 1898, reprints all the documents, with introduction.

in spite of an excellent dissuasive letter from Balzac, appealed to the recently founded Academy. Chapelain had based the Unities, not on Aristotle but on reason, the *à priori* reason by which Descartes was preparing to explain the universe. Richelieu himself was a disappointed author. Accordingly a committee was appointed, and a report drawn up by Chapelain, almost at the dictation of Richelieu, in which the *Cid* was condemned on the principles of that "art" which Jonson told Drummond "Shakespeare wanted," and for wanting which Lope de Vega had to defend himself on the ground of popular taste.

Corneille never admitted that he accepted the decision of the Academy, but it was impossible to ignore the opinion of such a body at a time when cultured and polite circles had become the sole arbiter of letters. The observance of the Unities was not a rule of art—Corneille is never weary of showing the improbabilities they involve—but it had become a *convenance*, a proof of decency and good tone. He accepted it; he dedicated his next play to Richelieu; and in accordance with the same academic taste he turned from Spanish subjects to classical and historic themes. The result was not entirely a gain. The tradition of the stage under Spanish and Italian influence, as well as that of the romances, had made "l'amour" the supreme dramatic motive. Corneille, who was not, like Racine, a subtle student of emotions, never outgrew the conception of love he had learned from Spanish plays and heroic romances,—a conception in full harmony with the romantic theme and

[margin: Corneille accepts the Unities.]

spirit of plays like *Le Cid* and *Don Sanche d'Aragon,*
—much less so with more essentially tragic themes.
But with this qualification it may be admitted that
the next three tragedies which Corneille produced—
Horace (1640), *Cinna* (1640), and *Polyeucte* (1643)—
are the flower of his work in interest of situation
and character. His heroes or heroines have not yet
become monsters of will, following their perverted
ideals through labyrinths of subtle and distorted
reasoning. If they rise above the normal, it is in
virtue of qualities that have their root in what is
best in human nature, qualities on whose occasional
manifestation the welfare of the race depends.

In *Horace* he sketches the fierce, almost monstrous,
patriotism of a small state conscious of its great
destinies, yet still in the throes of the
first struggle for bare existence. The
ideal Roman of the seventeenth century is not quite
a real person, but in the light of more recent history
it is difficult to say that excesses of patriotism, such
as the older and younger Horace are guilty of, must
be untrue to nature. The criticism which Corneille
passes upon his own play, that it lacks unity because
the life of the hero is twice exposed, is strangely
pedantic. It is not the life or death of Horace which
constitutes the crucial interest of the play, but the
whole moral situation and its issue in action.

Horace.

From Rome in the throes of birth he passed to
the equally idealised period of the early
empire. Transcendent virtue shines here
in Augustus with a mellower light. The mutual

Cinna.

passion of Cinna and Æmilie does not interest. "L'amour" in Corneille's tragedies is merely a conventional pretext for desperate resolutions and subtle casuistry. It is the wisdom and eloquence, combined with dramatic propriety and impressiveness, of the two great scenes between Augustus and Cinna, which lend the play a singular elevation and charm. The Senecan drama had cultivated argument and eloquence on moral and political themes, but never with a dramatic effect. When Corneille himself essayed it again in *Sertorius* he saved a poor play from complete failure, but was unable to give the scene any real dramatic justification.

In *Polyeucte* Christian zeal takes the place of moral wisdom. This play and *Théodore*, with Rotrou's *St Genest*, like Vondel's *Maeghden, Peter en Pauwel*, and *Maria Stuart*, are a result of the Catholic revival, and the quickened enthusiasm for the martyr and virgin reflected in so much of the poetry and the literature of the day. There is no reason to suppose that Corneille's work has—even so much as Vondel's — any direct relation with the mediæval drama. Each dramatises his saint's legends in the form he uses for other subjects. Neither makes any reference to the Mysteries, but both justify their choice of sacred subjects by the authority of Buchanan, Grotius, and Heinsius. Corneille's saint is almost as outrageous as his Roman patriot, but around him, and coming under the influence of his exalted character and triumphant death, stand three peculiarly interesting figures—Pauline, Sevère, and Félix. In variety of character-interest the play is superior to any of its predecessors. *Pompée*, which followed *Polyeucte* immediately, is wanting in distinct, intelligible purpose, but Cornélie is a very characteristic figure.

After *Pompée*, Corneille turned aside for a moment from tragedy to try his hand once again at comedy.

Le Menteur. He found his inspiration and model in a Spanish play. *Le Menteur* (1642) is a clever adaptation to the not always congenial conditions of the classic stage of a comedy of character and intrigue by Juan Ruiz de Alarçón y Mendoza. Viguier's analysis in Marty-Laveaux's edition brings out clearly his main contention, that as an elaborate and yet naturally evolved intrigue the play has suffered from being forced into the rigid Unities, but that as a study of a "humour" Corneille's comedy has preserved, and at times heightened, all that is most piquant and delightful in the original. In the history of French comedy it marks the highest limit attained before Molière. Corneille's earlier plays, though original in design, are somewhat colourless. In *Le Menteur* we have happy touches of contemporary manners set off by humour of character and situation; while the dialogue, especially between Dorante the liar and his amazed valet Cliton, is sparkling and witty. *La Suite du Menteur* (1643) is not a "suite" at all. Corneille has merely spoiled a fine romantic comedy of Lope de Vega's by attempting to connect it with the brilliantly successful predecessor. The Dorante of the second play has as little to do with the hero of the first as the Falstaff of the *Merry Wives* with the hero of *Henry IV*.

In *Rodogune* (1644) there is no sign of any abatement of Corneille's power. The brilliance of his oratorical verse is in its zenith; but the elaborateness with which the main situation is constructed, and the characters balanced against one another, marks a recession from the tragedy of character which the *Cid* had inaugurated towards tragi-comedy or melodrama. Both Cleopatra and Rodogune are monsters, and the virtuous twins a trifle absurd. As thrilling melodrama it would have gained from the more complete catastrophe with which an Elizabethan dramatist would indubitably have closed the fifth act. *Théodore* (1645), a saint-play on the trying subject of the virgin who, to preserve her vow, will submit to dishonour, rather than to marry the man whom she loves, was deservedly a failure. *Heraclius* (1646-47), from which Calderon borrowed suggestions for *Life is a Dream*, with its confusion of persons and consequent perils of incest and death, is frankly melodrama—that is, drama which thrills us not by the vivid and adequate presentation of the chances and sorrows to which life is inevitably exposed, but by the accumulation of improbable horrors. *Don Sanche d'Aragon* (1650)—which Corneille entitled a "comédie héroïque" because of the exalted rank of the characters—is a delightful romantic play inspired by the same chivalrous and gallant spirit that animates the *Cid*. It was immediately preceded by *Andromède*, a mythological piece written merely for elaborate spectacular presentation; and it was followed in 1651 by *Nicomède*, which, though entitled a tragedy, is almost as romantic in spirit as *Don Sanche*, though more entirely a play of character. It is a kind of counterpart to Mairet's *Sophonisbe*. Barbaric virtue here proves victorious over Roman policy. *Pertharite* (1652), which was apparently intended to magnify the power of marital affection, failed rather ludicrously, and Corneille withdrew for a time from the stage.

When he returned in 1659 a new spirit was beginning to make itself felt. The high ideals of the Hôtel de Rambouillet, of the first age of gallantry and refinement, were yielding to an increasing regard for nature and truth. Corneille's exaltation of the will, the power to choose and follow at all costs ideals lofty or perverted, had conduced to a neglect or conventional treatment of the normal passion of the heart. A reaction set in. In the plays and operas of Philippe Quinault sentiment — "tendresse" — is supreme. From extravagance in this direction the drama was saved by Racine, not by any reversion to the heroic, but by a more truthful and beautiful delineation of the passions of the heart and their power to make, or more often to mar, the destinies of men and women. Corneille, when he was tempted back to the stage by Fouquet in 1659, found himself out of touch with the prevailing taste. His own style had grown harder. In *Nicomède* he had already shown his tendency to portray an almost passionless strength of will. In his later political

Change of taste.

plays, such as *Sertorius, Sophonisbe, Bérénice,* the treatment of the feelings is frigid and unreal to the last degree, with the result that it is impossible to follow with any interest the high and subtle volitions they inspire. Bérénice sacrifices herself in much the same language as Chimène.

> "C'est à force d'amour que je m'arrache au vôtre,
> Et je serais à vous si j'aimais comme une autre,"

is very like

> "Tu t'es, en m'offensant, montré digne de moi,
> Je me dois, par ta mort, montrer digne de toi."

But the old ardour is gone, and Bérénice leaves us cold. At the same moment Racine was tracing the movements of the heart with a beauty and force of which Corneille had never at his best been capable. It was not to be wondered that his star declined. But this was the case only as regards the plays he was producing. His masterpieces still held the stage. He still had his champions, who preferred the moral grandeur of his characters to the impassioned frailty of Racine's. In one work of his old age, too, Corneille showed an unexpected capacity for delineating tender feeling. The little ballet play of *Psyche,* which he finished for Molière, has a freshness and charm hardly to be expected in the work of an old man. It was by deliberate choice, not from want of ability, that Corneille refused to become the rival of Quinault, to make "tendresse" the principal motive of tragedy, but remained faithful to the higher and more romantic traditions of his youth.

Whatever place French classical tragedy holds in the history of the drama, Corneille was undoubtedly its creator. As we have said at the beginning of this chapter, it is only a superficial criticism which could bring under one name the tragedy of the sixteenth century and that of Corneille and Racine. Undoubtedly there was a continuous tradition handed on by Hardy and Mairet which made classical tragedy the model for French tragedy. But in that tragedy as it finally took shape, the influence of tragi-comedy, as it flourished during the early years of the century, is not less apparent than that of classical tragedy.

French classical tragedy.

It was from tragi-comedy that French tragedy inherited the predominance of "l'amour" as a motive. Love had not been the principal moving passion in the sixteenth-century tragedies; it was rather revenge. And in Elizabethan tragedy, which grew up also under Senecan influence, love found its proper place in romance and comedy more often than in tragedy. It was because French tragedy sprang so directly out of plays the spirit of which was derived from Spanish tragi-comedies, Italian pastorals, and the romances of the day, that "l'amour" became its principal motive. In Corneille and his contemporaries the "amour" is still the high-flown conventional passion of the romances. Racine made it at once a more natural and a more essentially tragic passion, influenced doubtless by the study of Virgil and Euripides as well as of the human heart, but he did not depose love from its tragic supremacy.

L'Amour.

And if we turn from the spirit of French tragedy to its form, we can see equally clearly the influence of tragi-comedy with its highly-wrought interest of suspense and surprise. In the sixteenth-century tragedy there was little or no interest of plot. The story is taken as known. The play foreshadows it in dreams, describes it in the speeches of messengers, laments it in passionate and eloquent speeches, and moralises on it in choral odes. With the *Cid* all this is changed. Henceforward everything is made to help forward the action. All that is lyrical or elegiac in character is eliminated. On nothing does Corneille lay more stress than this in his theoretical writings. In no drama is there really so little idle declamation as in the French. Soliloquies occur in Shakespeare's tragedies which express character, and arise quite naturally from the action, but do not in any way further it. There are none such in French tragedy. Every soliloquy is a deliberation which ends in a choice. Every word from the beginning to the "Hélas!" at the close helps the action forward a step. And to the end the issue of the action remains uncertain. What differentiates this uncertainty from that of the story in a tragi-comedy is that it does not depend on elaborate intrigue and surprising recognitions,—at least, not in the best plays,[1]—but on the evolution of character. We are kept in suspense as to the issue of a tragedy by Cor-

---

[1] In his weaker plays Corneille falls back on the uncertainty and suspense which depend not on character but on intrigue and recognition—*e.g.*, in the *Œdipe*.

neille because we can never tell to what unexpected resolution subtle moral reasoning may lead a character of unusual strength and elevation. In Racine the same uncertainty attends the fluctuating course of violent and absorbing passion. Such a type of action is not Greek, no more than it is Shakespearean. French tragedy owes it to its evolution through tragi-comedy. And to the same cause it owes the frequent preference — almost universal in Corneille — for the happy close, the peril escaped. The adoption of the Unities was made possible by their suitability for an action of this peculiar character. Corneille, indeed, never escaped from a sense of restraint in their rigid application. The perfecting of tragedy under the limitations they imposed was left to Racine, who saw in them a signal not only for concentration of action, but for simplification, drawing closer thereby to the structure of Greek tragedy.

Corneille not only fixed the mould of French tragedy, he gave it also appropriate vesture. The *Corneille's style.* language of the drama in the first years of the century had oscillated between the bald and tasteless barbarism of Hardy's plays and high-flown "préciosité." Corneille's poetry is not without a touch of the prevalent taste for conceit,—

"Son sang sur la poussière écrivait mon devoir."

But this is not characteristic. He carried forward the movement inaugurated by Malherbe towards poetry logical in structure, rhetorical in style and verse. Corneille's poetry is not lyrical and it is not picturesque, and in both these respects differs from that of Garnier and Montchrestien. It is in closely-reasoned, eloquent declamation, in sonorously cadenced lines, that he has perhaps no rival. Dryden is our nearest parallel in English, and Corneille strikes a higher note than Dryden: his eloquence is less colloquial, and though his style varies with his inspiration, he was a more careful workman. In spirit Corneille stands closer to Jonson, even to Milton, than to Dryden. He is a characteristically French product of the same epoch, the early seventeenth century, with its high if somewhat narrow, somewhat pedantic, somewhat conventional ideals, religious, civic, and literary. Greatly as they differ from one another, there are links of community between the poet of *Paradise Regained* and the poet of *Polyeucte*. Both alike idealise the power and independence of the will. There is nothing of which man's will is not capable, no poetry too elevated and sonorous to portray its sublimity; and for both the highest and purest manifestation of this power and freedom is its consecration to the service of God. With Racine French tragedy draws closer to ordinary human nature with all its passions and frailties.

The movement towards regular tragedy, which was begun by Mairet's *Sophonisbe*, was accelerated by *Le Cid*. All the dramatists whose names are given on an earlier page turned more and more from tragi-comedy to tragedy. La Calprenède's *Mort de Mithridate* (1635) and *Comte d'Essex* (1639),

Contemporaries —Rotrou.

Scudéry's *Mort de César* (1636) and *Didon* (1636),[1] Tristan l'Hérmite's *Mariamne* (1636) and *Panthée* (1639)—embellished recasts of Hardy's plays,—Pierre du Ryer's *Alcinée* and *Scévole* (*circ.* 1644), are a few of the most notable. They are by no means all regular in the strict French classical sense of the word; and *l'amour* — the *amour* of the romances, "postiche, froid et ridicule" in Voltaire's words— is in all, or nearly all, the motive which determines the course of history at the most critical moments. This radical fault is unredeemed in them by Corneille's finer psychology of the will and the splendid eloquence of his verse. One only of Corneille's contemporaries has escaped oblivion, in virtue of a vein of imagination and naturalness which sets his work in pleasing contrast to that of most of his rivals.

Jean de Rotrou[2] (1610-1650), the son of a merchant in Dreux, for some years like Hardy and Théophile a *poète à gages*, released from this patronage by the generosity of patrons among whom was Richelieu, was traditionally the friend of Corneille, and seems to have tried to play the part of a mediator between him and Scudéry in the quarrel of *Le Cid*. He retired in

[1] A comparison of Scudéry's tragedies with those of Hardy will show clearly how tragi-comedy modified in motive, style, and characters the tragedy of the sixteenth century as that was transmitted by Hardy. Scudéry's Æneas is a model of high-flown gallantry, and his speeches of "préciosité."

[2] *Œuvres, &c.*, ed. Viollet-le-Duc, 5 vols., Paris, 1820-22. *Théâtre choisi, &c.*, ed. L. de Ronchaud, Paris, 1882, and F. Hémon, 1883. Rotrou's indebtedness to Spanish and Italian sources has been very fully worked out by A. Stiefel, *op. cit.*, and Georg Steffens, *Rotrou als Nachahmer Lope de Vegas*, 1891.

1639 to his native town, though continuing to write for the stage, and died there bravely discharging during a pestilence his duty as a magistrate.

The researches of scholars, French and German, have deprived Rotrou of much claim to originality of invention. His earlier tragi-comedies are translated more or less closely from the Spanish of Lope de Vega or the Italian of Da Porta. But while Corneille was attracted by the chivalrous spirit of the Spanish drama, what Rotrou reproduces most happily is its fancifulness and naturalness. Rotrou's imagination plays round the situations in his stories in a way that occasionally reminds an English reader of the Elizabethans. The feelings his characters express are natural, not merely conventional and stilted, and his style generally simple and flowing. In *Laure Persécutée* (1638), the feelings of a lover who has cast off his mistress yet cannot forget her, are described in a manner worthy of Dekker when most natural and felicitous; and in *L'Heureux Naufrage* (1633) are some touches that recall Shakespeare. Floronde, a princess disguised as a boy, attends Cléandre, who for her love has been banished. She is questioned regarding herself by Céphalie, who also loves Cléandre, and replies almost in the words of Julia to Silvia in the *Two Gentlemen of Verona*—

> "Pour vous la peindre mieux, vous savez qu'à la cour
> On représente en vers des histoires d'amour;
> La jeunesse nous porte à ces jeux de théâtre
> Et sur tous autrefois j'en étais idolâtre:
> Mon visage en ce temps et plus jeune et plus frais,
> Sous les habits de fille avait quelques attraits;

> Je faisais Amarante, ou Cloris, ou Sylvie,
> Et de mes actions la cour était ravie.
> Alors, il me souvient que mille fois le roi
> A fait comparaison de Floronde et de moi.
> Dieux ! disait-il à tous, la ressemblance extrême
> Voilà son même geste, et son visage même."

Rotrou's best known plays were written after the appearance of *Le Cid*, and are tragedies with a good many elements of tragi-comedy. *Le Véritable Saint Genest* (1645), adapted from *Lo fingido verdadero* of Lope de Vega, is a martyr-tragedy which catches in a simpler way some of the ardour and elevation of *Polyeucte*. There are no subtle cross-currents of feeling, however, and our attention is concentrated on the actor-martyr. *Venceslas* (1647), taken from a Spanish play by Francisco de Rojas, and *Cosroès* (1648) have more of the characteristically Corneillean conflict of motive managed, if not with the greater poet's strength and eloquence, with very considerable sincerity and dignity. The later contemporaries of Corneille who connect him most closely with his great successor, as his brother Thomas and Quinault, lie outside the range of this essay.

The salient features in the history of comedy [1] have been touched in passing. Represented at the beginning of the century by farce, not by the academic comedy of the sixteenth century, it made a fresh departure about 1629 in the work of Mairet, Corneille,

[1] Several of the comedies of this period, including Mairet's *Duc d'Ossonne*, Rotrou's *La Sœur*, and Saint-Sorlin's *Les Visionnaires*, have been reprinted, with biographical introductions, in *Le Théâtre Français au XVIe et au XVIIe Siècle*, ed. M. Édouard Fournier, Paris, n.d.

and Rotrou. Corneille's experiment was the most interesting—an endeavour to paint the life of Paris, not satirically, but realistically and comically, suggestive of one aspect of Jonson's comedies and of the *Tatler*. Pierre du Ryer's *Les Vendanges de Suresnes* (1635) was an experiment in the same direction, a study of the manners of the rich bourgeois class framed in the improbable plot of the pastoral drama. Once revived, however, comedy came under the prevailing influence of the Spanish drama. Corneille himself in *Le Menteur* and its successor, Rotrou in *La Bague d'Oubli* and *Diane*, Scarron in his burlesque *Jodelet ou le Maître valet* and *Don Japhet d'Arménie* and others, translate and adapt from the Spanish; and the general trend of this comedy is towards burlesque, the study of humours more extravagant but presented with less accumulation of detail than Jonson's. An excellent example is *Les Visionnaires* (1640) of Desmarests Saint-Sorlin, the confidant and useful servant in onerous offices of Richelieu. It is a comedy quite in the style of Jonson, from the preface explaining the "humours" of the characters to the interesting discussion of the Unities between the lady whose passion is the stage and the Ronsardising poet. But Saint-Sorlin's boasting captain is more like the captain of the *Commedia dell' Arte* than Boabadil. The scene of the play would require for probability to be the inside of an asylum. It was not to these burlesque polite comedies that Molière's work is most closely akin, but to the native and older farce, as is set forth in the next volume.

CHAPTER VIII.

ITALY AND GERMANY.

"SECENTISMO." MARINO—'LA LIRA'—'L'ADONE.' FOLLOWERS. CHIABRERA—THE ITALIAN "CANZONE" AND THE CLASSICAL ODE—BERNARDO TASSO — CHIABRERA'S PINDARICS AND "CANZONETTE." TESTI. TASSONI — CRITICISM OF ARISTOTLE AND PETRARCH—'LA SECCHIA RAPITA'— PROSE — GALILEO — D'AVILA — BENTIVOGLIO. GERMANY — LATE INFLUENCE OF RENAISSANCE. PRECURSORS. OPITZ — THEORY AND PRACTICE. FOLLOWERS — FLEMING. HYMNS. DRAMA—GRYPHIUS. SATIRE—LOGAU.

IN studying the poetry of Italy [1] in the seventeenth century, one finds oneself face to face with a phenomenon to which that much abused term decadence can be more intelligibly and legitimately applied than to anything in English or French poetry of the same period. In the affectations of Marino and his contemporaries — and one may not except altogether Chiabrera and Tassoni— we see an art which, whatever its limitations, had

[1] *Storia Letteraria d'Italia Scritta da una Società di Professori. Il Seicento*, Antonio Bellini, Milano. D'Ancona e Bacci: *Manuale della Letteratura Italiana*, vol. iii., Firenze, 1904. For other histories with comments see Elton, *Augustan Ages*, p. 382, note, and add *La Vita Italiana nel Seicento*, an issue of "conferenze tenute a Firenze nel 1894." Important periodicals are *Il Giornale Storico della Letteratura Italiana*, and *La Nuova Antologia*.

reached perfection, running to seed in the strained and feverish pursuit of novelty undirected by any new and fruitful inspiration. In "secentismo," one might venture to say, nothing is new but everything is novel. To startle and amaze was the motive of each new departure in form or verse or conceit. As Marino says—

> "È del poeta il fin la maraviglia,
> Parlo dell' eccellente e non del goffo,
> Chi non sa far stupir vada alla striglia."

But the only method of surprising that Marino and his contemporaries discovered was to heighten the notes, to make the conceits of compliment and flattery more far-fetched and hyperbolical, the descriptions more detailed and flamboyant, the horrors more hideous and grotesque, the mock-heroic more satirical and prosaic in spirit. They added no single new note or form to Italian poetry.

In lyrical poetry, despite the impatience of Petrarch's influence expressed by Marino, his work, and that of his imitators, is only the last phase in the progressive decadence which had invaded the Italian sonnet and lyric at least from Petrarch onwards. Indeed the courtly poets of the close of the fifteenth century, Cariteo, Tebaldeo, and Serafino Dall' Aquila, developed in their sonnets and *strambotti* all the extravagances of mere compliment latent in their great predecessor's work, all that tasteless pseudo-metaphysics of love, begotten of the frigid elaboration of metaphor (Addison's "mixed wit"), which M. Vianey has paraphrased from the poems

Decadence of Lyrical Poetry.

of Serafino. "Pending the fatal issue of this duel Serafino is the benefactor of his kind. Carry him into the desert and he will supply water from his eyes, fire from his heart. If a besieged castle is in want of water, call for him. Does a mariner desire wind to fill his sails, bring the poet. Is an unfortunate person freezing in winter, let him draw near. Love has put water in his eyes, the wind in his mouth, fire in his heart. And the proof that he is all fire is just that he is all water. He is like green wood which gives out water when it burns." In this poetry at the same time the more ideal conception of love gave place to the classical and sensual.[1]

Lorenzo de' Medici and Poliziano endeavoured to give new life to the Italian lyric by refining and enriching the fresh and living songs of the people; but the inspirer of cinquecentist lyric poetry was Cardinal Bembo, who revived a purer but still quite artificial Petrarchian tradition which — except in the sonnets of Michael Angelo — was little more than an exercise in style.[2] Marino's hyperboles and ingenuities are not more extravagant than those of many of his predecessors, and the prettiness which is their characteristic had appeared already, at any rate in Tasso's poetry.

Nor, although he boasted that like his townsman

[1] See Flamini, *L'Italianismo a Tempo d'Enrico III.* in *Studi di Storia Letteraria*, Livorno, 1895, and Joseph Vianey, *L'Influence Italienne chez les Précurseurs de la Pléiade* in *Annales de la Faculté des Lettres de Bordeaux*, Avril-Juin 1903. Vianey refers to Alessandro D'Ancona, *Del secentismo nella poesia cortigiana del secolo XV.* in *Studj sulla letteratura italiana de primi secoli*, Ancona, 1881.

[2] See Mazzoni, *La Lirica del Cinquecento* in *La Vita Italiana nel Cinquecento*, Milano, 1901.

Columbus he would find a new world or drown, do the experiments of Chiabrera reveal anything new in spirit or form. To reproduce the classical ode, to substitute classical imagery and sentiment for the more metaphysical and ideal strain of Petrarchian poetry, had been essayed by several poets, including Bernardo Tasso, before Chiabrera; while to make the main theme of poetry the praise of princes and heroes instead of love, was not a striking departure in a country and an age so prone to flattery.

In epic poetry, in like manner, what is novel in Marino's and Tassoni's experiments is either negation or exaggeration. In the *Adone* the chief novelty is the entire extinction of the heroic spirit which in Ariosto had never quite departed despite the prevalent tone of irony. All the ornaments of style with which that poem is overlaid can be found in the romantic-epic poems of his predecessors.[1] What Marino eviscerated, his friend and admirer Tassoni assailed with ridicule. The *Secchia Rapita* is the most original poem of the seventeenth century in Italy. Yet the heroic and burlesque had been mingled before. Tassoni has only heightened and intensified the strain of satire with which the mock-heroic is pervaded. The poetry of earlier burlesque is gone. And in all Tassoni's attacks upon the ideals of his day he was prompted more by spleen than by any clear perception of new ends and new ideals.

Of Epic.

---

[1] *Lo Stile del Marino nell' Adone ossia Analisi del Secentismo:* Sac. Dott. Enrico Canevari. Pavia, 1901.

The causes of the decadence of "secentist" literature are too complex and subtle to be discussed here.[1]

Causes. It would be rash to attribute them too entirely to the political condition of the country and the depressing influence of Jesuitism. To the latter is due rather the fact that the poetry of the "Seicento" proper was succeeded by the tame and conventional work of the "Arcadia," that Italy notwithstanding her great men of science did not share fully in the rationalist movement of the later seventeenth and of the eighteenth century, and that she therefore found no new and great inspiration until Rousseau awakened her to the enthusiasm for nature and humanity.

Of the poets mentioned, the most popular and the most influential both in Italy and abroad was Giovanni Battista Marino,[2] the Neapolitan

Marino. (1569-1625). His work excited as great enthusiasm in Italy as had Tasso's, or greater. Lope de Vega declared that he was the day to which Tasso had been the dawn; just as Denham considered that Jonson's and Shakespeare's graces were united and perfected in Fletcher. In France he was the idol of Richelieu and of the critical Chapelain, who

[1] See an interesting article by Professor Graf of Turin, *Il Fenomeno del Secentismo*, in the *Nuova Antologia*, October 1905.

[2] M. Menghini, *La Vita e le Opere di Giambattista Marino*. Roma, 1888 (a life and critical study). *Opere*, ed. G. Zirardini, Napoli, 1861. Palermo, 1864. Old editions of *La Lira*, &c., are procurable. Different editions of the *Lira* vary in details as to content, not all having, *e.g.*, the *Canzone Dei Baci*. A sumptuous edition of the *Adone* in four vols. is the Elzevier, 1678. Cheap editions are numerous. Sonnets in the *Parnaso Italiano*, tom. 41. 1784.

wrote a laudatory preface to the *Adone*, as well as of the Hôtel de Rambouillet. His influence is the predominant one in the refined work of the Scottish Drummond, and was not unfelt by Crashaw and Cowley; while in Holland, Hooft placed Petrarch and Marino at the head of Italian poets. A writer of such widespread influence deserves more careful study than has always been given to him, and fuller treatment than can be allowed here.

The son of a Neapolitan lawyer, Marino was turned out of doors by his father for debt, dissipation, and devotion to poetry. At the age of twenty he had already made himself famous throughout Italy by his voluptuous and musical *Canzone dei Baci*, and he had no difficulty in finding patrons, including the Marquis of Manso, at whose house he made the acquaintance and won the esteem of Tasso. His share in a scandalous abduction drove him to Rome, where he found fresh patrons in Crescenzio, the Pope's chamberlain, and Cardinal Aldobrandini. From Rome he accompanied the latter to Ravenna, and thence to the Court of Savoy, where his reputation as a poet and panegyrist gained him the favour of Carlo Emanuele. His quarrel with the poet Murtola, the scurrilous sonnets they wrote on one another, the attempt Murtola made on Marino's life, and the imprisonment of the latter, need not be detailed. In 1615 he left Milan for Paris, whither he had been invited by Margaret of Valois, and where he was granted a pension by Maria de' Medici. Here he enlarged, completed, and published the *Adone* in 1623.

He returned to Italy in the same year, and was received with the utmost enthusiasm in Rome, and in Naples where he died two years later.

It is clear from any careful study of the references to Marino's work that his poems circulated in manuscript before they were published. When he came to Rome he was already a well-known poet, yet he had printed only a single sonnet. In 1602 he collected and issued his earliest verses in two parts, the first consisting of sonnets (*amorose, marittime, boscherecce, lugubri, sacre e varie*), the second of madrigals and *canzoni*. The *Rime* of 1602 was enlarged by a book in 1614 and given the title of *La Lira*. The other works published in his lifetime, besides some panegyrics, and the sonnets on Murtola, were the *Galleria* (1619), a collection of madrigals on pictures and characters, mythical and historical, many of which are translated from Lope da Vega's *Epitafios*; the *Sampogna* (1620), a series of diffuse, operatic idylls; and the *Adone*. A sacred poem, the *Strage degli Innocenti*, was issued after his death, but of the long list of works which Claretti, in his preface to the third book of the *Lira*, described as finished and awaiting immediate publication, some were never issued, others would seem to have been melted down into the *Adone*.

The *Lira*—especially the first two parts—and the *Adone* are Marino's most representative works, the one of his earlier, the other of his later manner, and a just criticism would distinguish them in passing sentence on the writer. In the sonnets of *La Lira* there is not only technical perfection but beauty of description, as well as freshness and delicacy of feeling. Conceits abound, but the sensuous and voluptuous Neapolitan has few of the tasteless, pseudo-metaphysical extravagances of Tebaldeo, Cariteo, and Serafino. Marino's conceits are objective and pretty. A fair estimate of his best manner may be formed by remembering that a large number of Drummond's sonnets,[1] amorous, moral, and divine, are translated from or suggested by Marino's, and that if the Scotch poet's manner is the larger and nobler, the Italian's technique is the more perfect. A characteristic and beautful sonnet is the original of Drummond's "Alexis! here she stayed,"—

> "Quì rise o Thirse e qui ver me rivolse
> Le due stelle d' Amor la bella Clori :
> Quì per ornarmi il crin de' più bei fiori
> Al suon de le mie canne un grembo colse.
> Quì l' angelica voce in note sciolse
> C' humiliaro i piu superbi Tori :
> Quì le Gratie scherzar vidi, e gli Amori
> Quando le chiome d' or sparte raccolse.
> Quì con meco s'affisse, e quì mi cinse,
> Del caro braccio il fianco, e dolce interno,
> Stringendomi la man, l' alma mi strinse,
> Quì d' un bacio ferrimmi, e'l viso adorno
> Di bel vermiglio vergognando tinse.
> O memoria soave, ò lieto giorno!"

---

[1] See William C. Ward's edition (*Muses Library*), which prints several of the sonnets and madrigals translated. Mr Ward has not noticed "Run Shepherds" and "Alexis here." Probably others are translations. Mr Purves (*Athenæum*, Feb. 11, 1905) pointed out that *Forth Feasting* is suggested by Marino's *Tebro Festante*.

Beyond the hyperbole in the sixth line there is nothing in such a sonnet which is not purely charming, and the art is superior at every turn to Drummond's. For the delightful image of the Graces and the Loves dancing with joy when she gathered her golden hair, Drummond has only the conventional

> "Here did she spread the treasure of her hair,
> More rich than that brought from the Colchian mines;"

and Marino's closing sigh is lost in the Scotchman's platitude—

> "But ah! what serv'd it to be happy so,
> Sith passed pleasures double but new woe?"

Both the pastoral and maritime sonnets contain picturesque descriptions, such as the following of the bay of Naples:—

> "Pon mente al mar Cratone hor che'n ciascuna
> Riva sua dorme l' onda, e tace il vento:
> E notte in ciel di cento gemme, e cento
> Ricca spiega la vesta azurra, e bruna.
> Rimira ignuda, e senza benda alcuna
> Nuotando per lo mobile elemento
> Misto, e confuso l' un con l' altro argento,
> Trà le ninfe del Ciel danza la Luna.
> Vè come van per queste piagge, e quelle
> Con scintille scherzando ardenti, e chiare
> Volte in pesci le stelle, i pesci in stelle:
> Si puro il vago fondo à noi traspare
> Che frà tanti dirai lampi, e facelle
> Ecco in Ciel christallin cangiato il mare."

The hyperbolical, ingenious prettiness of the last thoughts is the characteristic of "secentismo" in

Marino's sonnets and madrigals. One gets it usually in the compliment which is the point of the poem. The following pastoral sonnet, for example, opens delightfully—

> "Pon giù l' urna gravosa ò bionda Spio,
> Ah troppo lunge è del volturno il fonte :
> Ti mostrero (se vuoi) di quà dal monte
> E men lontano, e più tranquillo un rio";

but instead of closing—as the sonnet quoted above does—in an appropriate and natural sentiment, passes into a conceit hyperbolical and ingenious, but cold as the frost-work on a window-pane—

> "vedrai poi
> Volto il fiume in argento, e l' acqua in foco
> S' avvien che specchio ei sia de' gli occhi tuoi."

And in another suggested by Theocritus's beautiful idyll, which tells how he fell in love with the young girl as she gathered fruit beside her mother, the passionate cry which Virgil translated

> "Ut vidi, ut perii ! ut me malus abstulit error !"

becomes a poor conceit—

> "Io stava in parte rimirando, e quante
> Cogliea la bianca man rose e ligustri
> Tante m' erano al cor facelle e piaghe."

Marino rehandles all the hackneyed images of the sonneteers — fire and ice, love's arrows and nets, hearts which migrate, mirrors, and little dogs; but even when absurd his conceits are both ingenious and pretty, and in the graver sonnets they are sometimes more. Those who think of Drummond as a refined and thoughtful poet, and of Marino as a decadent manufacturer of extravagant conceits, might not have suspected, till Mr Ward pointed it out, that the following and other philosophical sonnets were translations from Marino:—

> Of this fair volume which we world do name,
>   If we the sheets and leaves could turn with care,
> Of him who it corrects, and did it frame
>   We clear might read the art and wisdom rare :
> Find out his power which wildest powers doth tame,
>   His providence extending everywhere,
>   His justice which proud rebels doth not spare,
> In every page, no, period of the same :
>   But silly we, like foolish children, rest
> Well pleas'd with colour'd vellum, leaves of gold,
>   Fair dangling ribbons, leaving what is best,
> On the great writer's sense ne'er taking hold ;
>   Or if by chance our minds do muse on aught,
>   It is some picture on the margin wrought.

Of the madrigals and *canzoni* which fill the second book of the *Lira*, grace and elegance are the prevailing characteristic. Marino is a master in the art of carving heads upon cherry-stones, a Waller with more of fancy and invention, a Herrick without the classical strain which the latter got from Jonson, and without his happier choice of rural subjects.

It has seemed worth while dwelling on the prettiness and even charm of Marino's poetry, because it is frequently spoken of as though it abounded in the tasteless ingenuities of Serafino's; whereas there is more of such tasteless pseudo-metaphysics as have been exemplified above in Cowley's *Mistress* than in Marino's *Lira*. It is not in virtue of his conceits that the latter is a decadent. Marino's conceits are not worse than Shakespeare's can be. It is the absence from his poetry of any other quality than prettiness and cleverness—its barrenness of any interest of content beyond an appeal to prurience and love of flattery; and this barrenness is not so apparent in his earlier lyrical poetry as in his later idylls and epics.

For Marino's experience as the favourite poet of Italy, caressed and flattered by cardinals and princes, did not improve his poetry in spirit or form. His eulogies are vapid and rococo; his *Sampogna* a collection of idylls which suggest nothing so much as the libretto of an opera; the *Galleria* a further series of elegancies. The great work of these years was the *Adone*, which had been begun at Rome as an idyll, and consisted in 1614 of four books. It was, apparently, the adulation Marino received in France, the desire to vie with Tasso in an heroic poem, the inability of his lyrical and idyllic genius to rise to the height of a *Gerusalemme Distrutta* (of which one book was composed), that induced him to fall back on the line he had made his own — the line of voluptuous, facile, ornate description,—but to expand the *Adone* into an epic by the addition of other idylls planned for the *Sampogna*, of the astronomy and philosophy which were to have been the subject of a

The Adone, *&c.*

Polinnia,[1] by a series of pictures which might have enriched the *Galleria*, and by fresh variations on the endless theme of kisses and roses, versions in *ottava rima* of the *Canzone dei Baci* and *La Rosa* (*Lira* II.) The outcome was a poem of over forty thousand lines, in which a voluptuous and licentious story is expanded by endless digressions and diffuse, facile, irrelevant descriptions. All the conventional ornaments of cinquecentist poetry are heaped upon one another in Marino's glittering and fluent stanzas —conceits, antitheses, alliterative and other artificial sound-effects, gorgeous descriptions in which nature is embellished by art (trees have emerald leaves and golden fruit, teeth are pearls and lips are rubies), hackneyed and allegorical personifications and frigid hyperboles.[2] The taste for detailed picturesque description which had come down to the Italian poets from medieval romance, and had been intensified by the influence of classical idyll and contemporary art, divorced from everything else became a mania in

[1] This is one of the numerous works enumerated in the preface to the third book of the *Lira*, and was apparently to be a scientific poem, dealing with the structure of the universe from the elements up to God, in hymns in the style of Pindar, and of the choruses in tragedy. In the same preface the *Sampogna* is said to consist of fifty or sixty idylls. The *Polinnia*, if ever written, was never published: the *Sampogna* as published contains only twelve idylls, to which some additions were made in a second part. What I venture to suggest is that some of the material of these poems passed into the *Adone*, into whose texture are woven many myths besides that of Adonis, and which contains two allegoric-scientific cantos, the tenth and eleventh (*Le Maraviglie* and *Le Bellezze*), in which the hero visits the heavens and is instructed by Mercury.

[2] See Canevari, *op. cit*.

the *Adone*, the last Italian poem which was an event in European literature. The decline of Italy had begun half a century earlier, but the *Aminta* (1573), the *Gerusalemme Liberata* (1581), the *Pastor Fido* (1590), and the *Lira* (1602) were all works whose influence was felt far beyond Italy. The *Adone* was the last of such; though both the *Secchia Rapita* and Marino's posthumous *Strage degli Innocenti*—in which the grotesquely horrible and the sentimental are exaggerated in the same way as the romantic in the *Adone* — begot several imitations. Marino's popularity in France was short-lived, and later criticism was disposed to include Tasso and Italian poetry generally in its condemnation of "points" and tinsel.

Marino's followers were numerous. Both in verse and prose ingenious and extravagant conceit was the fashion, not least among the preachers.
Followers.
Marino boasted that he had succeeded in carrying a single metaphor through each of his prose *Dicerie Sacre*, discourses on painting, music, and the heavens. Of the Marinist poets the best known are Claudio Acchillini (1574-1640), Girolamo Preti (died 1626), whose conception of love, however, is—except in his early idyll *Salmace*—purely neo-platonic and spiritual, and Antonio Muscettola, who, besides Marinistic love-verses, composed some happier imitations of Anacreon, and a few odes which won the praises of Testi. The "sudate o fuochi" with which the first opened an ode to Richelieu has remained in literary histories as a type of "secentistic" conceit.

A purer if hardly less artificial taste than that for Marinistic love-poetry was ministered to by the elaborate and tumid odes of Gabriello Chiabrera[1] (1552-1638), a native of Savona, and fond of comparing his adventures into new regions of poetry with the achievements of his townsman Columbus. Chiabrera visited most parts of Italy in his lifetime, and enjoyed the patronage of cardinals and princes, including Carlo Emanuele; but though he was eager to have his compliments repaid with pensions, he shunned the complete immersion in court life which demoralised Marino, and the diplomatic career that gave Testi so much trouble. His works include heroic poems, tragedies, and pastorals, but his reputation rests upon his Pindaric odes, the *scherzi* and *canzonette* in which he followed Anacreon and Ronsard, his dignified epitaphs, and genial satires.

In the *canzone* of Dante and Petrarch the Italians possessed a noble and elaborate lyric which was so firmly established that, like the sonnet and the epic, it was modified but not superseded at the Renaissance by classical models. The *canzoni* of the cinquecento may be divided into those which, as Cariteo's and Tasso's, fill the Petrarchian form with the sentiments, imagery, and mythology of classical elegy, and others, such as those of Sannazaro, Bembo, and Ariosto, which

The Canzone and the Ode.

[1] *Delle Opere di G. C.*, &c. Venezia, 1730-57-82. *Rime*, Savona, 1847. *Poesie liriche scelte da F.-L. Polidori*, Firenze, 1865 (with introd. by Carducci). *Id. scelte ed annotate da G. Francesia*, Torino, 1872. *Canzoni, Parn. It.*, tom. 41, 1784, and Mathias, *Componimenti Lirici dei Piu Illustri Poeti d'Italia*, tom. II., 1802.

retain the "concetti metafisici ed ideali" of Italian poetry.[1] Efforts were made, however, to adopt the form and also the themes of the classical ode. Trissino, Alamanni, and Minturno experimented in the Pindaric structure, writing laudatory odes to the French King or the Emperor divided into *volta, rivolta,* and *stanza,* just as Ben Jonson later addressed "that noble pair Sir Lucius Cary and Sir H. Morison" in a Pindaric ode with *turn, counter-turn,* and *stand.* These experiments were isolated and unsuccessful. Better results were achieved in the moralising Horatian ode by Bernardo Tasso, the father of Torquato, whose epic has been mentioned in a previous volume. His *Odi,*[2] written in short stanzas of mingled hendecasyllabics and septenars, are too often artificial addresses, in the style of Horace, to gods and goddesses; but one of them is a moving description of his own sorrows, and two—that on the Dawn, which has the colour and sentiment of Drummond's "Phœbus arise!" and that on the Shepherd's Life—are finely conceived and executed. Bernardo Tasso's *Odi* were the first decisive movement from the *canzone* in the direction of the ode of Chiabrera, Testi, Redi, and a line of descendants down to Leopardi, Carducci, and D'Annunzio.

Chiabrera's first Pindaric odes were published seventeen years after Bernardo Tasso's. It was only in his later work that he made any serious effort to reproduce

[1] See the interesting article *Dello Svolgimento dell' Ode in Italia,* by Giosue Carducci, *Nuova Antologia,* June 1902. The article has been republished in the selections from Carducci's prose works, 1905.

[2] Published in the *Rime di Messer B. Tasso,* 1560.

the correct Pindaric structure. His odes are Pindaric because he departs from the regular structure of the *canzone;* because the sentiments and imagery are borrowed from Pindar, not from Petrarch; and because their theme is not love but the praise of dead and living Italian heroes and princes.

Chiabrera's Pindarics.

The receipt for writing classical odes which Chiabrera used was supplied by Bernardo Tasso in the preface to his *Odi.* "Sometimes I make the construction full of a shining obscurity as Horace does; at times I depart from the principal subject in a digression and return again; but at times I come to a close in the digression in imitation of the good lyric poets." Artificial obscurity, and artificial digressions into classical mythology, are Chiabrera's recurrent devices for giving the appearance of rapt elevation to his strain, and the result is tumid and artificial. A poem on Enrico Dandolo is occupied with the story of Eteocles and Polyneices. Chiabrera is at his best in dignified moral commonplaces, but he had not the "gran temperamento lirico" which made the torch even of pastoral elegy vibrate so fiercely in Milton's hand,[1] and lends so quickening an effect to Vondel's far less elaborately constructed pæans. There is fire

[1] Of the various forms which Milton indicated as suitable for great poetry, "doctrinal and exemplary to a nation," the only one which he never essayed in English was the strict Pindaric ode with strophic arrangement, and laudation for its theme. Had he done so he would, as in epic and tragedy, while giving the form fresh content and motive, have drawn his inspiration directly from the Greek, which Chiabrera did not. See G. Bertolotto, *G. Chiabrera ellenista?* Geneva, 1891, and *Il Ch. davanti all' ellenismo* in Gior. ligust. 21, 271, quoted by D'Ancona and Bacci.

enough in "Avenge, O Lord!" to burn up the whole of Chiabrera's *canzoniere*.

Chiabrera was happier, and perhaps rendered as great a service to Italian poetry, in his lighter *scherzi* and *canzonette*. Stimulated by the new developments in music, and taking Ronsard for his model, he found a midway "tra la via grece e'l bel cammin francese." He released the Italian lyric from its somewhat slavish bondage to the hendecasyllable and the septenar, experimenting in shorter lines and sonorous masculine rhymes. Tripping trochaic cadences like the following were comparatively new in Italian verse:—

Canzonette.

> Belle rose porporine
> Che tra spine
> Sull' aurora non aprite:
> Ma, ministri degli amori
> Bei tesori
> Di bei denti custodite;
> Dite, rose prezïose
> Amorose;
> Dite, ond' è che s' io m' affiso
> Nel bel guardo vivo ardente,
> Voi repente
> Discioglete un bel sorriso?

Unusual also, though they had been used by Dante, are the rhymes in the second, fourth, and sixth lines of each verse in the following:—

> "O man leggiadra, o bella man di rose;
> Rose non di giardin,
> Che un oltraggio di sole a mezzo giorno
> Vinte conduce a fin;
> Ma rose che l' Aurora in suo ritorno
> Semina sul mattin.

Per adornarti, o man, non tesser fregi
  Nè di perle nè d' òr.
Per tutte l' altre mani, o man, s'apprezza
  Di Gange il gran tesor :
È per te sola, o man, somma ricchezza
  Il tuo puro candor.

Dunque, leggiadra e bella man di rose,
  Che di te dir si può ?
Lodi altere diran lingue amorose,
  Io le mi tacerò ;
Perchè la tua bellezza, o man di rose,
  Il cor mi depredò."

In these delightfully fresh and varied strains Chiabrera brought cultured poetry back into closer touch with popular song. The dignified moralising, which is the best thing in his Pindarics, is shown to better advantage in the *sermone* and *epitaffii*. Of the latter some are familiar to English readers from Wordsworth's translations.

Testi. Leopardi and Carducci are at one in assigning the highest place among the writers of classical odes in the seventeenth century, early and late, to Fulvio Testi[1] (1593-1643), the servant of Cesare d'Este, Duke of Modena, and the friend of Tassoni, whose troubled and somewhat intriguing career closed in prison at Modena, but not as was believed by violence. Testi's earliest *Rime* (1613) were Marinistic, and he was accused by Claretti, speaking for Marino, of plagiarism. But he came under the influence of the patriotic sentiment evoked

---

[1] *Poesi . . . con alcune aggiunte . . . divise in quattro parti,* Milano, 1658. *Canzoni, Parn. It.,* tom. 41, 1784. Mathias, *op. cit.*

by the war between Savoy and Spain, and he turned to the ode to express his more masculine and elevated sentiments. He was almost certainly the author of the famous *Pianto d'Italia*, which in dignified and vibrating octaves portrayed the misery of Italy, and invoked the deliverance of Carlo Emanuele. In his first *Poesie Liriche* (1621) he was equally outspoken, and was in consequence banished from Modena. He found it safer formally to recant his too candid utterances, but his poetry remained thenceforward moral and elevated in cast. In an ode on the death of Lope de Vega he deplores the decadence of Italian song under the influence of Marino—

"Non hà dunque Elicona
Per dilettar altro, ch' amplessi e baci ?
Che Salmace nel fonte, Adon nel bosco ?"

And his own odes, Horatian in form rather than Pindaric,—being composed, like Bernardo Tasso's, in verses of intermingled hendecasyllabics and septenars, with a preference for the longer line,—are on moral themes, the vanity of court life and delights of retirement, the dignity of virtue, and the consolations of song. Simplicity, sincerity, ardour, and clear effective evolution are the qualities which distinguish Testi's odes from Chiabrera's. In evolution, the essential quality of the elaborate and elevated ode, Chiabrera's are singularly weak. Ambitious flights are followed by prosaic lapses. Testi warms to his theme, and carries the reader easily forward through his swelling stanzas. The digressions are relevant, the close

natural and effective, the phrasing felicitous and
dignified. There are not many poems in which figure
and thought are more happily matched than in the
"Ruscelletto orgoglioso," which excited Leopardi's
enthusiasm, an Horatian ode on overweening vanity,
in which the poet contrasts the noisy babbling of a
rain-swollen stream with the silent and stately flow
of the river Po bearing onward its freight of vessels.

One of the most learned, acute, and paradoxical
writers of the century was Alessandro Tassoni[1] (1565-
1635), whose life was a continuous literary
warfare. Educated at Bologna and Ferrara,
he was a member of the most famous academies,
while, in the service of Cardinal Ascanio Colonna, he
twice visited Spain. He supported the Duke of Savoy
in 1615 by two fiery *Filippiche contra gli Spagnuoli*,
which he had afterwards to repudiate; and although
some barren honours were bestowed on him, it seems
doubtful if he was ever a *persona grata* with Carlo
Emanuele. He died at Modena, where his statue has
been erected.

Tassoni.

Tassoni had a large measure of Dr Johnson's dislike of cant, and the tendency to be carried by that
dislike into the defence of paradox. In his earliest
work, the *Parte de' quesiti di A. Tassoni* (1608)—
which was expanded afterwards into the *Pensieri
Diversi*—he criticised Aristotle more from impatience

[1] *Rime*, Bologno, 1880. Old editions of the separate works are procurable. The *Secchia Rapita* is frequent—*e.g.*, *Parn. It.*, tom. 34.
Class. Ital., tom. 163. 1804; Barbèra, Firenze, 1861 (with preface
by Carducci); *La Secchia Rapita, L'Oceano e le Rime aggiuntevi le
Prose Politiche a cura di Tom. Casino*, Firenze, Sansoni, 1887.

of his tyranny in the schools than with any inkling of newer methods in science. He tested the *Iliad* by the rules of the "heroic poem" and found it wanting, which did not suggest to him any doubt of the rules, but was explained by the assertion that Homer was a rude natural genius who wrote wonderful verses for his time. For Tassoni was, also like Johnson, sceptical of the superiority of early to more cultivated ages, and devoted one whole book to the defence of the moderns.

In the *Considerazioni sopra le Rime del Petrarca* (1609), Tassoni disclaimed any prejudice against "il Petrarca Re di Melici"; but he was impatient of the imitators of that poet who said he could not err, and accordingly submitted his work to a minute and not always respectful examination, somewhat in the style of Malherbe's notes on Desportes, but much more discriminating, and with a great deal of caustic humour, interesting elucidation, and quotation from Provencal poets.[1] This candid treatment of Petrarch provoked a literary warfare which thoroughly roused Tassoni's bile, and it was primarily to avenge himself on his foes, and in the second place to attack still another idol, the epics written in imitation of Tasso's *Gerusalemme*, that he composed the *Secchia Rapita*, which, after circulating for some years in manuscript, was published at Paris in 1622. A political motive has been ascribed to the work, but without probability.

The idea of describing a war between two Italian

[1] For a full study of the *Considerazioni* see Orazio Bacci, *Le Considerazioni*, &c. Firenze, 1887.

cities, provoked by a trifling cause (the carrying off of a well-bucket during a raid), waged by realistic everyday Italians of the seventeenth century, in a style in which the dignified and picturesque diction of epic is interchanged with coarse and dialectal colloquialism, and with all the machinery of the heroic poem, was undoubtedly suggested to Tassoni by *Don Quixote*, to which he more than once makes reference. There is little of Cervantes' sympathetic humour, however, in the dry crackling laughter with which Tassoni describes the exploits of the Potta and his followers and foes. His characters are utterly unattractive, and the episodes in which the Conte di Culagna (who stands for the poet's chief enemy, Alessandro Brusantini) is proved "a coward and a cuckold-knave" are more malevolent than amusing. But the scheme of a mock-epic is sustained with the greatest skill, and Tassoni, who evidently had read the romantic epics with the same pleasure that Cervantes read romances, does not let the intention of parody prevent his describing the battles with vigour and gusto; and he has two episodes in the picturesque, voluptuous style of Marino. With a larger purpose and a little of Cervantes' humanity Tassoni might have written a great as well as a clever poem. His strangely critical and negative mind touched with acid all the literary idols of Italy, but he indicated no fresh direction and descried no new ideals.

[margin: La Secchia Rapita.]

Mellifluous verse is the most unequivocal excellence of Marino's *Sampogna* and *Adone*, and it was in the linking of flowing verse of no very high poetical quality to more and more elaborate music that Italy achieved her most notable success in the seventeenth century. This linking of poetry and music in melodrama and opera was a consequence, partly of the enormous advance made in music as a vehicle for the expression of feeling and picturesque representation, partly, like so many other things at the Renaissance, of the study of antiquity. It was while endeavouring to discover in what way the Greeks recited their tragedies, in song and to the accompaniment of music, that Vincenzio Galilei, father of the astronomer, devised, with others, the system of expressive recitative, and set to music the Ugolino canto in the *Divina Commedia*, and the *Book of Lamentations*. Once discovered, the new method was soon applied to other works, especially the favourite pastoral and mythological idylls and plays, and the first complete musical drama, *La Dafne*, written by Ottavio Rinuccini (1562-1621) and set by Corsi and Jacopo Peri, was performed in 1595. Rinuccini's *Euridice* and Chiabrera's *Rapimento di Cefalo* soon followed, and opera, growing always more elaborate musically, was started on its long career, — a career which belongs to the history of music, not of literature, for in Addison's words "the poetry of them is generally as exquisitely ill as the music is good."

Poetry and Music.

The literary drama of the seventeenth century in Italy is only a decadent continuation of the already decadent drama of the sixteenth—tragedies, religious and secular, modelled on Seneca, and abounding in horrors; comedy classical also, but

Drama.

in general following the line indicated by Giambattista
Della Porta (1553-1613), and freshening the interest
of the hackneyed scheme with incidents borrowed
from the *novelle;* pastoral plays in endless profusion,
the source of all of which is the *Aminta* and the
Pastor Fido. Despite its classical form, sacred tragedy
in Italy was, as regards theme and spirit, directly descended from the *Sacre Rappresentazioni* of the fifteenth
century, and the older allegorical characters and irregular structure reappear in some plays which are
interesting also inasmuch as they reveal the influence
of opera upon tragedy. These are the *Adamo* (1613)
and the *Maddalena* (1617) of Giambattista Andreini
(1578-*c.*1650), leader, after his father, of the famous
company of comedians, the *Gelosi,* and author of some
religious poems and literary comedies. The *Adamo*,
with its strange blend of morality, tragedy, and opera,
has been claimed by Voltaire and subsequent critics
as the source of *Paradise Lost*, on the ground especially
of the element of allegory which appears in Milton's
first sketches of a drama. The closest resemblance
to *Paradise Lost* is, perhaps, in the seventh scene of the
fourth act, where Death and Despair circle round in a
large hospital which contains all human diseases.
This may be the original of Milton's "Lazar-house,"
where

"Over them triumphant Death his dart
Shook, but delayed to strike."

If tragedy and pastoral found a serious rival in
opera, literary comedy suffered the same fate at the
hand of the popular comedy of improvisation (the

Commedia dell' Arte), which before the end of the six-teenth century had been launched by the *Gelosi* on its triumphant career. The captain, the doctor, the pantaloon, harlequin, and scaramouch were soon as popular in France and Spain as in Italy, and have left their mark on the comedy of Molière— even perhaps of Shakespeare and Jonson. Their effect in Italy was to make motley the only wear; and when the Spanish drama found its way through Naples into the Italian theatre, it was larded with buffoonery and indecency. Nay, when Addison witnessed a performance of the *Cid* at Venice in 1700, he found that noble tragedy also enlivened by interludes of the pantaloon and the harlequin. The whirligig of time brings its revenges. A living drama must have its roots in popular taste. The country which had rendered most obsequious reverence to classical authority in drama and criticism, had to allow a blend of kinds more inharmonious and inartistic than that at which tragi-comedy aimed, and which Shakespeare achieved in so many different ways.

Comedy.

Of prose writers Italy in the seventeenth century produced abundance, whose work in science, theology, history, and travels can be but touched on. Much of the prose of the period, especially in sermons, was affected by the same taste for conceits as the poetry, but there were writers of pure and eloquent Italian.

Prose.

The greatest Italian of the century, Galileo Galilei[1]

[1] *Opere di G. G. Linceo*, Bologna, 1655-56; Firenze, 1842-56 (in 16 vols.) A national edition, in 20 vols., is nearly or just completed.

ITALY AND GERMANY. 351

Galileo. (1564-1642), the story of whose life and discoveries in physics belongs to a history of science rather than of literature, wrote on the form, situation, and dimensions of Dante's Inferno, and also *Considerazioni al Tasso* (c. 1590, pub. 1793), notes on his phraseology not unlike those of Tassoni on Petrarch's *Canzoniere*. But Galileo's finest compositions are his scientific dialogues, notably the *Saggiatore, nel quale con bilancia esquisita e giusta si ponderano le cose contenute nella Libra astronomica e filosofica di Lotario Sarsi Sigensano* (1623), which D'Ancona and Bacci describe as "un vero gioiello di stile polemico"; the *Dialogo dei Massimi sistemi del Mondo* (1632), for which he was arraigned; and the *Dialoghi delle nuove scienze* (1638). In all of these the lucidity, strength, and freedom from all rhetoric of Galileo's prose are the vivid reflection of his acute and powerful mind. And his style is more than merely lucid and strong—it is dignified and harmonious.

Historians. Of historians the best known are Paolo Sarpi (1552-1623), the Venetian antagonist of the Inquisition and historian of the Council of Trent; Enrico Caterina D'Avila[1] (1576-1631), also a servant for a great part of his life of the Republic of Venice, author of the *Historia delle Guerre*

[1] *Historia*, first ed., Venezia, 1631; Londra, 1801-2 (6 vols. and 8 parts); Firenze, 1852 (6 vols.) *Class. It.*, tt. 178-183, 1804. Davila's *Historie of the Civil Warres of France* (1647) was translated under the eye of Charles I. at Oxford by William Aylesbury (1615-1656), brother-in-law of Clarendon, and Sir Charles Cotterel, the translator of *Cassandra*.

civili di Francia (1631), in fifteen books; and Guido Bentivoglio[1] (1579-1644), author of a history in twenty-four books, *Della Guerra di Fiandra* (1632-9). Sarpi's great work is not free from prejudice and passion, yet is an invaluable contribution to history, based on numerous contemporary sources, and written in a style which is clear, exact, and lightened by a vein of genial irony. D'Avila's history was translated into many other languages, and was one of the works most studied and admired by Clarendon. According to the classical Italian tradition, it is elaborate in its descriptions and very full in its report of councils, and of the pros and cons advanced — an example that Clarendon, statesman as well as historian, was able to follow. Bentivoglio was a great admirer of Marino, of whose *Sampogna* he exclaims, "O che vena! O che purità! O che pellegrini concetti!" And his own style is not free from antitheses, affectations, and what the French call the "cheville," the use of otiose epithets to secure balance and rhythm. It is, however, clear and easy.

Germany.

While the poetry of the Renaissance was expiring in Italy in the scintillating extravagances of Marino and his school, and in the tumid grandeur of Chiabrera's classical odes, it was making its first endeavour to find a footing in

---

[1] *Della Guerra*, &c., Colonia, 1632-9. *Class. It.*, tt. 182-188, 1804. *Englished by Henry Earl of Monmouth*, London, 1654.

ITALY AND GERMANY.

Germany,[1] where its advent had been delayed by the more national and vivifying influence of the Reformation. The endeavour, unfortunately, came at a time when social conditions made almost impossible any leisurely and fruitful culture of art and letters.

The way for new experiments had been prepared by the Humanists, who did so much for German culture, and had made the school Latin drama so living and interesting a product. But, as elsewhere, a new literature came, not from the direct imitations of the classics, but from the living influence of Italy, and, more directly, from countries which had already transplanted and naturalised the Italian flower, such as France and Holland. Pioneers in the movement to introduce new forms, and give poetry a new grace and elegance, were Paul Schede or Paulus Melissus (1539-1602), who translated Marot's *Psalms*; Julius Wilhelm Zincgref (1591-1635), author of some stirring war-songs modelled expressly on the poems of Tyrtæus, and a collection of *Scharpfsinnige Kluge Sprüch* or *Apothegmata* containing anecdotes and proverbs; and Georg Rodolf Weckherlin (1584-1653), who spent a considerable portion of his life in England, and whose Horatian *Oden und Gesänge* (1618-19) have the courtly grace and musical rhythm which are the most unmistakable features of Renaissance poetry.

Preparation.

---

[1] W. Scherer, *History of German Literature*, transl. by Mrs F. C. Conybeare, Oxford, 1896; John G. Robertson, *A History of German Literature*, Edin., 1902; Karl Goedeke, *Grundriss zur Geschichte der Deutschen Dichtung*, Dritter Band, Dresden, 1887. Many of the works mentioned have been reprinted in *Neudrucke deutscher Litteraturwerke des xvi. und xvii. Jahrhunderts*, Halle, 1880.

But the Ronsard or Hooft of German poetry was Martin Opitz (1597-1639). Born in Silesia, educated in Breslau, and in the Universities of Frankfurt and Heidelberg—the cradle of the Renaissance movement,—Opitz led a wandering life. He visited Holland, and imbibed the critical doctrines of Heinsius, two of whose Dutch poems— hymns to Bacchus (1614) and Christ (1616) — he translated into German in 1622. In Paris, he met Hugo Grotius; in Denmark, he wrote his *Trostgedicht in Widerwärtigkeit des Krieges*; at Vienna, the emperor laureated and ennobled him. Though a zealous Protestant he was for a time in the service of Graf Hannibal von Dohna, the Catholic persecutor of Silesia. After his death (1633), Opitz entered the service of Ladislaus of Poland, where he died in 1639.

Opitz set himself deliberately to introduce new forms and an improved metre into German poetry—

"Ich will die Pierinnen,
Die nie nach teutscher Art noch haben reden können,
Sampt ihrem Helicon mit dieser meiner hand
Versetzen biss hieher in unser Vaterland."

With him began, says Goedeke a little bitterly, "the dependence of German literature, which has continued ever since, now on Dutchmen, Italians, and Spaniards; then on Frenchmen and gallicised Englishmen; then on Romans, Greeks, and Englishmen; thereafter on the Middle Ages; the East and the extreme West; and lastly, on an eclectic selection from the world's literature."

Following in the wake of the Pleiad, and drawing

ITALY AND GERMANY.

his precepts from Du Bellay, Scaliger, and Heinsius, Opitz sketched the plan of his reforms in his *Buch von der Deutschen Poeterey* (1624). With some just and fruitful remarks on purity of language, and on versification (some of which he had anticipated in his earlier *Aristarchus sive de contemptu linguæ Teutonicæ* (1617)), he combines the usual discussion of the "kinds"—epic, tragedy and comedy, eclogues, sylvæ, lyrics, &c.—and singles out for commendation Petrarch, Sannazaro, Ronsard, Sidney (whose *Arcadia* he translated), Heinsius, and the tragedies and comedies of those Dutchmen, Hooft, Brederoo, and Coster, who had established Coster's Academy, a few years before, with the same reforming intention as Opitz.

Theory.

Opitz's own contributions to the carrying out of his ambitious programme—epics, tragedies, pastorals, and odes—have proved of no enduring value. All that lives of his poetry are some of the more graceful and simple of his songs—lyrics like

> "Sei wohlgemuth, lass Trauern sein,
> Auf Regen folget Sonnenschein,
> Es giebet endlich doch das Glück
> Nach Toben einen guten Blick,"

and

> "Ich empfinde fast ein Grauen
> Das ich, Plato, für und für
> Bin gesessen über dir;
> Es ist Zeit hinaus zu schauen,
> Und sich bei den frischen Quellen
> In dem Grünen zu ergehn,
> Wo die schönen Blumen stehen
> Und die Fischer Netze stellen."

The opening verses recall Wordsworth's "Up! up my friend, and quit your books," but the German proceeds to confess that Nature is not for him a sufficient stimulant—

> "Holla, Junge, geh' und frage,
> Wo der beste Trunk mag sein,
> Nimm den Krug und fülle Wein."

What is true of Opitz is true of his followers. The ambitious societies, imitations of the Italian academies, which sprang up with the declared purpose of carrying out Opitz's principles ("Die Fruchtbringende Gesellschaft" under Prince Ludwig of Anhalt, "Der gekrönte Blumenorden" of Nürnberg, known also as "Die Gesellschaft der Schäfer an der Pegnitz," &c.), produced nothing of value beyond works on language and metre; but some of Opitz's imitators wrote good songs, secular and religious. Among them was the Königsberg poet, Simon Dach (1605-1659), author of

Followers.

> "Jetz schlafen Berg' und Felder
> Mit Reiff und Schnee verdeckt,"

and

> "Der mensch hat nichts so eigen,
> Nichts steht so wohl ihm an,
> Als dass er Treu erzeigen,
> Und Freundschaft halten kann,"

as well as the delightful *Aenchen von Tharau*. Jacob Rist (1607-1667) wrote the sublime hymn, "O Ewigkeit du Donnerwort"; but the best of Opitz's followers was Paul Fleming (1609-1640), who, after being educated in Leipzig, accompanied his friend Adam Olearius on an embassy to Russia and to Persia. Fleming composed Latin poems, and translated from Latin, French, Dutch, and Italian. His German poems are in the classical forms which Opitz recommended—odes, songs, sonnets, epithalamia, epicedes,—and are amorous, religious, and occasional. But the spirit of Fleming's poetry is not pedantic, but sincere and natural. "An heitrer Naturwahrheit," says Goedeke, "steht er allen Dichtern des Jahrhunderts voran." His is the beautiful

Fleming.

> "Lass dich nur nichts dauren
> Mit Trauren,
> Sei stille,
> Wie Gott es fügt,
> So sei vergnügt,
> Mein Wille."

There is more fire in Fleming's songs than in those of the elegiac Dach, and the lines he wrote on his death-bed have the confidence without the arrogance of Landor's

> "Mein Schall floh über weit, kein Landsman sang mir gleich,
> Von Reisen hochgepreist, für keiner Mühe bleich,
> Jung, wachsam, unbesorgt. Man wird mich nennen hören
> Bis dass die letzte Glut dies Alles wird verstören."

In religious poetry, strengthening, consoling, and at times mystical, the spirit of the German people found its most natural expression during years of endless war and suffering. Some of it shows the influence of Opitz's artificialities and refinements, as for example the religious pastorals of

Hymns.

Silesius (of whom the next volume speaks) and
Friederich von Spee (1591-1635), and the religious
sonnets of Andreas Gryphius. But the best has the
simplicity and strength of folk-song. The greatest
of these hymn-writers is the author of "Befiehl du
deine Wege" and "Nun ruhen alle Wälder," Paul
Gerhardt (1607-76), who also has been included in
the subsequent volume of this series.

The dramatic preparation of the sixteenth century,
which has been described in a previous volume,[1] produced no adequate result in the seven-
teenth. No Shakespeare arose to harmonise the popular and learned elements in a
drama vital and artistic. The school Latin drama of
the preceding century remained Germany's greatest
achievement in drama till the appearance of Lessing,
Goethe, and Schiller. For a Shakespeare or a Corneille, Germany produced only an Andreas Gryphius
(1616-1664).

Drama.

A native of Glogau, in Silesia, Gryphius had a
troubled early life, in which he made himself master
of all the languages which the confusion
of the Thirty Years' War brought together
in Germany, as well as composing the usual epic
poem. A patron gave him the means of proceeding
to Leyden to study, where he brought out two books
of sonnets, *Son- und Feyrtags Sonnete* (1639), accomplished in form, and full of passionate religious zeal.
He visited Italy and many parts of Germany, and
died at his native town in 1664.

Gryphius.

---

[1] *Early Renaissance*, cc. 5 and 6.

Gryphius' plays show the influence of the tragedies of Seneca and Vondel, and of the English plays which had already affected the ruder work of Jacob Ayrer (1595-1605), who "grafted the English dramatic style" (with its abundance of action and striking situations) "on to the style of Hans Sachs." Gryphius' tragedies — *Leo Arminius, Catharina von Georgien, Ermordete Majestät oder Carolus Stuardus*, &c., *Cardenio und Celinde, Gross-muttiger Rechts-Gelehrter* — breathe the same Christian spirit as Vondel's (three are, like so many of the Dutch poet's, martyr-plays), but Gryphius' are in the more melodramatic Senecan style, which Vondel outgrew as he became familiar with Greek tragedy. They are full of ghost scenes, atrocities, and bombast. The *Cardenio und Celinde*, an Italian *novella* tragedy, is written in a simpler and more effective style.

But Gryphius' best plays are his two comedies, *Peter Squenz* and *Horribilicribrifax*. The first deals with the comic episodes, the acting of Bottom and his friends, in *A Midsummer Night's Dream;* the second is more a comedy of humours—the bragging soldier, the pedant, and the Jew. Both are written in prose.

In Friedrich von Logau (1605-1655) the early seventeenth century produced a satirical epigrammatist who was scantly appreciated in his lifetime. In 1638 he published *Erstes Hundert Teutscher Reimen-Sprüche*, and, in 1654, *Salomons von Golaw Deutscher Sinn-Gedichte Drey Tausend*. They were little noticed till republished in 1759. Logau was a patriot, and was not a great

Satire.

believer in Opitz's rules. He expresses bitterly his sense of the subservience of Germany in literary and other fashions—her unhappy lot at this period, when Spain and France, England and Holland, had such rich and such national literatures—

> "Wer nicht Französisch kann,
> Ist kein gerühmter Mann;
> Drum müssen wir verdammen
> Von denen wir entstammen,
> Bey denen Herz und Mund
> Alleine deutsch gekunt."

The mass of artificial and occasional verse produced by the admirers of Opitz is consigned to oblivion. To the rich harvest of Renaissance poetry—especially rich in lyric and drama—Germany's contribution is practically limited to some drama not of the first order, some graceful courtly song, epigrams, and some passionate and simple hymns.

CHAPTER IX.

CONCLUSION.

FORCES AT WORK—END OF THE RENAISSANCE—THE COUNTER-REFORMATION—RATIONALISM AND CLASSICISM.

ON no period in the history of European literature is it more difficult to generalise with profit than that
Introduction. which has been briefly reviewed in the foregoing chapters. Since human thinking began, it has been said, there has been no greater revolution in thought than that which was effected, in men's conception of the world and its laws, in the course of the seventeenth century. To give any complete account of that revolution, and of the eddies which retarded, obscured, or advanced its progress, is beyond the scope of the present work. Indeed, to give a sketch of the intellectual activity, in all its aspects, of even the first sixty years of the century, such as Hallam attempted in his *Introduction*, would require another volume as large as the present, the subject of which is exclusively literature conceived as an art. Philosophers, theologians, historians, and men of science have been included only

in so far as they were also distinctly and admittedly men of letters. It is therefore on one or two of the larger aspects of the literature of the period alone that it is necessary in closing to dwell briefly, mainly with a view to defining as clearly as possible the relation of the period under consideration to those which precede and follow.

In certain aspects the literature of the early seventeenth century is a continuation of the literature of
End of the Renaissance. the Renaissance, the present volume a third chapter in the history whose first and second chapters are contained in Professor Saintsbury's *Earlier Renaissance* and Mr Hannay's *Later Renaissance*. This is notably the case as regards Holland and Germany, where the early years of the seventeenth century correspond, in the most important respects, to the last half of the sixteenth in France and England; although, of course, the very fact that the Renaissance movement came late in these countries was not without consequences for the literature which that movement produced. It came from the beginning under the influence of the religious agitations of the century.

It is especially in lyrical and dramatic poetry that the impulse of the Renaissance is still traceable in
Lyrical Poetry. wellnigh all the literatures touched on here. The lyrical poetry of the Renaissance, that wonderful product, stimulated in its growth from Italy, but in all the countries north of the Alps striking a deeper root into the health-giving soil of

popular song, blooms in full splendour and fragrance throughout these years in England and Holland, blossoms even in Germany despite adverse circumstances, and in Italy puts forth late flowers, somewhat waxy and gaudy but not without charm. The songs of Jonson and Carew, of Milton's *Comus* and Herrick's *Hesperides*, are not less beautiful than anything of the kind which the sixteenth century produced in France or England, and no whit less redolent of the Renaissance worship of beauty. The poetry of Holland is, as has been seen, above all things a lyrical poetry. In drama and epic, Holland, even in this "Heldenperiode," achieved little of enduring value, but the harvest of lyric poetry which she brought forth is rich indeed, and in nothing more surprising than in the range and variety of its metres. It is difficult to do justice to it in this respect without appearing to exaggerate, which, in dealing with Dutch literature, I have been specially anxious to avoid. Some indication of its range has been given in the opening chapters, from the playful

> "Tesselschaedtje
> Kameraedtje"

of Huyghens, to the roll of Vondel's

> "Wie is het, die zoo hoogh gezeten,
> Zoo diep in 't grondelooze licht;"

but it must be remembered, that the long Alexandrine itself is used by Vondel with a wonderful lyrical effect. There are lines in his pæans and tragedies which have the sweep and glitter of waves in mid-ocean:—

> " De koesterende zon, tot 's avonts van den morgen,
>   Voltreckt haer ronde, toont elk een haer aengezicht
> En straelen, dagh op dagh, blijft nimmermeer verborgen,
>   En begenadight elk met warmte, en heilzaem licht.
> Zy schijnt rondom den ringk des aerdtrijcks, naar elks wenschen,
>   Een ieder even na, een ieder even schoon,
> Gewelkomt, en onthaelt bij dieren, en bij menschen,
>   En planten, waerze blinckt uit haeren gouden troon."

That is Vondel at his most flamboyant, a Rubens in lyrical poetry. But he can change his rhythm, when the subject requires, to the quiet flow of a pastoral stream, as in his beautiful rendering of the twenty-third psalm—

> " D' Almaghtige is mijn herder, en geleide.
>   Wat is er datme schort ?
> Hij weit my, als zijn schaep, in vette weide,
>   Daer gras noch groen verdort."

Besides this wealth of metrical effect, the Dutch lyrical poetry has most of the beauties and affectations of Renaissance poetry,—the flamboyant mythology, the pastoral and amorous conventions, the conceits, Petrarchian and Marinistic in Hooft, Dubartist in Vondel, and touched in Huyghens with the intellectuality and obscurity of Donne,—

> " De Britse Donn'
> Die duistre zon,"—

"that obscure sun," as Vondel calls him. But this taste for conceit does not conceal the sincere, personal, natural note which distinguishes Dutch poetry, as it does Dutch art.

CONCLUSION.

Even in Italy, where better than anywhere else one may study the poetry of the Renaissance in decadence,—decadence undisturbed by the emergence of new forces,—lyrical poetry still lingers. All that is best in Marino's sonnets, and madrigals, and the octaves of the *Adone*, is musical and picturesque lyric. Chiabrera's pompous odes show little genuine inspiration, but Testi's have ardour and flow; and in Chiabrera's *canzonette* France repaid some of her debt to Italy.

Only in France herself is this lyrical spirit already wellnigh extinct when the century opens. Malherbe, or the spirit of which Malherbe is the first representative, comes, "like an envious sneaping frost," killing the plant which had borne beautiful if delicate blooms in the songs of Ronsard and Du Bellay. The sonorous eloquence of Corneille is a fine thing of its kind, but a lover of pure poetry would give a good deal of it for "Mignonne allons voir si la rose," and "À vous troupe légère." Théophile is the last of the French poets who preserves some of the lyrical inspiration of an older generation.

The chief symptom of decadence in this final flowering of Renaissance lyric is the phenomenon, which has attracted so much attention, of "con-
Conceit. ceit" — the "accutezze" or Marinism of Italy, Gongorism of Spain, "préciosité" of French and "metaphysical wit" of English poetry. The time is past for speaking of seventeenth-century "wit" or "conceit" as though it were some sudden and inexplicable phenomenon, some startling epidemic in European letters. For it is clear that seventeenth-

century "wit" is only an exaggeration of what had been a complaint, and a beauty, of Renaissance poetry throughout. Euphuism is older than *Euphues*, and *Secentismo* than the seventeenth century. Their characteristic artifices have been traced through the rhetorical studies of the Middle and Dark Ages back to classical models. And if the Renaissance, in its general heightening and embellishment of style in verse and prose, often accentuated rather than corrected artifice, was it not because the first enthusiasm for the classics flowed quite naturally in the traditional rhetorical channels? It was only gradually that taste discriminated between more florid beauties and those deeper and purer qualities which we associate with the word classical.[1] In the poetry of the first half of the seventeenth century we have the final phase of this phenomenon, but the form which it took in different countries was determined by special circumstances. The extravagant conceits of Marino and his followers in Italy were the result of that exaggeration of a fashion which so frequently precedes its disappearance, the search for novelty, undirected by a new inspiration, and issuing merely in the bizarre and outrageous. In France and Holland, Germany, and even England (as we have seen in cases such as Drummond, Crashaw, and Cowley), the cultivation of conceit was in part an outcome of the admiration of Italian literature. But in France the aberrations of the "précieux" and "précieuses" were part of the movement towards the refinement and dignify-

[1] See Professor Ker, *The Dark Ages*, pp. 34-36. John Dover Wilson, *John Lyly*, Camb., 1906.

ing of style which issued in classicism; while in England, the peculiarly intellectual and erudite character of Donne's "metaphysical wit" is a symptom of the theological and scholastic direction given to English thought and learning by the trend of the second great force in the history and literature of the period—namely, religious polemic.

The other literary kind in which the free artistic spirit of the Renaissance survives is the drama. The tale of the modern drama, opened by Professor Saintsbury in the *Earlier Renaissance*, taken up by Mr Hannay's chapters on Spanish and Elizabethan literature in the *Later Renaissance*, is continued here by an account of the English drama under James and Charles, and of the dramatic experiment in Holland, and by a chapter on French drama introductory to that which follows in Professor Elton's *Augustan Ages*. Of the three dramas dealt with here, that which retains most of the free artistic spirit of the Renaissance is the English, and the reason is not difficult to discover. The French drama, though it sprang from the same roots as the English, developed later, and when the rigid influence of classicism was in the ascendant. The serious drama of Holland, on the other hand, never emancipated itself sufficiently from the didactic spirit of the sixteenth century Morality and the Latin school drama. It has been sometimes argued that the decay of the English drama was due to the withdrawal from the theatre of the serious middle classes. The example of the Dutch drama is a useful reminder that a drama which did enjoy the full approval of serious and

Drama.

pedantic persons—the extreme Puritans were opposed to the stage on principle, and may be left out of the question—could never have portrayed life with the fulness and freedom which is the glory of the drama of Shakespeare and the Elizabethans. From Marlowe to Shirley, the English dramatists owed this freedom to the protection extended to them against Puritan mayors by the Court, and to the fact that the audience for which they wrote was the Court and the populace, not the serious middle classes. They were thus enabled to portray life without squeamishness, and without the too oppressive intrusion of didactic purpose. What pressure there was in this direction came from pedantry rather than respectability.

This volume has dealt only with the English playwrights of the second class, the first being occupied by Shakespeare alone. But perhaps the freshness and greatness of the lesser Elizabethans, as we may still call them, are more readily acknowledged when that overshadowing figure is temporarily excluded. To do justice to Jonson and Webster, Beaumont and Fletcher, not to mention Dekker, Middleton, Massinger, and Ford, let a reader take them up, not immediately after studying Shakespeare, but after a course, say, of the lesser Dutch and French dramatists, their contemporaries. He will find the latter trying to do the same thing, to dramatise the same or similar Italian and Spanish novellas; and he cannot fail to realise the difference in the handling, the difference between the colourless atmosphere, the stock characters, the style *banale* or precious on the one hand, and the resolute effort made by the Elizabethans to realise their scene, be it London or Italy, and to give life and individuality to the characters; as well as the poetry with which their plays overflow. And even if one passes from the second- to the first-rate dramatists, the Elizabethans maintain their position. Fletcher and Webster are more dramatic, and not less poetic, though in a somewhat different way, than Hooft and Vondel. And even in the work of the great Corneille himself, despite scenes of eloquent argument and declamation, and dramatic touches such as "Moi! et c'est assez" or "Qu'il mourût," where can one find scenes to surpass in subtle and thrilling dramatic power the interview between Beatrice and De Flores in Middleton's *The Changeling*, or that in *The Duchess of Malfi*, already referred to, when the brother cries—

"Cover her face: mine eyes dazzle: she died young";

and Bosola replies in even more thrilling words—

"I think not so: her infelicity
Seemed to have years too many"?

There is more in such a scene to evoke the Transcendental Feeling, the solemn sense of the immediate presence of "that which was and is and ever shall be," to induce which is, Professor Stewart tell us, the chief end of poetry, than in a whole tragedy of Corneille.

In sustained and finished workmanship, Corneille's plays are doubtless infinitely superior to the mass of minor Elizabethan work. It is rare, indeed, that an Elizabethan play is wrought out in a completely satisfying manner. *The Virgin Martyr* is a rude, inchoate piece when set beside the shining workmanship of *Polyeucte*. But the Elizabethans had moments of dramatic insight that seem to me beyond the range of Corneille; and the wild, natural beauties of their poetry have, at any rate for an English reader, a charm that his great and admirable eloquence lacks.

The artistic freedom and variety of the English dramatists are not more striking on a broad survey than is the fundamental soundness of their morality. They are certainly not squeamish, whether in comedy or tragedy, though there is nothing in English to equal the coarseness of Dutch, the cynicism of French farce. There are doubtless signs of decadence, in Fletcher and some of his followers, which forecast the tone of the Restoration plays. Not all are equally sound. Middleton is somewhat brutal, Fletcher callously indecent, and Ford is attracted by the morbid. But taking a broad view; allowing for the demands of a popular audience in the way of amusement; remembering the general tone of plays like Dekker's *The Honest Whore*, Webster's *Vittoria Corrombona* and *Duchess of Malfi*, even of Tourneur's tragedies, of Massinger's plays despite a needless indecency of language, and of comedies which might easily have been only cynical like *Northward Ho* and *Westward Ho*,—it is impossible not to admit that the complete freedom the dramatists enjoyed, limited by the general exclusion of political subjects and occasional edicts against strong language, only illustrates the fundamental soundness of their morality, their reverence for virtue in men and women.

CONCLUSION.

The second great factor in the literature which has been under survey is the religious, the currents and counter-currents of religious passion which agitate the century from first to last. The Protestant Reformation had spent its full force before the sixteenth century closed, and was entering on a struggle for existence with the forces of the Catholic reaction, which followed the Council of Trent, the rise of the Jesuits, and the setting in order of the Roman Church. Orthodox Protestantism left no great mark on the pure literature of this time, with the notable exception of the writings of Milton, whose orthodoxy was in a constant process of disintegration, and of Bunyan later. It is otherwise with the so-called Counter-Reformation, and the eddies which it produced in other than Roman Catholic countries and churches. To it is due, in the first place, the definite ending in Italy of the anti-religious and anti-clerical current which had flowed since the Renaissance. In the change of tone which took place there was a good deal of hypocrisy as well as sincerity.[1] Tasso's pure and pious *Gerusalemme Liberata* having to establish its orthodoxy, while Marino's lascivious *Adone* poses as a moral allegory, is not an edifying example of clerical influence in literature, and Milton has described, in ever-memorable words, the condition of Italy under the Inquisition. But the more interesting results of the reaction

The Counter-Reformation.

---

[1] For full treatment consult Dejob, *De l'Influence du Concile de Trent sur la Littérature et les Beaux-Arts chez les Peuples catholiques.* Paris, 1884.

are to be seen in the literature produced north of the Alps. It is where the strongest currents meet that the most complex eddies are produced. To the sincerity and ardour of the Catholic reaction in France, and Holland, and England, we owe some beautiful and interesting literature in prose and verse.

In France, the scepticism and libertinism of the Renaissance pass rapidly away. Catholicism and classicism advance hand in hand. Corneille's *Polyeucte*, and Racine's later *Athalie* and *Esther*, are not less characteristic of the age than *Cinna* and *Britannicus*, Arnauld's *La Fréquente Communion* than the *Discours de la Méthode*. For the Jansenist movement, which produced the *Lettres Provinciales* and the *Pensées*, though it came into conflict with Jesuit influence and ecclesiastical authority, is only an incident in the general spiritual history of the period, and was not without influence even on those who opposed it, and on the great preachers of the period which follows.

In Holland, the result of the dissensions in Protestantism and of the Catholic reaction is seen in the strange phenomenon, that the greatest and not least representative poet of a Protestant country is an ardent Catholic, using the stage to set forth Catholic doctrine, and pouring out his heart in poetic apologetics, and hymns to the Virgin and saintly martyrs. And a deep religious strain runs through all the Dutch poetry of this period. Hooft alone has the blended epicureanism and stoicism which mark the pure child of the Classical Renaissance. Huyghens and Cats, Camphuysen and Van der Wiele, are all in different ways religious poets, bent on edification; even Brederoo wrote pious as well as humorous songs, and Luiken's secular songs are his earliest.

But it is in England that the effects of the religious currents are most complex and striking, whether in verse or prose, in poets or divines. The reason is to be found in the position of the Anglican Church, the *via media* which she strove to make her own, between pure Bible Protestantism on the one hand and traditional Roman Catholicism on the other. The consequence of this peculiar position—the value of which was recognised by foreigners like Casaubon and Grotius—was that, when the reaction against Protestantism came, it did not necessarily drive a Crashaw, as it did Vondel, into the arms of Rome at once; nor, on the other hand, was it impossible for a Roman like Donne to justify himself in conforming. Whatever any one may think of the religious value of the Anglo-Catholic movement, there can at any rate be no doubt of the mark which it has left on English literature. The greatest preachers of these years are Andrewes and Donne and Taylor; and Donne and Herbert, Vaughan and Crashaw, Traherne and King, are not the least interesting of the poets.

A direct result of the controversy between Canterbury and Rome, of the revival of theological and ecclesiastical studies, was a recrudescence of scholasticism; and one of the strangest phenomena in literature is the combination in Donne's poetry of the emancipated, moral and artistic, tone of the Renaissance with the erudition and subtlety of a controversialist of the Counter-Reformation. Metaphysics was not something new in love-poetry; but since the time of Dante and some of his imitators, it was little more than a rhetorical dressing. In Donne's love-poetry there is a real metaphysical strain, while the range of erudition from which he draws his imagery was something altogether new. Donne's followers are none of them either so metaphysical or so erudite as himself. The metaphysics in the poetry of most of them is simply an ingenious and often far from beautiful rhetorical device. In the religious poets, however, the erudite imagery ministered to their theological didactic, as well as to that love of symbolism which has always belonged to the catholic religious temper.

The field of religious thought and feeling was not left entirely to Roman Catholics, Anglo-Catholics, and orthodox Protestants—Calvinist and Lutheran. From the internecine conflict of churches and creeds some minds turned towards a more liberal thought, or a more mystical pietism. Hales, Chillingworth, and Jeremy Taylor sought to widen the basis of Anglicanism by reducing the essentials of unity in faith; and a little later, when Presbyterian orthodoxy had taken the place of Anglican, and when, despite Presbyterian effort, sects had begun to abound, a similar movement was initiated in the Puritan shades of Cambridge by the liberal and charitable Benjamin Whichcote (1610-1683), and the more philosophic and Platonic John Smith (1618-1652), whose *Select Dis-*

courses (1660) contain some of the most interesting religious thought of the century—an attempt to form a deeper conception of reason, and its operations in the spiritual sphere, than was possible either for narrow orthodoxy, or for rationalism in its earliest phases. His followers, the most systematically metaphysical of the Cambridge Platonists, More and Cudworth, belong to the subsequent period. Pure mysticism is represented most strikingly by the German Jacob Boehme (1575-1624), on whose work I have not had courage to venture, but mystical piety found representatives in most Protestant countries.

The consideration of the appearance of a liberal strain in seventeenth-century theology brings us naturally to the third great force whose influence is traceable in the literature of the early seventeenth century,—that revolution to which we have referred in the opening chapter, the growth of a new, rationalistic conception of the world. In the years which this volume covers, rationalism is shaping and asserting itself, but is far yet from having become the recognised and omnipresent force it proved in the period which follows. Bacon, at the opening of the century, heralds and proclaims its advent, but he was not able to formulate its principles adequately; and it was not until the end of the Forties that Bacon and Descartes began to be studied at the English universities. English thought is still scholastic; still most active in theological and historical studies; and science is only gradually emancipating itself from

Growth of Rationalism.

mediævalism. Its confused transitional condition is obvious in the work of writers like Burton and Browne, even in the poetry of Donne and Milton. It is with Hobbes that rationalism appears in English thought, as an organised method and an aggressive force.

Hobbes, if not a Cartesian, yet follows the deductive, mathematical methods of Descartes rather than the experimental, inductive method adumbrated by Bacon, which was not applied in philosophy till Locke wrote. The first formulator of rationalism was Descartes; and the chief thinkers of the century, as Spinoza and Leibnitz, derive from Descartes. And as it was in France that rationalism was first formulated,—a consequence of the advance of mathematical studies, in which England lagged behind,—it was in France that rationalism first became a force in letters. It is in our period that the classicism of the Augustan ages is taking shape; and the two shaping forces are the organisation of polite society, and the rationalist ideal of precision in the use of words, logical and lucid order. From the opening of the Hôtel de Rambouillet dates the organisation of polite society as a conscious force in life and letters, the beginning of the process which was to make literature, poetry and prose, the finest flower of social intercourse, its greatest beauties that elegance and dignity which are the adornment of aristocratic manners. It is only a beginning that we have in these years. In the literature of the period there is still much of the ruder, freer, larger spirit of the sixteenth century. In the *badinage* of the Hôtel there is a good deal of coarseness; in the refinements of style which they cultivate, a large admixture of the precious and fantastic. But before the first sixty years of the century are over, modern French prose has taken shape. In moulding it, the two great influences of classicism are at work. Balzac represents the one, the influence of society and its conscious pursuit of dignity and elegance; Descartes stands for the other, the rationalist requirement of precision and order; Pascal combines the two. It may be that the actual influence of Descartes' own style on French prose has been exaggerated. Even so, it would not affect the claim of the new scientific method to have been the principal shaping influence. For Pascal, about whose importance all critics are at one, was educated in that method, and was fully conscious of what right thinking requires of the medium it is to use—precision in the definition of words, and logical order. The method of right thinking is "de n'employer aucun terme dont on n'eût auparavant expliqué nettement le sens: l'autre, de n'avancer jamais aucune proposition qu'on ne démontrât par des vérités déjà connues." When Pascal opened his attack on Arnauld's judges in the *Lettres Provinciales*, it was by showing the ambiguity of the terms in use, and how, in consequence, the innocence or guiltiness of a doctrine was made to depend not on its meaning but on the person who uttered it. But Pascal was not merely a philosopher. Before he wrote the *Provinciales* he had been a man of the world; and he knew how little capable the *honnête homme* is of appreciating logical argument, how much a creature of tastes and prejudices. And the method he adopted in the *Provinciales*, as he proceeded, was that which he thought most likely to appeal to the average man. To combat prejudice he evoked prejudice. To the help of argument he brought irony and eloquence. Before Addison and Steele, he realised that, even on religious matters, the man of the world must be addressed in a different tone from that which suits the *savant*. Pascal made French prose a fit instrument, at once for the precise expression of scientific thought and for the more delicate and varied uses of social intercourse and letters.

The history of English prose, and of the less important Dutch prose, of the period, is not quite the same as that of French. It was not till later that rationalism and classicism united in the shaping of modern English prose; and Van Effen's *Hollandsche Spectator* is generally regarded as the first work in Dutch prose that is distinctly modern. For England on a large, for Holland on a smaller scale, the earlier seventeenth century is a period of enrichment rather than of settling and uniformity; and the chief influence in each is Latin oratorical and historical prose. Hooker and Bacon, Donne and Taylor, Milton and Browne, enriched the resources of English prose in vocabulary, in structure, and in harmony, so much that, despite the work done by Dryden and his followers, the greatest prose writers, from Johnson to Ruskin, have never failed to go back to the study of these great models. On a much smaller scale, something of the same kind was done for Dutch prose by the pedantic, but dignified and harmonious, work of Hooft.

Yet even in this period the simpler, directer prose of Dryden and Swift is heralded; and, as might be expected, it is among those in whom the spirit of reason, of the *Aufklärung*, is at work. The prose of the moderate divines, Hales and Chillingworth, is comparatively simple and straightforward, though Taylor is still diffuse and ambiguous; and Hobbes's style, in everything but ease and grace, is as modern as Dryden's — precise, orderly, and regular in construction.

These are the chief forces at work in this period, a period to which the title of transitional might be applied quite as fittingly as to the fifteenth century. But the transition is not marked by the slow decay of an old tradition and the gradual birth of a new, —rather by the confused conflict of great and active forces. The Renaissance, the Reformation, the Counter-Reformation, all are potent and shaping influences. Even the prophetic vision of a Bacon could hardly have descried at the opening of the century how completely all these would yield place before it closed to the spirit of rationalist inquiry.

INDEX.

Abuses Stript and Whipt, 146.
Académie Française, 252.
Acchillini, Claudio, 338.
Adamo, 349.
Adams, T., 218 note.
Addison, Joseph, 102, 139, 283, 348, 350.
Address to Cromwell, 188.
Adone, 143, 328, 330, 331, 336, 338, 347.
Advancement of Learning, The, 206, 207.
Aenchen von Tharau, 356.
Æneas, 321 note.
Alamanni, 340.
Alcestis, 295.
Alchemist, The, 96, 98, 100, 102.
Alcinée, 322.
Amadis of Gaul, 260 note, 262, 265.
Aminta, 144, 183, 262, 293, 296, 300, 338.
Amours Tragiques de Pyrame et Thisbé, 295.
An Advertisement touching the Controversies of the Church, 206.
Anatomy of Melancholy, 226.
Andreini, 192, 193 note, 349.
Andrewes, Lancelot, 174, 212, 213, 214, 216, 217.
Andromède, 314.
Animadversions on the Remonstrants' Defence against Smectymnuus, 221.
Ansloo, 42.
Antonio and Mellida, 104.
Apology for Smectymnuus, 221.
Appius and Virginia, 118.

Arcadia, 262, 263.
Arden of Feversham, 112.
Areopagitica, 221, 224.
Argenis, 264.
Ariadne, 295.
Ariosto, 182, 328, 339.
Aristotle, 211, 259, 300, 310.
Arnauld, 277, 372.
Arnold, M., 139, 204.
Artamène ou le Grand Cyrus, 267.
Asselijn, Thomas, 83.
Atheist's Tragedy, 119, 120.
Ayrer, Jacob, 359.

Bacon, Francis, 203, 204, 205 and note, 207, 210, 211, 212, 224, 237, 239, 379.
Ballad upon a Wedding, 177.
Balzac, Jean-Louis de, 111, 182, 204, 272-274, 276, 295, 310.
Bang, Prof., 89 note.
Barlaeus, 81.
Baro, Balthasar, 297.
Barry, Dr Alfred, 215 note.
Bartholomew Fair, 96, 99.
Basse, W., 148.
Baxter, Rich., 167.
Beaumont, Francis, 85, 120-127.
Beaumont, Sir John, 152.
Beaumont, Joseph, 149, 186.
Beeching, Canon, 154 note, 213 note.
Beets, Dr Nicholas, 79, 193 note, 194.
Behemoth, 237.
Bellarmine, 212.
Bellini, A., 193 note, 325 note.

INDEX. 381

Bembo, Cardinal, 327, 339.
Benlowes, 186.
Benserade, Isaac, 256.
Bentivoglio, Guido, 352.
Bérénice, 316.
Bergerac, Cyrano de, 271.
Bernagie, Pieter, 82.
Bijns, Anna, 9.
Blake, W., 172.
Blurt, Master Constable, 108.
Boas, Mr F., 85 note, 87, 88 note.
Boehme, Jacob, 375.
Boileau, 195, 260, 267, 283.
Bondman, The, 128.
Bonducca, 123.
Bourgogne, Hôtel de, 251, 290.
Boutroux, M., 277 note.
Boyle, R., 121 note.
Brandt, Geraert, 25, 42, 45, 46-48.
Brathwait, Rich., 148.
Brederoo, Gerb. Adriaensz., 4, 18-20, 21, 57-60, 82, 83.
Breton, M. le, 260 note.
Brink, Prof. Ten, 2 note.
Britain's Ida, 141.
Broken Heart, The, 131.
Browne, Sir T., 204, 223, 228-233.
Browne, W., 134, 144, 145.
Browning, Rob., 159.
Brunetière, F., 244 note.
Buchanan, G., 73, 76, 312.
Buddensieg, Rudolf, 193 note.
Bullen, A. H., 105, 134.
Bunyan, John, 218, 371.
Burke, Edmund, 214.
Burns, Robert, 147.
Burton, Robert, 226-228.
Busken-Huet, 2 note.

Calderon, 314.
Calvin, John, 219.
Camphuysen, 39, 40.
Camus, Jean-Pierre, 263.
Canevari, 337 note.
Canzone dei Baci, 330, 337.
Cardinal, The, 133.
Carducci, 339 note, 340, 343, 345 note.
Carew, T., 165, 175, 176.
Cariteo, 326, 332, 339.
Carlyle, 198.
Carmen deo Nostro, 170.
Caroline Court Poetry, 164.
Cartwright, Rich., 122, 134.
Cassandre, 266.

Castara, 180.
Catiline, His Conspiracy, 99.
Cats, Jacob, 4, 28, 38, 39.
Centuries of Meditation, 172.
Cervantes, 3, 109, 264, 268, 294.
Chamberlayne, W., 191.
Chambers, E. K., 135 note.
Chambers's *Encyclopædia of English Literature*, 202 note.
Changeling, The, 110.
Chapelain, 274, 313, 329.
Chapman, G., 85 and note, 88, 105, 118, 137, 138, 139, 204.
Character writings of seventeenth century, 224.
Characters of Virtues and Vices, 224.
Chaste Maid in Cheapside, A, 109.
Chateaubriand, 277.
Chiabrera, Gabriello, 325, 328, 339, 340, 343, 344, 365.
Chillingworth, William, 27, 216, 219 and note.
Chriséide et Arimande, 298.
Christian Ethics, 171.
Church, Dean, 205 note.
Cinna, 311.
City Madam, 129.
Clarendon, E. Hyde, Lord, 46, 187, 189, 240-242, 280, 352.
Claretti, 343.
Clélie, ou Histoire Romaine, 267.
Cléopâtre, 266, 306.
Cleveland, Ed., 176, 186.
Clitandre, 304.
Cœlum Britannicum, 175.
Colours of Good and Evil, 205.
Comédiens du Prince d'Orange, 303.
Comédiens du Roi, 303.
Commedia dell' Arte, 324, 350.
Complete Angler, The, 243.
Comus, 144, 180, 182, 183, 201.
Confrérie de la Passion, 289, 290.
Considerazioni sopra le Rime del Petrarca, 346.
Cooper's Hill, 188.
Coornhert, D. V., 11, 12.
Coriolan, 292.
Corneille, P., 81, 128, 253, 257-259, 285, 287, 292, 302-320, 321, 322-324, 369, 370.
Corneille, Thomas, 295.
Corsi, 348.
Cosroès, 323.
Coster, Dr Samuel, 56, 63, 64, 65.

Counter-Reformation, the, 371-375.
Courthope, Prof., 84 note, 119, 135 note, 152, 153, 156, 159, 196.
Cowley, Abraham, 174, 181, 189, 190, 191, 199, 330, 336, 366.
Craik, Sir H., 202 note.
Crashaw, Rich., 27, 31, 167, 169-171, 174, 177, 178, 180, 189, 198, 330.
Crépet, 244 note, 245.
Cynthia's Revels, 92, 105.
Cypress Grove, A, 150.
Cytherée, 266.

Da Porta, 322.
Dach, Simon, 356, 357.
D'Ancona e Bacci, 325 note.
Daniel, S., 138, 152, 239, 288.
D'Annunzio, 340.
Dante, 339, 342.
D'Aubigné, 258.
Davenant, Sir W., 134, 186, 190, 191.
Davideis, 182, 190.
D'Avila, Enrico Caterina, 240, 351.
De Casteleyn, 8.
Defensio pro Populo Anglicano, 222.
Dekker, 85, 103, 106-108, 111, 125, 322.
Delights of the Muses, 170.
Denham, Sir John, 186, 187, 188, 191, 329.
Descartes, 204, 230, 237, 273, 274-276, 310, 376, 377.
Desgilberts, G., 303, 307.
Desportes, Malherbe's notes on, 346.
Devil is an Ass, The, 99.
Devil, The White, or the Hypocrite Uncased, 219.
Dicerie Sacre, 338.
Dictionary of National Biography, 84 note, 135 note, 218.
Dictionnaire des Précieuses, 253.
Didon, 306, 321.
Discours de la Méthode, 275, 276.
Discourse of Friendship, 216.
Discoveries, 111.
Dobell, B., 171.
Doctrine and Discipline of Divorce, 192, 222.
Dodsley, 21 note.
Don Japhet d'Armenie, 324.
Don Quixote, 268, 269, 270, 347.

Don Sanche d'Aragon, 311, 314, 315.
Donne, John, 35, 140, 144, 152, 153, 154-160, 164, 166, 168, 169, 170, 174, 175, 176, 178, 180, 181, 187, 188, 190, 204, 213 and note, 214, 216, 217, 367, 373, 374.
Dorland, Pieter, 54.
Dort, Synod of, 219.
Dowden, Prof. E., 244 note.
Dowry, The Fatal, 128.
Drayton, Michael, 137, 138, 140, 144.
Drummond, William, 96, 149-152, 171, 181, 234, 239, 310, 330, 332, 333, 335, 340.
Dryden, John, 120 note, 122, 152, 178, 190, 201, 204, 320.
Du Bartas, 23, 193, 195.
Du Bellay, 244, 246, 355, 365.
Duchess of Malfi, 113, 117.
Ductor Dubitantium, 216.
Dutch Courtezan, The, 105.
D'Urfé, Honoré, 260-263, 270.

Earle, John, 225, 226.
Eastward Ho! 105.
Edmundson, The Rev. George, 193 note, 199.
Edward IV., 111.
Edwards, Rich., 223.
"Eglantine," The, 12, 14, 19, 34, 55, 56, 62.
Eikonoclastes, 222.
Elegy on Harvey, 189, 190.
Elton, Prof. O., 91, 325 note, 367.
Endymion, 265.
England's Worthies, 236.
English Traveller, The, 112.
Eniautos, 216.
Epigrammata Sacra, 169.
Episcopacy Asserted, 220.
Euphormio, 268.
Euphues, 262.
Euridice, 348.
Evelyn, John, 242.
Everaert, Cornelis, 54.
Every Man in his Humour, 90, 92.
Every Man out of his Humour, 90, 92.
Eymael, H. J., 37.

Faerie Queene, 189, 203.
Faguet, M. Emile, 244 note, 272.
Fair Quarrel, The, 110.

INDEX.

Fairfax, Edward, 187.
Falkland, Lord, 187, 189, 220.
False One, The, 123.
Faramond, 266.
Felismène, 294.
Fielding, Henry, 271.
Filippiche contro gli Spagnuoli, 345.
Firth, Prof. C. H., 240 note, 242 note.
Flaming Heart, The, 171.
Flamini, Francesco, 327 note.
Fleay, Rev. F. G., 84 note, 94 note, 121 note.
Fleming, Paul, 356, 357.
Fletcher, Andrew, 103, 128, 175, 183, 329.
Fletcher, Giles, 140, 142, 198.
Fletcher, Phineas, 142.
Ford, John, 85, 124, 128, 130-132.
Forest, The, 160.
Fragments d'une Histoire Comique, 268.
Francisco de Rojas, 323.
"Fronde, The," 281-284.
Fuller, Thomas, 235-236, 239.
Furetière, 270.

Galilei, Galileo, 207, 208, 230, 350, 351.
Galilei, Vincenzio, 348.
Galleria, 331, 336.
Game at Chess, 109.
Gangræna, 223.
Garden of Cyrus, 232.
Gardiner, Dr S. R., 127, 205 note.
Garnett, Dr Richard, 180 note, 193 note.
Garnier, Robert, 285, 288, 289, 290, 306, 320.
Gaspary, Prof. A., 157.
Gautier, Théophile, 244 note.
Gelosi, 349.
Gerhardt, Paul, 358.
Germany, literary academies in, 356.
Gerusalemme Liberata, 338, 346, 371.
Giambattista Della Porta, 349.
Gilbert, W., 208.
Glapthorne, H., 134.
Go, lovely Rose, 188.
Godeau, 259.
Goedeke, Karl, 353 note, 354, 357.
Golden Age, The, 111.
Gombauld, Jean-Ogier de, 265.

Gondibert, 191.
Gosse, Edmund, 2 note, 15, 135 note, 154 note, 215 note, 228 note, 229.
Gournay, Mlle. de, 245, 250.
Graf, Prof., 163, 329 note.
Great Exemplar, The, 215.
Greek tragedy, 199, 200.
Green, T. H., 236 note.
Greene, Robert, 103.
Grimeston, E., 87.
Grotius, 15, 44, 66, 69, 76, 17, 193 and note, 194, 195, 312, 354.
Gryphius, Andreas, 358, 359.
Guarini, 253.
Guevara, 253.
Guizot, 302 note.
Gunpowder Treason, Sermon on, 215.

Hadewijch, Zuster, 6.
Hales, John, 27, 216, 219 and note, 220.
Hall, Bishop, 221, 224, 225.
Hallelujah, or Britain's Second Remembrancer, 146.
Hannay, Mr D., 250, 262, 268, 362, 367.
Hardy, Alexandre, 286, 288, 289, 300, 312, 319, 321.
Heber, Bishop, 215 note.
Heinsius, 44, 103, 111, 274, 300, 312, 354, 355.
Henslowe, 90, 106, 108, 113.
Heraclius, 314.
Herbert, George, 165-167, 168, 169, 174, 177, 178, 180.
Herbert of Cherbury, Lord, 239, 242.
Herodes Infanticida, 111, 274.
Herrick, Robert, 122, 177, 178, 363.
Hesperides, 178.
Heylin, 239.
Heywood, T., 111, 112.
Histoire Comique des États et Empires de la Lune, 271.
History of Henry VII., 209.
Hobbes, T., 191, 203, 204, 223, 231, 236-239, 280, 283, 376.
Holy Dying, 216.
Holy Living, 216.
Honest Whore, The, 106, 107.
Hooft, Pieter Cornelisz., 4, 13-18, 19, 26, 29, 43, 44, 45, 60-62, 64, 65, 70, 84, 288, 330, 372.

INDEX.

Hooft, William Diederickz., 82, 83.
Hooker, Richard, 202, 203, 212, 223, 241.
Horatian Ode to Cromwell, 179.
Horribilicribrifax, 359.
Hôtel de Rambouillet, 330.
Humble Remonstrance in favour of Episcopacy, 220.
Hutcheson, Mrs, 242.
Huyghens, Const., 4, 14, 30, 34, 38, 363.
Hydriotaphia, 231, 232.

Ibrahim, ou l'illustre Bassa, 266.
Il Penseroso, 182.
Inventorie of the Historie of France, 87.

Jodelet, ou le Maître valet, 324.
Jodelle, 285, 290-292.
Johannes de Boetgezant, 199.
Johnson, Samuel, 156, 183, 184, 185, 227, 378.
Jonckbloet, Dr, 2 note, 9 note, 52, 75, 79.
Jonson, Ben, 85, 86, 88-103, 105, 112, 115, 118, 120, 122, 129, 140, 152, 153, 160-162, 163, 164, 176, 179, 187, 188, 189, 190, 200, 206, 210 and note, 226, 300, 310, 320, 324, 329, 340.
Jusserand, J. J., 84 note, 135 note.

Kalff, Prof., 2 note, 5, 7 note, 9 note, 10, 11 note, 14 note, 18 note, 21 note, 22 note, 34 note, 38 note, 39 note.
Keats, John, 139, 145.
Kepler, 207, 208, 230.
Ker, Prof., 366 note.
King and No King, A, 11, 123, 125.
King, Edward, 183.
Knight of the Burning Pestle, The, 122, 126.
Knollys, Richard, 239.
Koeppel, Dr Emil, 84 note, 120 note.
Koerting, Prof., 260 note, 263, 270.
Kyd, Thomas, 114, 196.

L'Allegro, 182.
L'Astrée, 251, 260, 261, 262-264, 295, 296.
La Bague d'Oubli, 324.

La Belle Égyptienne, 294.
La Calprenède, 264, 266, 267, 297, 320.
La Chrysolite, ou le Sécret de Romans, 270.
La Dafne, 348.
La Force du Sang, 294.
La Galerie du Palais, 304, 305.
L'Illusion, 304, 305.
La Lira, 331-336.
La Mort de César, 306.
L'Orphise de Chrysante, 268.
La Place Royale, 304, 305.
La Pucelle, 259.
La Rosa, 337.
La Savoysiade, 261.
La Suite du Menteur, 313.
La Suivante, 304.
La Veuve, 304.
Lady's Trial, The, 131.
Lafayette, Marie de, 267.
Lamb, Charles, 119.
Lanson, M., 244 note, 276, 286 note, 302 note.
Larivey, 286, 304.
Laud, Archbishop, 214, 216, 218, 219, 220.
Laure Persécutée, 322.
Le Berger Extravagant, 268, 269.
Le Cid, 272, 274, 286, 293, 298, 301, 307-311, 314, 320, 321, 323.
Le Menteur, 313, 324.
Le Prince, 273.
Le Véritable St Genest, 312, 323.
Lecomte, Valleran, 251, 289, 290.
Lefranc, Prof. A., 260 note.
Lemaitre, Jules, 302 note.
Leopardi, 340, 343.
Leroy, Marie, 264.
Les Bergeries, 249.
Les Galanteries du Duc d'Ossone, 298.
Les Visionnaires, 324.
Letter to a Friend, 232.
Lettres Provinciales, 272, 277, 278.
Leviathan, 237-239.
Liberty of Prophesying, The, 215, 216.
Lightfoot, Bishop, 213 note.
Lo fingido Verdadero, 323.
Locke, John, 283.
Logau, Friederich von, 359, 360.
Lope de Vega, 288, 293, 297, 310, 313, 322, 329, 344.

INDEX.

Lorenzo de' Medici, 329.
Lovelace, Richard, 176.
Love's Sacrifice, 131.
Lucifer, 194.
Luiken, 42, 43.
Lycidas, 165, 183-185, 200, 221.

Machiavelli, 113, 114, 196, 208, 209.
Maeghden, 312.
Maerlant, Jacob van, 5.
Magnetic Lady, The, 99.
Maid's Tragedy, The, 123.
Mairet, 292, 297, 298-302, 309, 317, 323.
Malcontent, The, 104, 113, 114.
Malherbe, 245-248, 249, 250, 251, 254, 257, 273, 275, 276, 295, 302, 319, 365.
Mander, Karl van, 10.
Marc Antonie, 386.
Maria Stuart, 312.
Mariamne, 321.
Marino, 150, 151, 162, 163, 170, 171, 184, 196, 199, 253, 256, 295, 325, 326, 338, 344, 347, 365.
Marlowe, C., 18, 85, 87, 88, 123, 125, 156, 196, 288, 289, 368.
Marnix, P. van, 11, 12.
Marprelate controversy, 220.
Marston, John, 85, 103, 104-106, 114, 119, 140.
Martyr, The Virgin, 106, 128, 369.
Marvell, A., 179.
Masque of Hymen, 100.
Masque of Queens, 100.
Massinger, Phil., 85, 121, 127-130.
Masson, Prof. D., 180 note.
May, T., 239.
Maynard, François, 248.
Mayne, Jasper, 234.
Mazzoni, 327 note.
Médée, 306.
Médicis, Marie de, 250.
Mélite, 303, 304.
Meres, F., 86.
Metamorphosis of Tobacco, 152.
Metaphysical poetry, 156-158, 162, 163, 367, 374.
Mezières, A., 84 note.
Michaelmas Term, 109.
Microcosmographie, 225.
Middleton, T., 85, 103, 106, 107, 108-111, 124, 126, 226, 369.
Milan, Duke of, 128.

Milton, 3, 28, 65, 72, 74, 80, 90, 95, 137, 138, 163, 180-186, 192-197, 198, 201, 203, 204, 220-224, 258, 259, 320, 341 note, 349.
Minto, Prof., 84 note, 202 note.
Minturno, 340.
Mistress, The, 189, 336.
Mithridate, 306.
Molière, Fr. de, 83, 98, 101, 102, 103, 253, 264, 313, 316, 324.
Moltzer, Prof., 18, 32, 50.
Montaigne, 17, 226, 273, 276, 277, 278.
Montchrestien, Antoine de, 286, 306, 320.
Montemayor, Jorge de, 262, 294.
Moolhuizen, J. J., 193 note.
Moralities (Dutch), 53.
More, Henry, 149, 375.
Morley, H., 225 note.
Mort de César, 321.
Motley, J. L., 11 note.
Motteux, P. A., 234.
Moyse Sauvé, 190, 259.
Muller, Aug., 193 note.
Muscettola, Antonio, 338.

New Atlantis, 207.
New Inn, The, 99.
New Way to Pay Old Debts, A, 129.
Newcastle, Duchess of, 242.
Nicol, Prof., 205 note.
Nicomède, 315.
Noble Numbers, 178.
Northward Ho! 106, 107.

Ode to Hobbes, 189.
Ode on the Morning of Christ's Nativity, 182.
Of Prelatical Episcopacy, 221.
Of Reformation in England, 221.
Of the Sacred Order of Episcopacy, 215.
Ogier, François, 300.
Old Fortunatus, 106, 107.
Old Law, The, 110.
Olor Iscanus, 168.
On a Girdle, 188.
On the Assumption, 171.
On the Death of a Fair Infant, 181.
Opitz, Martin, 354-356.
Ossone, Duc de, 304.
"Oude Kammer, The." *See* "Eglantine, The."
Overbury, Sir Thomas, 225.

INDEX.

Page disgracié, 270.
Panthée, 321.
Paradise Lost, 183, 185, 192, 194, 195, 198, 199, 259.
Paradise Regained, 198, 199, 201, 320.
Parasitaster, or The Fawn, 104, 179.
Parfaict, Frères, 285 note.
Pascal, Blaise, 17, 204, 206, 229-231, 237, 260, 277-279, 377, 378.
Pastor Fido, 262, 293, 296, 300, 338, 349.
Pater, W., 228 note, 229.
Patin, Guy, 268.
Pattison, M., 180 note.
Pensées, 278.
Pensieri Diversi, 345.
Pepys, S., 133, 242.
Peri, Jacopo, 348.
Peter en Pauwel, 312.
Peter Squenz, 359.
Petit de Julleville, 244 note, 275 note, 286 note, 302 note.
Petrarch, 150, 326, 330, 339.
Pharonnida, 191.
Phœnix, The, 109.
Pianto d' Italia, 344.
Pindariques (Cowley), 189, 190.
Piscatorie Eclogues, 141.
Platonists, Cambridge, 374, 375.
Pleasure reconciled to Virtue, 100.
Pleiad, 4, 178, 200, 244, 248, 250, 354.
Plutarch, 265, 292.
Poetaster, The, 93, 94, 95, 102, 104.
Poetic diction, 182.
Poetical Blossoms, 189.
Polexandre, 265, 266.
Polinnia, 337 and note.
Poliziano, 327.
Polyandre, 268, 270.
Polyeucte, 311, 312, 323, 370.
Pompée, 313.
Pope, A., 147, 178.
"Port Royal," 277.
Potter, Dirk, 6.
"Précieuses," 284.
"Préciosité," 163, 253, 257, 366.
Preti, Girolamo, 338.
Prideaux, Col., 143, 148 note.
Promus of Formularies and Elegancies, 205.
Prudhomme, S., 277 note.
Pseudodoxia Epidemica, 231.

Pseudo-Martyr, 214.
Psyche, 316.
Puritanism, 200, 217, 218.
Purple Island, 141.
Purves, Prof. J., 332 note.
Pyramus and Thisbe, 189.

Quarles, F., 148.
Quinault, 315, 316, 323.

Rabelais, F., 226, 234, 235.
Racan, Seigneur de, 247, 249, 296.
Racine, 285, 308, 309, 315-319.
Raleigh, Prof. W., 180 note.
Raleigh, Sir W., 239.
Rambouillet, Hôtel de, 164, 251-253, 255, 260, 262, 263, 267, 273, 284, 303, 315, 376.
Rambouillet, Monseigneur de, 251.
Randolph, 134.
Rapimento di Cefalo, 348.
Rationalism, 251, 275, 276, 375-379.
Ready and Easy Way to Establish a Free Commonwealth, 232.
Reael, Laurens, 65.
Reasons of Church Government urged against Prelaty, 199, 221.
Régnier, Mathurin, 247, 250.
Religio Medici, 229.
Renaissance, 1, 10, 44, 190, 200, 293 note, 362-370.
Renegado, The, 128.
Retreat, The, 172.
Return from Parnassus, 93.
Retz, Cardinal de, 281.
Reure, Abbé, 261.
Revenger's Tragedy, 119.
Rhetoric, Chambers of, 7, 26, 54, 55.
Richelieu, 310, 322, 329.
Rigal, Eugène, 285 note, 288 note.
Rist, Jacob, 356.
Robertson, Prof. G. Croom, 236 note.
Robertson, J. G., 353 note.
Rochefoucauld, Duc de la, 267, 281, 282-284.
Rodogune, 314.
Roelandt, H., 64.
Roman Comique, 270, 271.
Roman Forgeries, 171.
Roman Satyrique, 270.
Ronsard, 150, 245, 246, 289, 292, 342, 365.

INDEX.

Rossetti, D. G., 157.
Rotrou, Jean de, 297, 298, 306, 321, 324.
Rousseau, J.-J., 329.
Rowley, W., 108, 110.
Royal Society, 190.
Ruskin, J., 215.
Ryer, Pierre du, 297, 324.

Sablé, Madame de, 284.
Saggiatore, 351.
Saint-Amant, 190, 254.
Saint-Louis, 259.
Saint Patrick for Ireland, 132, 133.
Saint Paul, 259.
Saint-Sorlin, 324.
Sainte-Beuve, 244 note, 274, 277 note, 289.
Saintsbury, Prof., 84 note, 138 note, 202 note, 244 note, 362, 367.
Sales, S. Francis de, 263, 274.
Salmacis and Hermaphroditus, 121, 338.
Salmasius (Saumaise, C.), 222.
Sampogna, 331, 336, 347.
Samson Agonistes, 199.
Sannazaro, 150, 339.
Sarpi, Paolo, 351, 352.
Satiromastix, 93, 106.
Scaliger, 300, 355.
Scarron, P., 255, 271, 324.
Scévole, 322.
Schede, Paul, 353.
Scherer, W., 353 note.
Schism and Schismatics, 220.
Scott, Sir W., 126.
Scudéry, G. de, 259, 266, 274, 297, 309.
Scudéry, Madeline de, 264, 266.
Secchia Rapita, La, 347.
"Secentismo," 325, 326, 366.
Sejanus, His Fall, 95, 99.
Select Discourses, 375.
Senecan tragedy, 286, 287, 306.
Serafino, 326, 332, 335.
Sertorius, 312, 316.
Sévigné, Mdme. de, 262, 267.
Shakespeare, W., 3, 84, 86, 88, 93, 98, 103, 114, 115, 117, 118, 120, 122, 137, 156, 182, 183, 196, 203, 211, 288, 289, 292, 300, 308, 310, 336.
Shepherdess, The Faithful, 127.
Shirley, James, 85, 103, 132, 133, 175, 368.

Sidney, Sir Phil., 140, 144, 262, 300.
Silent Woman, The, 96, 97, 98, 100.
Silex Scintillans, 168.
Silvanire, 298, 299, 300.
Silver Age, The, 111.
Sirène, 261.
Small, Roscoe A., 94 note.
Smith, Gregory, 53.
Smith, John, 374.
Smollett, Tob., 269, 271.
Socrate Chrestien, 273.
Song-books (Dutch), 18.
Songs and Sonnets (Donne), 160.
Sophonisba, The Tragedy of, 104.
Sophonisbe, 297, 298, 301, 302, 306, 315, 316, 320.
Sophy, The, 188.
Sorel, Charles, 268, 269, 270.
Spaccio della Bestia, 175.
Spanish Gipsy, The, 109.
Spedding, 205 note.
Speed, 239.
Spenser, E., 13, 135, 137, 140-143, 144, 182, 184, 201.
"Spenserians, The," 166.
Spieghel, H. Lz., 12, 13.
Staple of News, The, 99.
Starter, 20, 21.
Steele, R., 283.
Steffens, G., 321 note.
Stephen, Leslie, 236 note.
Steps to the Temple, 170.
Sterne, Laurence, 226.
Stewart, Prof. J. A., 369.
Stiefel, A. L., 87 note, 293 note, 321 note.
Strage degli Innocenti, 170, 190, 331, 338.
Struys, Jacob, 64.
Suckling, Sir J., 122, 134, 176, 177.
Swift, 211.
Swinburne, A. C., 86, 89 note, 90, 98, 120 note, 210 note.
Sylva Sylvarum, 207.
Sylvester, 181.
Sylvie, 298, 299.
Symonds, J. A., 89 note.

Taille, Card. de la, 290.
Tale of a Tub, A, 99.
Tasso, Bernardo, 340, 341, 344.
Tasso, T., 25, 119, 182, 184, 185, 192, 195, 196, 200, 327-329, 339, 371.
Tassoni, 255, 325, 328, 343, 345-347.

Tatler, The, 324.
Taylor, Jeremy, 204, 215 and note, 220.
Tebaldeo, 326, 332.
Temple, The, 165-167.
Tenure of Kings and Magistrates, 222.
Testi, Fulvio, 338, 340, 343-345, 365.
Théagène et Cariclée, 291.
Théodore, 312, 314.
Théophile, 321, 365.
Theophrastus, 224.
Thijm, J. A. Alberdingk, 2 note, 3, 42.
Thomson, James, 139.
'Tis Pity, 131.
To His Coy Mistress, 179.
Tourneur, Cyril, 119, 120.
Traherne, Thomas, 171-174, 374.
Traité des Passions, 253, 275.
Traitor, The, 133.
Trent, Council of, 377.
Trevelyan, G. M., 200.
Trissino, 340.
Tristan l'Hermite, 292, 297.
Triumph of Peace, 132.
Troubles of Queen Elizabeth, 111.
Tyr et Sidon, 300.

Underwoods, 160.
Unities, The, 297-299, 301, 304, 309.
Urquhart, Sir T., 234, 235.

Van der Eembd, 64.
Van der Goes, 42.
Van der Noot, Jan, 10.
Van der Wiele, Stalpert, 41, 42.
Van Effen, 48.
Van Noppen, L. C., 71 note.
Van Spee, Friederich, 358.
Vaughan, Henry, 167-169, 172, 174, 178, 179, 196, 197, 198.
Vaumorier, Pierre de, 264.
Venceslas, 323.
Vendanges de Surenne, Les, 324.
Verney, Sir E., 241.
Vianey, M. J., 326.
Viau, Théophile de, 254, 255, 268, 295, 296.
Virgidemiarium, 225.

Virgile Travesti, 271.
Virginie, 301.
Visscher, Anna, 13, 15, 27.
Visscher, Roemer, 12, 13, 19.
Visscher, Tesselschade, 13, 15, 19, 27.
Vivonne, Catherine de, 251.
Voiture, Vincent, 177, 255.
Vollenhove, 42.
Volpone, 96, 97, 101, 102.
Voltaire, 321, 349.
Vondel, 4, 17, 22-34, 36, 37, 42, 43, 46, 65-82, 165, 169, 171, 192, 193 note, 198, 312, 363, 364, 372.
Vondel and Milton, 81.
Vos, Jan, 81.
Vossius, 44, 69, 78.

Waller, Edmund, 156, 179, 186, 187.
Walton, Isaac, 213 note, 243.
Ward, Dr A. W., 121 note.
Ward, W. C., 332 note, 335.
Webster, John, 85, 110, 113-119, 124, 125, 130, 214, 369.
Weckherlin, G. Rodolf, 353.
Wendell, Prof. Barrett, 135 note.
Westward Ho! 106, 107.
What you Will, 105.
Whibley, C., 234 note, 235.
Whichcote, Benj., 374.
White Devil, The, 113, 116, 117.
Widow's Tears, 87.
Willcock, Rev. John, 234 note.
Wilson, John Dover, 366 note.
Winkel, Prof. Te, 76, 78.
Wither, George, 144, 145-147.
Woman killed with Kindness, A, 112.
Women Beware Women, 110.
Wordsworth, C., 243 and note.
Wordsworth, William, 172, 189, 343.
Wybrands, Aemstel, 52.

Your Five Gallants, 109.

Zedeprinten (Huyghens), 225.
Zegers, Gustaaf, 193 note.
Zincgref, Julius Wilhelm, 353.
Zinnespelen, 53.